3500
5 vol set
Joseph T. Okimoto, M.D.
AF737481

THE INTERNATIONAL
PSYCHO-ANALYTICAL
LIBRARY

No. 7

The International Psycho-Analytical Library
No. 7, edited by Ernest Jones, M.D.

SIGMUND FREUD

COLLECTED PAPERS

VOLUME 1

AUTHORIZED TRANSLATION UNDER THE SUPERVISION OF
JOAN RIVIERE

New York Basic Books, Inc. Publishers

FIRST AMERICAN EDITION 1959

Published by Basic Books, Inc.
by arrangement with
The Hogarth Press Ltd and
The Institute of Psycho-Analysis, London

ALL RIGHTS RESERVED.

LIBRARY OF CONGRESS CATALOG CARD NUMBER 59-8642
MANUFACTURED IN THE UNITED STATES OF AMERICA
EIGHTH PRINTING

COLLECTED PAPERS

VOLUME I

EARLY PAPERS

★

ON THE HISTORY OF THE PSYCHO-ANALYTIC MOVEMENT

EDITORIAL PREFACE

To write a preface is often a perfunctory matter, but in the preface to this series of Collected Papers we wish to direct the reader's special attention to two cardinal considerations.

In the first place it should be said that these Collected Papers, of which the present is the first volume, constitute the real basis of Psycho-Analysis. All Professor Freud's other work and theories are essentially founded on the clinical investigations of which these papers are the only published record. It is unfortunate that the English-speaking public should for years have had access only to what may be called the superstructure of his work, the application of his psycho-analytic method to the study of dreams, sexuality, totemism, and so on, while the basis of it all remained buried in a foreign tongue. It is now proposed to fill this central lacuna in English psycho-analytical literature by publishing, in four or more volumes, a translation of the *Sammlung kleiner Schriften zur Neurosenlehre*. Incidentally it may be said that the papers in this series have been re-grouped, in co-operation with Professor Freud, so that they do not follow the same order as that of the German original.

This brings us to the second consideration. If the reader wishes to extract the greatest profit from these volumes, it is quite essential that he should constantly bear in mind the *date* when each Paper was written. The only really satisfactory way of acquiring a knowledge of Professor Freud's writings is to follow the order of development of his work. It is hardly possible otherwise to obtain a coherent picture of the whole. To follow this development is not only a fascinating study in itself, disclosing as it does a beautiful example of the way in which ideas are gradually unfolded—and constantly extended and modified—under the pressure of widening and deepening experience. It also gives a conviction of the truly scientific nature of the author's work, for the tentative "feeling forward" here revealed—now in one direction, now in another, as occasion and opportunity present—is the very antithesis of the promulgation of an *a priori* philosophic system such as has sometimes been ignorantly imputed to him. One inflexible determination has always guided him, and that was the determination to keep ever in the closest contact with the actual material daily brought before his observation, and not to be tempted along side-tracks by speculations, however enticing these might appear. His path lay through a jungle hitherto completely unexplored. Rarely did his path follow a straight line for long: deviations, détours, fresh departures were often necessary, and occasionally even the retracing of his steps. No one will expect that in these circumstances of exploring an unknown territory the pioneer's trail would be orderly and regular in its progress, or that the path should be everywhere beaten equally smooth; but that the progress has been a real and inspiring one is attested by the host of workers now following in his steps.

In his preface to the first volume of the *Sammlung kleiner Schriften* Professor Freud writes:—"Whoever is familiar with the development of human knowledge will hear without astonishment that I have passed beyond some part of the views here presented and have learnt to modify some others. Still I have been able to retain unchanged the greater part, and do not really need to withdraw anything as completely erroneous and quite worthless". He probably had in mind here particularly the view that underwent most modification subsequently, that concerning the importance of sexual traumas in infancy. Few episodes in the history of scientific research provide a more dramatic test of true genius than the occasion on which Professor Freud made the devastating discovery that many of these traumas to which he had been obliged to attach ætiological significance had never occurred outside the imagination of the patients. The realization—so modestly related in the last of the Early Papers (p. 276)—that an imagined event could in certain psychological circumstances produce an effect exactly equivalent to that of an actual event was one that only an investigator gifted with a supreme feeling for psychology could have achieved. Initial error led to a profound discovery. Most of Professor Freud's alleged "inconsistencies" will be found to carry a similar moral.

In the work of organizing the translations I have had the invaluable assistance of Mrs. Riviere; they have also been carefully revised by her as well as by myself. In this Frl. Anna Freud was very helpful, and we wish to express our indebtedness to her.

CONTENTS OF VOLUME I

EARLY PAPERS

I

CHARCOT[1]

(1893)

In the person of J. M. Charcot whom, after a life of happiness and fame, a sudden death without suffering or illness took from us on the 16th of August the young science of neurology has lost its most active promoter, neurologists of all countries have been bereft of their teacher, and France has lost prematurely one of its leading men. He was only sixty-eight years of age; his bodily strength and mental vigour, together with the hopes he so frankly expressed, seemed to promise him that long life which has been granted to not a few of the thinkers of this century. The imposing nine volumes of his *Œuvres Complètes*, in which his pupils had collected his contributions to the science of medicine and of neuropathology, the *Leçons du Mardi*, the yearly reports of his clinic at the Salpêtrière, and other papers—all these publications, though they will remain precious to his pupils and to science, cannot take the place of the man who still had much to give and to teach, whose personality and whose work no one ever approached without learning from them.

He had a perfectly honest, human delight in his own great success and used to speak freely about his early days and the road that he had traversed. His scientific curiosity had been aroused early in life when he was but a young house-physician by the abundance of material, at that time utterly

[1] First published in the *Wiener Medizinische Wochenschrift*, 1893, No. 37. [Translated by J. Bernays.]

unintelligible, contained in the facts of neuropathology. At that period in his life, whenever he made the rounds in the wards of the Salpêtrière (the asylum for women) with his chief, when he saw all the wilderness of paralyses, tremors and spasms for which no name or proper understanding existed forty years ago, he would say, '*Faudrait y retourner et y rester*', and he kept his word. As soon as he had become *médecin des hôpitaux* (hospital physician) his goal was to get into the Salpêtrière, into one of the wards for nervous patients. Once there, he remained; instead of, as is the privilege of French physicians, transferring in regular order from hospital to hospital and from ward to ward, at the same time changing his speciality.

Thus his first impression and the resolution to which it led determined his whole future career. Having at his disposal a considerable number of patients afflicted with chronic nervous disease he was enabled to take full advantage of his peculiar talent. He was not much given to cogitation, was not of the reflective type, but he had an artistically gifted temperament—as he said himself, he was a '*visuel*', a seer. He himself told us the following about his method of working: he was accustomed to look again and again at things that were incomprehensible to him, to deepen his impression of them day by day, until suddenly understanding of them dawned upon him. Before his mind's eye, order then came into the chaos apparently presented by the constant repetition of the same symptoms; the new clinical pictures which were characterized by the constant combination of certain syndromes took shape; the complete and extreme cases, the 'types', were then distinguishable with the aid of a specific kind of schematic arrangement, and with these as a starting-point the eye could follow down the long line of the less significant cases, the '*formes frustes*', showing some one or other peculiar feature of the type and fading into the indefinite. He called this kind of mental work, in which he had no equal, 'practising nosography' and he was proud of it. He was heard to say that the greatest satisfaction man can experience is to see something new, that is, to recognize it as new, and he constantly returned with repeated observations to the subject of the difficulties and the value of such 'seeing'. He wondered how it happened that in the practice of medicine men could only see what they had already been taught to see, he described how wonderful it was suddenly to see new things—new diseases—although they were probably as old as the human race; he said that he often had to admit that he could now see many a thing which for thirty years in his wards he had ignored. No physician will need to be reminded of the wealth of new outlines which the science of neuropathology gained through his efforts, and of the much greater keenness and accuracy in diagnosis which was made possible by the aid of his observations. But to his pupils, who made the rounds with him through the wards of the Salpêtrière—that museum of clinical facts for the greater part named and defined by him—he seemed a very Cuvier, as we see him in the statue in front of the Jardin des Plantes, surrounded by the various types of animal life which he had understood and described; or else he reminded them of the myth of Adam, who must have experienced in its most perfect form that intellectual delight so highly praised by Charcot, when the Lord led before him the creatures of Paradise to be named and grouped.

Charcot never tired of defending the claims of the purely clinical task of seeing and classifying phenomena, as against the encroaches of theoretical medicine. One day a small group of foreign students brought up in the ways of German orthodox physiology annoyed him by raising objections to his clinical innovations. 'That cannot possibly be', one of us interrupted him, 'that contradicts the theory of Young-Helmholtz.' He did not reply, 'So much the worse for the theory, clinical facts rank first', and so forth. But he did say—leaving us deeply impressed '*La théorie, c'est bon, mais ça n'empêche pas d'exister.*'

For a long term of years Charcot held the chair of pathological anatomy in Paris, carrying on as a side-issue his neuropathological work and the lectures which rapidly made him famous abroad as well as at home. It was fortunate, however, for neuropathology that the same man could fulfil the functions of two incumbents; on the one hand he created the clinical pictures by observations, and on the other he proved that in the typical case as well as in the *forme fruste* the same anatomical changes were the foundation of the disease. It is generally known how great the success of this anatomical-clinical method was in the sphere of organic nervous disease, with tabes, multiple sclerosis, amyotrophic lateral sclerosis, and so on. With these chronic, not immediately fatal diseases, patient years of waiting were often necessary before proof of the organic changes could be established, and only in a hospital for incurables like the Salpêtrière was it possible to keep and to watch the patients for such long periods. As it happened, Charcot made his first discovery in this field before he was in charge of a ward. During his student days chance brought him into contact with a charwoman who suffered from a peculiar form of tremor and could not get work because of her awkwardness. Charcot recognized her condition to be 'choreiform paralysis', already described by Duchenne, of the origin of which, however, nothing was known. In spite of her costing him a small fortune in broken plates and platters, Charcot kept her for years in his service and, when at last she died, could prove in the autopsy that 'choreiform paralysis' was the clinical expression of multiple cerebro-spinal sclerosis.

Pathological anatomy has to serve neuropathology in two ways: first, to bring proof of morbid alterations, and secondly, to determine the localization of these changes; we all know that in the last two decades the second part of the task has aroused greater interest and has been more actively advanced. In this field also Charcot co-operated brilliantly, although the pioneer work was not done by him; he followed to begin with the footsteps of our countryman Türck, who is said to have lived and worked among us in comparative obscurity. Later, after the two important discoveries which inaugurated a new epoch in our knowledge of the 'localization of nervous diseases'—namely, the stimulation tests of Hitzig-Fritsch and Flechsig's work on the development of the spinal cord—his lectures on localization were the best and most significant aid towards co-ordinating the new theories with the clinical side and making them available for clinical purposes. As regards the relation of the muscular system to the motor area of the cerebrum, I should like to remind the reader how long the specific mode and topography of this connection was a matter of conjecture (common representation of both extremities in the same areas, representation of the upper extremity in the anterior, of the lower in the posterior central convolution: that is, vertical disposition), until at last continued clinical investigations, with stimulation- as well as extirpation-tests on human beings during surgical operations, decided the matter in favour of Charcot's and Pitres' view, namely, that the middle third of the central gyri mainly serves the representation of the arm, while the upper third and the mesial portion serve the representation of the leg; in other words, that the disposition in the motor areas is a horizontal one.

It would not be possible to demonstrate Charcot's importance to the science of neuropathology by enumerating particular achievements, for during the last two decades there have been few questions of any significance to the formulation and discussion of which the 'school of the Salpêtrière' has not made contributions of signal importance. The 'school of the Salpêtrière' was, of course, Charcot himself; his wealth of experience, his power of plastic description, his transparent clearness of diction was easily recognizable in the papers of every one of his pupils. Some members of this circle of young men whom he gathered about him and made his partners in his work had attained to consciousness of their own individuality, and won celebrity on their own account, and one or other of them would now and then advance an opinion that seemed to the master clever rather than correct; this he would attack sarcastically enough in conversation and in his lectures without, however, in any way injuring his affectionate relation with the pupil. Charcot does indeed leave behind him a group of pupils whose intellectual qualifications and whose work are pledges that the practice of neuropathology in Paris will not readily descend form the high level to which it was brought by him.

In Vienna we have repeatedly found that an academic teacher of intellectual importance is not also as a matter of course gifted with that close personal influence on his students which expresses itself in the formation of a numerous and important 'school'. If Charcot was more favoured in this respect we must attribute it to his personal qualities as a man, to the magic of his aspect and his voice, to the gracious frankness of his manner after the first strangeness of a new relation had worn off, to the readiness with which he placed everything at the disposal of his pupils, and to his life-long loyalty to them. The hours he spent in his wards were hours of fellowship and interchange of ideas with his whole medical staff. He never shut himself off from them; the youngest assistant had an opportunity of seeing him at work and might interrupt him, and the same privilege was granted to the foreigners who were never absent from his rounds in later years. Finally, his pupils and assistants were regarded as part of his family in welcoming the guests on the evenings when Madame Charcot—assisted by a highly gifted daughter, not unlike her father—received a distinguished company in her hospitable house.

In the year 1882 or 1883 the circumstances of Charcot's life and work took on their final form. The idea had come to be generally realized that the activity of this man was part of the national '*gloire*', to be guarded all the more jealously since the unsuccessful war of 1870—1871. The government, headed by Charcot's old friend, Gambetta, created for him a chair of neuropathology at the Faculty of Medicine, which permitted him to give up his course in pathological anatomy, and, in addition, founded for him a clinic with auxiliary scientific departments at the Salpêtrière. '*Le service de M. Charcot*' now embraced (with the old wards of the chronic patients) several clinical halls where men also were received, a large out-patient department—the *consultation externe*—an histological laboratory, a museum, an electro-therapeutic department, an eye-and-ear department, and a special photographic studio. Each of these institutions offered opportunities for attaching former assistants and pupils permanently to the clinic in good positions. The two-storey-high, weather-beaten buildings and the courts they enclosed reminded the foreigner extraordinarily of our Allgemeines Krankenhaus in Vienna, but the resemblance did not go very far. 'It is perhaps not beautiful here', Charcot would say as he showed the visitor about his domain, 'but you can find room for everything you want to do.'

Charcot stood at the zenith of his career when this abundance of material for teaching and investigating was placed at his disposal. He was an indefatigable worker, always the most industrious of the whole group. His private practice, crowded with patients 'from Samarcand and from the Antilles', could not divert him from his activities as a teacher and investigator. This throng was assuredly not attracted merely by the famous scientist, but as much or more by the great physician, and by the sympathetic nature of the man, who always knew how to give counsel, and could surmise and guess in those cases where the present status of science did not permit him to know. He has often been reproached on account of his therapeuty, which with its multiplicity of prescriptions could not but offend a rationalistic conscience: he simply continued the current and local methods customary at that time and place, without deceiving himself much about their effectiveness. Incidentally, he was not pessimistic in regard to therapeutic results and was ever willing to encourage at his clinic experiments with new methods of treatment, which had but a short-lived success, as others were quick to point out. As a teacher, Charcot was positively fascinating; each of his lectures was a little masterpiece in construction and composition, perfect in style, and so impressive that the words spoken resounded in one's ears and the subject demonstrated remained before one's eyes for the rest of the day. He rarely made a demonstration with a single patient, but was accustomed to present a whole group or a number of contrasting types which he then compared with one another. In the hall in which he gave his lectures hung a picture of the 'citizen' Pinel, causing the poor insane of the Salpêtrière to be relieved of their chains; for after having been the scene of so many horrors during the French Revolution, the Salpêtrière had also witnessed this most humane innovation. Maître Charcot himself made a strange impression during these lectures; usually bubbling over with vivacity and cheerfulness, with witticisms always on his lips, he would appear at such moments solemn and serious, nay, even aged in his velvet cap; his voice seemed muffled, and we almost understood how malicious strangers could accuse the whole performance of theatricality. Those who expressed themselves in this manner were probably accustomed to the lack of form in German clinical lectures or else they forgot that Charcot, who gave only one lecture a week, could prepare it carefully.

Charcot was very probably following a tradition of long standing with this ceremonious lecture, in which everything was prepared and had to happen as planned; nevertheless he felt the need of displaying his activity to his pupils in a less artificial setting. For this purpose he made use of the out-patient department which he took charge of personally in the so-called *Leçons du mardi*. There he examined cases quite unknown to him, risked all the chance occurrences of an interrogation, laid his authority aside and confessed at times that in one case diagnosis was impossible, and that in another appearances had deceived him. Never did he appear greater to his students than on these occasions, when he thus did his best to lessen the distance between teacher and pupils by giving them a complete and faithful account of his own train of thought, by stating his doubts and misgivings with the utmost frankness. The publication, at first in French, now also in German of these improvised lectures of the years 1887 and 1888 has extended the circle of his admirers indefinitely; nor has any other neuropathological work ever achieved greater success among the medical public.

About the time that the clinic was instituted and the course in pathological anatomy given up, there occurred a change in Charcot's scientific interests to which we owe the best part of his work. He explained that the theory of organic nervous diseases was for the present fairly complete, and he began to turn his attention almost exclusively to hysteria, thus suddenly focussing general attention on this subject. This most enigmatic of all nervous diseases—no workable point of view having yet been found from which physicians could regard it—had just at this time come very much into discredit, and this ill-repute related not only to the patients but was extended to the physicians who treated this neurosis. The general opinion was that anything may happen in hysteria; hysterics found no credit whatsoever. First of all Charcot's work restored dignity to the subject; gradually the sneering attitude, which the hysteric could reckon on meeting when she told her story, was given up; she was no longer a malingerer, since Charcot had thrown the whole weight of his authority on the side of the reality and objectivity of hysterical phenomena. Charcot had repeated on a small scale the act of liberation commemorated in the picture of Pinel which adorned the lecture hall of the Salpêtrière. Now that the blind fear of being fooled by the poor patient which had stood in the way of a serious study of the neurosis was overcome, the question arose which mode of procedure would most speedily lead to the solution of the problem. The wholly unprejudiced observer might have found an opening in the following reflection: If I find a person in a condition bearing all the marks of a painful affect, crying, screaming, raving, I am led to surmise that a mental process is going on in him of which these bodily phenomena are the adequate expression. In such a case the normal person is capable of telling us what is troubling him, but the hysteric would answer that he did not know; and the problem at once arises: How comes it that the hysteric is subject to an affect of the causes of which he claims to know nothing? If we adhere to the conclusion that there must exist a corresponding psychic process, and at the same time believe the patient's assertion when he denies its existence, if we assemble all the manifold signs which indicate that the patient nevertheless behaves as though he knows the cause, if we search into the patient's life and find therein a cause—a trauma—likely to create such an affective expression—then indeed the solution is forced upon us that the patient is in a peculiar mental condition in which his impressions or memories are no longer all linked up one with the other, and in which it is possible for one memory to express its affect by means of bodily phenomena without the other mental processes—the ego—knowing about it or being able to interfere; and the recollection of the well-known psychological difference between sleep and the waking state might have lessened the strangeness of such an hypothesis. Let no one object that the theory of dissociation of consciousness as a solution of the enigma of hysteria is too far-fetched to suggest itself to the untrained and unprejudiced observer. In fact the Middle Ages had chosen this very solution, in declaring possession by a demon to be the cause of hysterical manifestations; all that would have been required was to replace the religious terminology of those dark and superstitious times by the scientific one of to-day.

Charcot did not choose this path in his explanation of hysteria, though he drew plentifully from existing records of witchcraft trials and of possession in order to show that the manifestations of neurosis were the same then as they are now. He treated hysteria like any other theme of neuropathology, gave the complete description of its manifestations, showed that these had their own laws, and taught his pupils to recognize the symptoms which make the diagnosis of hysteria possible. He and his pupils occupied themselves in most careful tests with the disturbances of sensibility caused by hysteria on the skin and the deeper tissues, with the behaviour of the sense organs, peculiarities of hysterical contractures and paralyses, trophic disturbances and alterations of metabolism. The manifold forms of the hysterical attack were described and a scheme drawn up which represented the typical configuration of the attack of '*grande hystérie*' in four stages, and permitted the correlation of the commonly observed attacks of '*petite hystérie*' with the type. They also investigated the localization and frequency of the so-called hysterogenic zones and their relation to the attacks, and so on. Equipped with all this information about the manifestations of hysteria it was possible to make a number of surprising discoveries; it was found that hysteria was far commoner among men than had been suspected, especially among working-men, and that certain conditions which had been ascribed to alcoholic or lead poisoning were hysterical. It was possible to include a large number of hitherto unintelligible, unclassified affections under the head of hysteria, and to distinguish the part played by hysteria in cases where the neurosis was combined with other diseases, forming a complex clinical picture. Most far-reaching in its influence was probably that research work concerning the nervous diseases following upon traumas—the traumatic neuroses—the conception of which is still under discussion to-day; in all these affections Charcot successfully presented the case for hysteria.

Since the latest extensions of the conception of hysteria had so frequently led to a rejection of any ætiological diagnosis, the need arose to investigate the ætiology of hysteria. Charcot laid down a simple formula for this: heredity is the unique originating cause of hysteria, which is therefore a form of degeneration, a member of the '*famille névropathique*', all other ætiological factors playing the part of precipitating causes, of '*agents provocateurs*'.

The building up of this great structure of doctrine was not, of course, achieved without violent opposition. This was, however, nothing but the barren objection of an older generation which disliked making any change in its views. The younger group of neuropathologists, in Germany as well, accepted Charcot's theories to a greater or lesser extent.

Charcot himself was quite convinced of the success of his teaching in regard to hysteria; if objections were raised that the four stages of the attack, or that hysteria among men, etc., were not observable outside France, he pointed out that he had himself overlooked these things for a long time, and reasserted that hysteria was the same everywhere and at all times. He disliked to hear the French accused of being a far more nervous nation than other peoples, and hysteria spoken of as their national foible; he was delighted when a paper on a case of 'reflex epilepsy' in a German grenadier could be diagnosed by him at a distance as one of hysteria.

At one point Charcot's work rose above the level of his general treatment of hysteria and took a step which gives him for all time the glory of being the first to elucidate hysteria. While he was occupied with the study of hysterical paralyses appearing after traumas, the idea occurred to him to reproduce by artificial means such paralyses as he had previously carefully differentiated from organic disturbances; for this purpose he took hysterical patients and placed them in a state of somnambulism by hypnotism. He succeeded in producing a faultless demonstration and proved thereby that these paralyses were the result of specific ideas holding sway in the brain of the patient at moments of special disposition. With this the mechanism of an hysterical phenomenon was for the first time disclosed, and on this incomparably fine piece of clinical research his own pupil Janet, and also Breuer and others, based their theories of the neurosis which, while agreeing with the mediæval view, replaces the 'demon' of priestly imagination by a psychological formula.

Charcot's application of the phenomena of hypnosis to hysteria enabled a very great advance to be made in this important sphere of hitherto neglected and despised facts, because the weight of his reputation put an end once for all to doubts of the reality of hypnotic manifestations. But this exclusively nosographic approach was not suited to a purely psychological subject. Limiting the study of hypnosis to hysterical patients, distinguishing between greater and lesser hypnotism, establishing three stages of 'greater' hypnosis distinguished by somatic signs—all these practices sank in the estimation of contemporaries when Liébeault's pupil, Bernheim, undertook the task of basing the theory of hypnotism on a broader psychological foundation and of making suggestion the nucleus of hypnosis. Only the opponents of hypnotism who content themselves with hiding their own lack of experience behind some recognized authority still cling to Charcot's pronouncements, and like to quote an expression uttered in his last years denying that hypnosis has any therapeutic efficacy whatever.

As for the ætiological theories which Charcot defended in his doctrine of the '*famille névropathique*' and made the cornerstone of his whole conception of nervous diseases, they too will probably soon need to be probed into and corrected. So greatly did Charcot over-estimate heredity as a cause that no loophole was left by which nervous disease could be acquired; to syphilis he allotted only a modest place among the '*agents provocateurs*'; nor did he, in ætiology or elsewhere, differentiate sharply enough between the organic nervous affections and the neuroses. The progress our science has made in additions to its knowledge will inevitably diminish the value of much that Charcot has taught us, but neither the passing of time nor the changing of ideas will diminish the glory of the man whom we—in France and elsewhere—are mourning to-day.

II

ON THE PSYCHICAL MECHANISM OF HYSTERICAL PHENOMENA[1]

(In collaboration with Dr. Joseph Breuer, 1892)

I

Stimulated by a chance observation, we have for a number of years been investigating the most varied types and symptoms of hysteria with reference to the exciting cause, the event which evoked the phenomenon in question for the first time, often many years before. In the great majority of cases it is impossible to discover this starting-point by straightforward interrogation of the patient, be it ever so thorough; partly because it is often a matter of experiences which the patient finds it disagreeable to discuss, but chiefly because he really does not remember and has no idea of the causal connection between the exciting occurrence and the pathological phenomenon. As a rule it is necessary to hypnotise the patient and under hypnosis to arouse recollections relating to the time when the symptom first appeared; one can then succeed in revealing this connection in the clearest and most convincing manner.

In a great number of cases this method of examination has yielded results which appear to be valuable theoretically as well as practically. From the theoretical point of view the results are valuable because, for the pathology of hysteria, the accidental factor is decisive to a far greater extent than is

[1] First published in the *Neurologisches Zentralblatt*, 1893, Nos. 1 and 2. [Translated by John Rickman.]

known or acknowledged. In regard to traumatic hysteria it is obviously the accident which has evoked the syndrome; and when we learn from the utterances of patients in hysterical attacks that they invariably hallucinate in every attack a repetition of the original occurrence which evoked the first, the causal connection then also becomes perfectly clear here. The question is more obscure in the case of other phenomena.

Our experience has shown us, however, that the most varied symptoms, usually regarded as spontaneous and, so to speak, idiopathic products of hysteria, have just as strict a connection with the exciting trauma as those mentioned above in which the relation of the two sets of facts to one another is transparent. To exciting causes of this kind we have been able to trace anæsthesias as well as neuralgias of the most varied kind, often of many years duration, contractures and paralyses, hysterical attacks and epileptoid convulsions which all observers had taken for genuine epilepsy, *petit-mal*, symptoms of the nature of tics, chronic vomiting and anorexia carried to the point of refusal of food, the most varied disturbances of vision, constantly recurring visual hallucinations—and the like. The disproportion between the many years duration of an hysterical symptom and the single occurrence which evoked it is similar to that which we are accustomed to see egularly in traumatic neurosis; it was quite frequently in childhood that the events occurred producing a more or less grave symptom which persisted from that time onwards.

The connection is often so clear that it is quite evident how the exciting event has happened to produce just this and no other manifestation; the phenomenon is determined in a perfectly clear manner by the cause; to take the most ordinary example, a painful affect, which was originally excited while eating but was suppressed, produces nausea and vomiting, and this continues for months as hysterical vomiting. A girl watching in harrowing anxiety at the bedside of a sick person falls into a twilight state and has a terrifying hallucination while her right arm which is hanging over the back of the chair 'goes to sleep'; from this develops a paresis of that arm with contracture and anæsthesia. She wants to pray but can find no words; finally she succeeds in repeating an English prayer which she learnt in childhood. Then later a severe and highly complicated hysteria develops in which she can speak, write and understand only English, while for a year and a half her mother-tongue remains unintelligible to her.—A child who is very ill at last falls asleep, and its mother tries her utmost to keep quiet and not to wake it; but just in consequence of this resolution (hysterical counterwill) she makes a clucking noise with her tongue. On another occasion when she wishes to keep absolutely quiet this happens again, and so a tic in the form of tongue-clicking develops which for a number of years accompanies every excitement.—A highly intelligent man assists while his brother's ankylosed hip is straightened under an anæsthetic. At the instant when the joint gives way with a crack he feels a violent pain in his own hip-joint which lasts for almost a year; and so on.

In other cases the connection is not so simple; there exists only what may be called a symbolic relation between the cause and the pathological manifestation, such as normal people also fashion in dreams; for example, a neuralgia links itself on to some mental distress, or vomiting accompanies a feeling of moral disgust. We have had under observation patients who habitually made extensive use of such symbolism. In yet other cases a determination of this kind is not at the first glance clearly intelligible; to these belong precisely the typical hysterical symptoms—hemianæsthesia, contraction of the field of vision, epileptiform convulsions and the like. The exposition of our theories concerning this group must be reserved for a more detailed consideration of the subject.

Such observations seem to us to prove the pathogenic analogy between ordinary hysteria and traumatic neurosis and to justify an extension of the concept of traumatic hysteria. In traumatic neurosis the active cause of illness is not the trifling bodily injury but the affect of fright—the psychic trauma. Similarly, our investigations of many, if not of the majority, of hysterical symptoms have revealed causes which must be described as psychic traumas. Any experience which rouses the distressing affects of fright, apprehension, shame, or psychical pain can have this effect and it obviously depends on the sensitiveness of the person concerned (as well as on a further condition which we will refer to later) whether the experience acquires the importance of a trauma. We not infrequently find in ordinary hysteria several partial traumas instead of one grand trauma—a group of causes—which can only achieve traumatic effectiveness by accumulation and which belong together only in so far as they form parts of a whole painful experience. In still other cases circumstances in themselves apparently indifferent have attained an otherwise unexpected importance as traumas, either on account of their conjunction with really effective experiences or because they occurred at a moment of special susceptibility. This importance they then retain henceforward.

But the causal connection between the exciting psychical trauma and the hysterical symptom is not of such a kind that the trauma (like an *agent provocateur*) sets going a symptom which then becomes independent and persists on its own account. On the contrary, we are of opinion that the psychical trauma, or the memory of it, acts as a kind of foreign body constituting an effective agent in the present even long after it first penetrated; and we see the proof of this in a highly remarkable phenomenon which also lends an important practical interest to these results of our observations.

The discovery that we made, at first to our own great surprise, was that when we had succeeded in bringing the exciting event to clear recollection, and had also succeeded in arousing with it the accompanying affect, and when the patient had related the occurrence in as detailed a manner as possible and had expressed his feeling in regard to it in words, the various hysterical symptoms disappeared at once, never to return. Recollection without affect is nearly always quite ineffective; the original psychical process must be repeated as vividly as possible, brought into *statum nascendi* and then 'talked out'. In the case of excitation phenomena—contractures, neuralgias, and hallucinations—the symptoms appear again during this repetition in full intensity and then disappear for ever. Defects in functioning, paralyses and anæsthesias disappear in the same way, the transitory exacerbation not being of course perceptible in those cases.[1]

[1] Delbœuf and Binet have clearly recognised the possibility of such a therapy, as the following quotations show. Delbœuf: *Le Magnétisme animal*, Paris, 1889: 'Since then it has been possible to understand how the magnetist helps in bringing about recovery. He restores the patient to the condition in which the illness established itself and then with his words he attacks the illness, now *in statu nascendi*.' — Binet: *Les Altérations de la personnalité*, 1892,

One may be inclined to suspect that the explanation lies in unintentional suggestion; the patient expects to be rid of his suffering as a result of the treatment, and this expectation might be the effective factor, not the 'talking out'. But this is not the fact; the first observation of this kind was a highly complicated case of hysteria having symptoms with distinct causes which were separately dispersed, and was analysed on these lines in the year 1881, that is, in the 'pre-suggestion' era. It was made possible by spontaneous auto-hypnosis on the part of the patient, and it occasioned the observer the greatest surprise.

Inverting the phrase '*cessante causa cessat effectus*', we may well conclude from these observations that the exciting experience continues in some way to be effective even years after, not indirectly by means of a chain of causes linking up with one another, but directly as the actual exciting cause—just as, for instance, the recollection of mental distress in full consciousness at some later period may stimulate tears; we thus conclude that *hysterical patients suffer principally from reminiscences.*[1]

II

It may at first appear strange that experiences long since past should operate with such intensity,

p. 243: '. . . Perhaps we shall see that by bringing back the patient by a mental device to the moment when the symptom appeared for the first time we make him more susceptible to suggestive therapy'. — In P. Janet's interesting book *L'Automatisme psychologique*, Paris, 1889, there is a description of a cure obtained in an hysterical girl by the employment of a method analogous to ours.

[1] In the text it is not possible to separate what is new in the content of this provisional communication from what is also to be found in other authors, e. g. Möbius and Strümpell, who have put forward similar views on hysteria. The nearest approach to our theoretical and therapeutic deductions is found in a few recently published remarks of Benedikt's which we propose to consider elsewhere.

and that the memory of them should not succumb to the fate which we see overtaking all our memories; perhaps these facts may become rather more comprehensible in the light of the following considerations.

The fading of a memory or of its affect depends on several factors. First and foremost it depends on whether an energetic reaction (discharge of feeling) supervened on the affective experience or not. By *reaction* we here mean the whole range of voluntary and involuntary reflexes, by which according to experience the affects are habitually worked off—from weeping up to an actual act of revenge. If this reaction occurs with sufficient intensity a great part of the affect disappears; common speech bears witness to these facts of every-day observation in the expressions 'to cry oneself out', 'to storm oneself out (*sich austoben*)'. If the reaction is suppressed the affect remains attached to the memory. An insult which is returned, if only in words, is remembered differently from one which had to be endured in silence. Common speech also recognizes this difference in the psychical and bodily consequences, and most characteristically designates silently endured suffering as a *Kränkung*,[1] wound, injury, mortification. The reaction of an injured person to the trauma has a really complete 'cathartic' effect only if it takes the form of a fully adequate reaction, such as an act of revenge. But man finds a surrogate for such an act in speech, by the help of which the affect may be almost as effectually 'abreacted'. In other cases talking is itself sufficient as a reflex, for example, complaining or relieving the burden of a secret (the confessional!). If a reaction of this

[1] [There is no satisfactory translation of this highly expressive German word, which is obviously allied to *krank* = ill.—Ed.]

kind by word or deed, or in the mildest cases by tears, does not ensue, the memory of the occurrence retains for a time its affective tone.

'Abreaction' is, however, not the only kind of solution at the disposal of the normal psychical mechanism in a healthy person who has met with a psychical trauma. Even if the memory is not abreacted it becomes merged in the great complex of associations, and is then ranged alongside of other experiences which perhaps contradict it; thus it undergoes correction by means of other ideas. After an accident, for example, the remembrance of the danger and the subsequent (weakened) reproduction of the terror is accompanied by the memory of the sequel, of the rescue and the consciousness of present security. The memory of an injury to the feelings is corrected by an objective evaluation of the facts, consideration of one's actual worth and the like, and thus the normal man succeeds by means of associations in dissipating the accompanying affect.

In addition to this there is also that general effacing of impressions, that fading of recollection called 'forgetting', which tends more than anything else to absorb ideas which have lost their affective tone.

Our observations have shown that those memories which give rise to hysterical phenomena are retained with wonderful freshness and with full affective tone for a long period. But we must mention as a further striking fact, to be turned to account later, that these recollections are not at the disposal of the patient in the way that his more commonplace memories are. On the contrary, when the patient is in his usual psychical condition these experiences are completely absent from his memory or are present to it only in the most summary manner.

Only when patients are questioned under hypnosis do these memories recur with the undiminished vividness of recent events.

Thus for six months one of our patients under hypnosis reproduced with hallucinatory vividness everything which had excited her on the corresponding day of the previous year (during an acute hysteria); her mother's diary, of which she knew nothing, attested the perfect accuracy of the reproduction. Another patient lived through with hallucinatory clearness—partly in hypnosis, partly in spontaneous attacks—all the experiences of an hysterical psychosis which she had suffered from ten years before, and in regard to which amnesia had been almost complete until the moment of the re-emergence. Several ætiologically important recollections dating back fifteen to twenty-five years were of astonishing integrity, and intensity of feeling; on reproduction their effect had the full force of new experiences.

As a reason for this we can only conjecture that these recollections have met with an exceptional fate in reference to all the ordinary processes of effacement discussed above, for we find that they relate to traumas which have not been sufficiently abreacted; closer investigation of the reasons which have prevented the operation of the latter then shows us at least two groups of conditions under which reaction to the trauma does not ensue.

In the first group we reckon those cases in which the patient has not reacted to the psychical trauma because its nature excluded the possibility of any such reaction, as in the case of the apparently irretrievable loss of a loved person, or when social conditions made a reaction impossible, or when the trauma concerned something which the patient wished to forget and therefore deliberately repressed[1] and excluded from his conscious thoughts. Under hypnosis we discover painful ideas of precisely this character underlying the hysterical phenomena (e. g. in the hysterical deliria of saints and nuns, of abstinent women and well-brought-up children).

The second group of conditions is not determined by the content of the recollection, but by the mental condition of the patient at the moment when the given experience occurred. That is to say, among the exciting factors of hysterical symptoms we also discover under hypnosis ideas which though not in themselves significant owe their preservation to the circumstance that they happen to coincide with a seriously disabling affect, for example, terror, or with a directly abnormal mental condition, such as the half-hypnotic twilight state of day-dreaming, auto-hypnosis, and the like. In these cases it is the nature of these conditions which made a reaction to the experience impossible.

Naturally both determinants may and often do occur together. This happens when a trauma effective enough in itself occurs during a state of seriously disabling affect or of altered consciousness; but it seems that in many persons an abnormal state of this kind is produced as the result of a psychic trauma which then in its turn makes a reaction impossible.

Both groups of determining conditions have this in common: that the psychical traumas which are not resolved by reaction will also fail of solution by means of associative absorption. In the first group the patient's intention to do so causes him to forget

---

[1] [This is the first occasion on which this term was used. Later it became the author's technical term for the *unconscious* process by which thoughts are excluded from consciousness.—Ed.]

the painful experiences and consequently to exclude them from association as far as possible. In the second group the associative absorption does not succeed because sufficient associative connection does not exist between the normal state of consciousness and the pathological state in which these ideas originally arose. We shall have immediate occasion to go more closely into these conditions.

Thus it may be said that the ideas which have become pathogenic are preserved with such freshness and affective force because the normal process of absorption by abreaction and by reproduction in a state of unrestrained association is denied them.

III

In describing the conditions which according to our experience are decisive for the development of hysterical phenomena from psychical traumas, we mentioned the abnormal states of consciousness in which such pathological ideas arise; and we laid stress on the fact that the recollection of the effective psychical trauma is not to be found in the normal memory of the patient, but in his memory under hypnosis. Indeed, the more we occupied ourselves with these phenomena the more certain did our conviction become that that splitting of consciousness, which is so striking in the well-known classical cases of *double conscience*, exists in a rudimentary fashion in every hysteria and that the tendency to this dissociation—and therewith to the production of abnormal states of consciousness, which may be included under the term '*hypnoid*'—is a fundamental manifestation of this neurosis. This view is in agreement with those of Binet and the two Janets; we have not had the opportunity, however, to confirm their highly remarkable discoveries in reference to anæsthetic patients.

We should like therefore to supplement the often-quoted phrase 'hypnosis is an artificial hysteria' with another—namely, 'the existence of hypnoid states forms the foundation and condition of hysteria'. There is one thing common to all these hypnoid states and to hypnosis, in spite of all their differences—namely, that the ideas which emerge in them are marked by great intensity of feeling but are cut off from associative connection with the rest of the content of consciousness. These hypnoid states are capable of association among themselves and the ideas belonging to them may in this way attain different degrees of psychical organization. Incidentally, however, the nature of these states and the degree of their inaccessibility to the rest of conscious processes would very probably vary in a fashion similar to that of hypnosis, which ranges from light sleepiness to somnambulism, from complete recollection to absolute amnesia.

If such hypnoid states exist before the manifest illness, they provide a foothold upon which the affect establishes itself with its pathogenic recollection and its subsequent somatic manifestations. This situation corresponds to dispositional hysteria. But our observations show that a severe trauma (such as that in a traumatic neurosis) or a troublesome suppression (for instance, of sexual affect) can effect a splitting of groups of ideas in people previously free from it, and this would constitute the mechanism of psychically acquired hysteria. Between the extremes of these two forms we must recognize a series within which the readiness to dissociation in the persons concerned and the volume of affect roused by the trauma varies inversely.

We have nothing new to say concerning the origin of dispositional hypnoid states. They often develop, we believe, from the 'day-dreams' so frequently met with also in healthy people, great opportunity for which is provided, for instance, in the feminine occupation of needlework. The question why the 'pathological associations' formed in such states are so strong and why they influence somatic processes so much more strongly than ideas habitually do is part of the problem of the operation of hypnotic suggestion in general. Our experiences teach us nothing new on this point; they do, however, illuminate the contradiction between the statement 'hysteria is a psychosis' and the fact that one finds among hysterics people with the clearest and most critical intellects, of great strength of character and will-power. These characteristics in such people are valid for their waking thoughts; in the hypnoid state they become alienated from their conscious personalities as we all are in dreams. But whereas our dream-psychoses do not influence our waking existence the products of hypnoid states intrude as hysterical phenomena into waking life.

IV

Almost the same conclusions that we have just formed concerning hysterical symptoms of long duration may be repeated concerning hysterical attacks. As is well known, we possess a schematic description of the '*grande attaque*', worked out by Charcot, according to which four phases may be recognized in a complete attack: (1) the epileptoid, (2) that of violent movements, (3) that of '*attitudes passionnelles*' (the hallucinatory phase), and (4) that of the concluding delirium. According to Charcot, all the various forms of an hysterical attack (which as a matter of fact are more frequently observed than the full *grande attaque*) are derived from a shortening, lengthening, omission or isolation of these separate phases.

Our attempt at explanation has to do with the third phase, the *attitudes passionnelles*. When this is well-marked it will reveal itself as an hallucinatory reproduction of a memory important for the outbreak of the hysteria, i. e. the memory of the one grand trauma in what is called κατ' ἐξοχήν traumatic hysteria, or of a series of inter-related partial traumas which lie at the root of ordinary hysteria. The remaining alternative is that the attack will reproduce those experiences which were raised to importance by happening to occur at a time of special sensitivity to traumas.

But there are also attacks which seems to consist of nothing but motor symptoms and in which the *phase passionnelle* is lacking. If we can succeed in establishing a *rapport* with the patient during such general clonic attacks, during tonic catalepsy, or during an *attaque de sommeil*, or, better still, if we succeed in summoning up an attack while the patient is under hypnosis, we find that these attacks too are based on the memory of a psychic trauma or series of traumas which usually finds expression in an hallucinatory phase. For instance, a little girl has suffered for years from attacks of general convulsions which might have been epilepsy and had in fact been taken for it. To establish a differential diagnosis she was hypnotised and was promptly seized by an attack. When asked: 'What do you see now?' she answered. 'The dog, the dog is coming!' Further enquiry revealed that the first attack of the kind had appeared after she had been chased by a mad dog. Therapeutic success later confirmed the diagnosis of a psychogenic malady.—A clerk who had become hysterical in consequence of being assaulted by his superior suffered from attacks during which he fell to the ground in a frenzy of rage, but without uttering a word or betraying any signs of an hallucination. An attempt to produce the attack under hypnosis proved successful, and the patient revealed that he was again living through the situation in which his superior had openly insulted him in the street and thrashed him with a stick. A few days afterwards he returned complaining that the same attack had occurred again, and this time he revealed under hypnosis that he had been living through the situation which provoked the actual outbreak of the disease, i. e. the trial in court where he failed to obtain compensation for the injury.

The memories which come to the fore in hysterical attacks, or can be wakened during them, correspond also in all other respects with the exciting occurrences which we have found at the root of hysterical symptoms of long duration. Like these, they relate to psychic traumas which have remained unresolved by abreaction or by associative mental operations; and like these, they—or at least their essential constituents—are absent from the store of memories of which normal consciousness is made up; they belong to the ideational content of hypnoid states of consciousness with their narrow fields of association. Finally, they also admit of the therapeutic test. Our observations have often demonstrated that a memory of this kind which had hitherto provoked such attacks lost this power as soon as it was brought during hypnosis to a reaction or to associative readjustment.

The motor phenomena of hysterical attacks are to be explained partly as a general mode of reaction to the affect which accompanies the memory, and may be compared, for example, with the beating movements of all the limbs which even an infant makes use of for this purpose; and partly as signifying direct emotional expressions of this memory; although they also elude this explanation to some extent as do the hysterical stigmata in chronic symptoms.

There is yet another aspect of the hysterical attack which reveals itself in the light of the theory we have just indicated: that in hysteria there are present ideational groups (arising in hypnoid states) which, cut off from associative relations with the remainder but associable *inter se*, establish a more or less highly organized nucleus of a second consciousness, a *condition seconde.* An hysterical symptom of long duration then corresponds to an intrusion of this *condition seconde* into the somatic innervations usually controlled by normal consciousness; an hysterical attack, however, gives evidence of a higher organization of this *condition seconde* and, when of recent origin, signifies the moment at which this hypnoid consciousness takes possession of the subject's whole personality (i. e. an acute hysteria); but recurring attacks which contain a memory signify a recurrence of this moment. Charcot has already suggested that the hysterical attack is probably the nucleus of a *condition seconde.* During the attack, control of the entire somatic innervation has passed to the hypnoid consciousness. Experience shows that in these cases normal consciousness is not always completely superseded; it may even perceive the motor phenomena of the attack while the psychic processes of the latter escape its notice.

The typical course of a severe hysteria is, as is well known, that first an ideational content is formed in hypnoid states, which then, when sufficiently developed, takes possession during a period of 'acute hysteria' of the somatic innervation and personality of the patient, creates chronic symptoms and attacks, and then recedes until mere vestiges of it are left. If therefore the normal personality can regain control, what remains of the hypnoid ideational contents then returns in hysterical attacks and again temporarily produces in the patient similar states, which are again susceptible themselves and predisposing to the influence of traumas. A sort of equilibrium between the psychical groups united in the same personality is then frequently established; attacks and normal life exist side by side without affecting one another. The attacks then arise spontaneously, as memories commonly do; but they may also be provoked, just as any memory may be aroused according to the laws of association. Provocation of an attack occurs either by stimulation of an hysterogenic zone or by a new experience resembling the pathogenic experience. We hope to be able to show that no essential difference exists between the two conditions, apparently so distinct; that in both cases a hyperæsthetic memory has been stirred. In other cases this equilibrium is very unstable; the attack appears as an expression of the vestiges of hypnoid consciousness whenever the normal personality is exhausted and powerless. It is not impossible that in such cases the attack may be divested of its original significance and may return as a motor reaction without content.

It remains a task for further enquiry to discover what are the conditions determining whether in any given patient an hysteria will take the form of attacks, or chronic symptoms, or a combination of both.

V

It is now clear how the method of psychotherapy which we have just described leads to recovery. By providing an opportunity for the pent-up affect to discharge itself in words the therapy deprives of its effective power the idea which was not originally abreacted; by conducting it into normal consciousness (in light hypnosis) it brings it into associative readjustment or else dispels it by means of the physicians' suggestion, as happens in cases of somnambulism combined with amnesia.

We regard the therapeutic effect achieved by employing this procedure as important. We naturally cannot cure that element in hysteria which is dispositional; we can do nothing against the return of hypnoid states. Even during the productive state of an acute hysteria our procedure cannot prevent the phenomena which have just been removed with such difficulty being forthwith replaced by new ones. But when the acute stage has passed off and its vestiges remain in the form of chronic hysterical symptoms and attacks our method will frequently remove them in turn, and the results are permanent because radical. It therefore appears to us that in this respect it far surpasses the effect of removal by direct suggestion which is now practised by psychotherapeutists.

Although, by thus disclosing the psychical mechanism of hysterical phenomena, we have now made a further step along the path which Charcot first opened up so successfully with his explanations and experimental imitations of hystero-traumatic paralyses, we nevertheless do not conceal from ourselves that it is only the mechanism of the hysterical symptom that has been brought within our grasp and not the inner causes of hysteria. We have but touched upon the ætiology of hysteria and have really only been able to throw light on the causes of its acquired forms—the significance of the accidental factor for this neurosis.

III

SOME POINTS IN A COMPARATIVE STUDY OF ORGANIC AND HYSTERICAL PARALYSES[1]

(1893)

In 1885 and 1886, when I was his pupil, Charcot was good enough to entrust me with the task of making a comparative study of organic and hysterical motor paralyses, based upon observations at the Salpêtrière, which might serve to discover some of the common characteristics of neuroses and lead to a conception of their nature. Accidental and personal reasons prevented me from following his suggestion for a long time; even now I only intend to give an account of some of the results of my work, omitting the details needed for a complete demonstration of my views.

I

I must begin with some remarks on the nature of organic paralyses, which incidentally represent generally accepted conclusions. Clinical neurology recognizes two forms of motor paralyses: periphero-spinal (or bulbar) and cerebral. This distinction is entirely in harmony with the facts of the nervous system, which show that there are only two segments in the course of the motor fibres: one extending from the periphery to the anterior horn cells of the spinal cord, and a second which proceeds from here to the cerebral cortex. Modern neuro-histology, based upon the work of Golgi, Ramón y Cajal, Kölliker, etc., formulates these facts as follows: The path of fibres

[1] First published in *Archives de Neurologie*, No. 77, 1893. [Translated by M. Meyer.]

conducting motor impulses consists of two neurones (a neuro-histological unit composed of a cell and its fibres) which meet in intimate relation at the so-called motor cells of the anterior horn. The essential clinical difference between these two types of paralysis is the following: *Periphero-spinal paralysis is a paralysis of individual elements while cerebral paralysis is a paralysis en masse.* Types of the former are the facial palsy of Bell, the paralysis in infantile anterior poliomyelitis, etc. Now in these diseases each muscle, we might say each muscle fibre, may be paralysed individually and in isolation. It depends only upon the site and extent of the nerve lesion; there is, moreover, no definite rule according to which one peripheral element escapes paralysis while another is permanently subject to it.

Cerebral paralysis, on the other hand, is always a disease affecting a considerable portion of the periphery, an extremity, a segment of it, or a complicated motor apparatus. It never affects one muscle alone, as for example, the biceps brachii or the tibialis; in any apparent exceptions to this rule (cortical ptosis, for example) it is evident that the muscles concerned are of the kind which in themselves fulfil a particular function—in which they are the sole agents.

It may be noted that in cerebral paralyses affecting the extremities distal segments always suffer more than proximal ones; the hand, for example, is more paralysed than the shoulder. As far as I know, there is no isolated cerebral paralysis of the shoulder in which the hand retains its motor power, while the reverse is the rule in incomplete paralyses.

In a critical study of aphasia, published in 1891 (*Zur Auffassung der Aphasien, Wien, 1891*), I attempted to show that the cause of this important difference between periphero-spinal and cerebral paralysis was to be sought in the structure of the nervous system. Each element in the periphery corresponds to one in the grey substance, which is, as Charcot expresses it, its neural terminus; the periphery is then, so to say, projected on to the grey substance of the spinal cord, point by point, element for element. I have proposed that the particularized periphero-spinal paralysis should be named 'projection paralysis'. The relation between the elements of the spinal cord and those of the cortex is, however, different. The number of conducting fibres would no longer suffice for a second projection of the periphery, to the cortex. We must suppose that the fibres coming from the spinal cord to the cortex no longer represent single peripheral elements, but rather a group of them; on the other hand, a peripheral element may correspond to several spino-cortical fibres. The change in arrangement occurs at the point where the two segments of the motor system meet.

Therefore I would say that the reproduction of the periphery in the cortex is no longer an accurate one, point for point; it is not a true projection. The relation is established so to say by representative fibres, and I propose therefore to name the cerebral form of paralysis 'representation paralysis'.

Naturally, when a projection paralysis is total and very extensive, it too becomes a paralysis *en masse* and its striking distinctive characteristic disappears. Cortical paralysis, on the other hand, which is differentiated from the other cerebral paralyses by a greater tendency to dissociation, nevertheless invariably presents the character of a representation paralysis.

The other differences between projection paralysis and representation paralysis are well known. Among them I may mention the preservation of nutrition and of electrical reaction in the latter. Although clinically very important, these signs have not the theoretical significance that is to be ascribed to the first differential trait mentioned, i. e., whether the paralysis be one of individual elements or *en masse.*

Hysteria has often been credited with the faculty of simulating the most varied kinds of organic nervous diseases. The question arises whether it can simulate accurately the characteristics of both types of organic paralysis, whether there are hysterical projection paralyses and hysterical representation paralyses, as in the organic symptomatology. An important fact at once confronts us here. Hysteria never simulates the periphero-spinal or projection paralyses; hysterical paralyses show the characteristics of organic representation paralyses only. This is indeed a very interesting fact, since Bell's palsy, musculo-spinal paralysis, etc., are among the most common diseases of the nervous system.

It should be noted in this connection, in order to avoid all confusion, that I am dealing only with flaccid hysterical paralyses and not with hysterical contractures. It seems to me impossible to apply the same rules to both hysterical paralyses and hysterical contractures. The contention that the paralysis never affects an isolated muscle (unless such a muscle be the sole agent of a function), that the paralysis is always *en masse,* agreeing in this respect with an organic cerebral representation paralysis, can only be maintained in respect of flaccid hysterical paralyses. Further, in regard to the nutrition and electrical reactions of the paralysed part hysterical paralysis shows the same characteristics as organic cerebral paralysis.

But although hysterical paralysis may be related in this way to cerebral and especially to cortical paralysis, which exhibits a greater aptitude for dissociation, important distinctive traits are not lacking between them. In the first place, it is not subject to the constant fixed rule of organic cerebral paralyses, namely, that the distal segment is always more extensively affected than the proximal one. In hysteria, the shoulder or the thigh may be more seriously paralysed than the hand or the foot. Movements may occur in the fingers while the proximal part is still absolutely motionless. There is not the least difficulty in producing artificially an isolated paralysis of the thigh, of the leg, etc., and clinically we quite frequently meet with these isolated paralyses which do not conform to the rules of organic cerebral paralyses.

In this important respect hysterical paralysis is, so to speak, intermediate in type between projection paralysis and representation paralysis. On the one hand it does not possess all the characteristics of dissociation and isolation proper to the former; on the other hand it is by no means subject to the rules which strictly govern the latter. With these reservations we may say that hysterical paralysis also is a representation paralysis, but one possessing a special manner of representation which remains to be dicovered.[1]

II

As a step in this direction I propose to study the other traits which differentiate hysterical paralysis

[1] I will state by the way that that important feature of hysterical paralyses of the leg emphasized by Charcot, following Todd—namely, that an hysteric drags his leg like a dead mass instead of performing the circumduction of the hip commonly carried out in hemiplegia—is easily explained by a characteristic of the neurosis already mentioned. In organic hemiplegia, the proximal part of the extremity is always more or less intact; the patient can move the hip and uses it to perform the circumduction movement that carries the leg forward. In hysteria, the proximal part (the hip) does not enjoy that privilege; the paralysis is as complete as in the distal part, and as a result the leg must be dragged *en masse*.

from the most perfect form of cerebral organic paralysis—namely, cortical paralysis. The first of these distinguishing characteristics has been mentioned, the fact that hysterical paralysis may be much more dissociated and systematised than cerebral paralysis. The symptoms of organic paralysis appear in hysteria as if apportioned. Hysteria reproduces the common organic hemiplegia (paralysis of the upper and lower extremities and of the lower half of the face) only to the extent of imitating the paralysis of the limbs; frequently it even splits off the paralysis of the arm from that of the leg, exhibiting with the greatest ease paralysis in the form of a monoplegia. It reproduces in an isolated form the motor aphasia seen in the syndrome of organic aphasia and, as I have observed in some unpublished cases, it can create a total aphasia (motor and sensory) for a given language, without affecting in the least the ability to understand and to speak another, a phenomenon unheard-of in organic aphasia. This power of dissociation is again manifested in those isolated paralyses in which one segment of a limb is affected while other portions of the same limb are entirely intact, and again, when one function is completely abolished (abasia astasia) while another function performed by the same organ is unaffected. The more complex the function in question, the more striking is this dissociation. In organic disease, whenever several functions are impaired in different degrees, it is always the most complex function, the one most recently acquired, that is most extensively affected by the paralysis.

In addition to the above, hysterical paralysis presents another characteristic, which is, as it were, the hall-mark of the neurosis. Indeed, as I heard Charcot say, hysteria is a malady with extravagant manifestations, with a tendency to produce its symptoms in the severest possible degree. This characteristic is not met with only in the paralyses but also in the contractures and anæsthesias. The degree of distortion that may be produced by hysterical contractures is well known and is hardly equalled in organic symptomatology. We also know how frequently hysteria exhibits the absolute, profound anæsthesias, of which the organic lesions only reproduce a faint sketch. The same is true of the paralyses; they are often as complete as is possible. The hysterical aphasic does not utter a word, while the organic aphasic almost always retains a few syllables, 'yes', 'no', an oath, etc.; the paralysed arm is absolutely inert, and so on. This characteristic is too well known to dwell on it at length. On the other hand, it is known that in organic paralysis partial paresis is always more common than complete paralysis.

Hysterical paralysis, then, shows an *exact delimitation* and an *excessive intensity*. It possesses these two qualities simultaneously, and it is in this respect that it contrasts most strongly with organic cerebral paralysis, in which these two characteristics are never associated. Monoplegias do exist in organic symptomatology also, but they are almost always monoplegias *a potiori* and not sharply delimited. If an arm is paralysed in consequence of a cortical lesion, there is almost always a minor concomitant affection of the face and leg; and if this complication is no longer visible at a given period, it existed nevertheless at the beginning of the disease. Cortical monoplegia is indeed always a hemiplegia, of which one part or another has been more or less effaced but still remains recognizable. To go further, let us suppose that the paralysis has affected the arm alone, that it is a pure cortical monoplegia; in such a case we shall see that the paralysis is one of moderate degree. As this monoplegia increases in degree, and as soon as it becomes a total paralysis, it at once loses its characteristic of being a pure monoplegia and will be accompanied by motor disturbances in the leg or the face. *It cannot become a complete paralysis and at the same time remain restricted in area.*

This is the very condition, however, that hysterical paralysis can easily accomplish, as we may see daily in clinical work. For example, it may affect the arm exclusively without showing a trace in the leg or the face. Further, in the arm it is as complete as a paralysis can possibly be, and this forms a striking contrast to organic paralysis, a difference that gives occasion for serious reflection.

There are, of course, cases of hysterical paralysis in which the degree of paralysis is not excessive and in which the dissociation offers nothing remarkable. Such cases are recognized by other traits; but they are cases that do not bear the typical stamp of neurosis and, since they cannot teach us anything about the nature of the latter, are of no interest for our present purpose.

Let me add a few remarks of minor importance, though they overstep the limits of my subject.

To begin with, I may recall the fact that hysterical paralyses are much more frequently accompanied by sensory disturbances than are organic paralyses; such disturbances are altogether more profound and frequent in neurosis than in organic disease. Nothing is more common than hysterical anæsthesia or analgesia. Recollect, in contrast to this, how obstinately sensation persists in cases of organic lesion. If a peripheral nerve is cut, the anæsthesia will be less extensive and intense than might be expected. When an inflammatory process attacks the spinal nerves or the spinal cord centres the result always is that motility suffers in the first instance, while sensibility remains or is merely diminished; for some part of the nervous elements which have not been completely destroyed always persists. With cerebral lesions the frequency and the permanency of motor hemiplegia is well known, while the accompanying hemianæsthesia is vague and transitory, and is not always present. Only a few special localizations can produce a marked and lasting sensory disturbance (*carrefour sensitif*), and even this fact is not free from doubt.

This difference in the nature of the sensory disturbances in organic lesions and in hysteria is scarcely explicable with our present knowledge. The solution of this problem would probably reveal the core of the whole matter.

Another point that seems to me worthy of mention is that there are some forms of cerebral paralysis which, just like the periphero-spinal projection paralyses, are not found in hysteria. Paralysis of the lower half of the face, the most frequent manifestation of organic brain disease, should be mentioned first in this connection, and, if I may be permitted to enter the field of sensorial disturbances, homonymus lateral hemianopsia. I know that I run a risk in stating that a given symptom does not exist in hysteria when the researches of Charcot and his pupils are almost daily discovering new and hitherto unsuspected symptoms. But I must take things as they are at the moment. The existence of an hysterical facial paralysis is seriously contested by Charcot, and, even if we believe those who vouch for it, it is a very rare phenomenon. Hemianopsia has not as yet been seen in hysteria, and I believe it never will be.

Now how is it that hysterical paralyses closely simulate cortical ones and yet differ from them in the distinctive characteristics that I have attempted to enumerate, and what is the special type of representation to which they conform? The answer to this question would embody a large and important part of the theory of this neurosis.

III

Not the least doubt exists about the conditions controlling the symptomatology of cerebral paralysis. They are the facts of anatomy—the structure of the nervous system, the distribution of its vessels and the inter-relation between these two sets of facts and the nature of the lesion. We have said that the basis of the difference between the projection paralysis and the representation paralysis lies in the smaller number of fibres proceeding from the spinal cord to the cortex in comparison with the number proceeding from the periphery to the spinal cord. Again, every clinical detail of a representation paralysis finds its explanation in some detail of cerebral anatomy and, *vicc versa*, we can deduce the structure of the brain from the clinical characteristics of the paralyses. We believe that a perfect parallel exists between these two series of facts.

Thus if cerebral paralysis does not show any great tendency to dissociation, it is because the fibres conducting motor impulses run too close together for a great part of their intra-cerebral course for them to be injured individually. If cortical paralysis shows a greater tendency to monoplegias, it is because the diameter of the conducting bundle, brachial, crural, etc., goes on increasing up to the cortex. If paralysis of the hand is the most complete of all the cortical ones, it is, I believe, because the contralateral relation between hemisphere and periphery is more nearly complete for the hand than for any other part of the body. If the distal segment of an extremity suffers a greater degree of paralysis than a proximal segment, it may be assumed that the representative fibres of the distal segment are more numerous than those of the proximal one, so that the influence of the cortex is more important for the former than for the latter. If moderate-sized lesions of the cortex do not succeed in producing pure monoplegias, we infer from this that the motor centres of the cortex are not cleanly separated from one another by indifferent areas, or that there are factors operating at a distance (*Fernwirkungen*) which nullify the effect of an exact separation of the centres.

Similarly, if disturbances of various functions are always found in a mixed form in organic aphasia, this is explained by the fact that branches of the same artery nourish all the speech centres, or, if the view expressed in my critical study of aphasia is accepted, it is because we are dealing, not with separate centres, but with a continuous association area. In any event, there is always some reason to be found in anatomy for these things.

The remarkable combinations which are so often observed in the symptomatology of cortical paralyses (motor aphasia and right hemiplegia, alexia and right hemianopsia) are explained by the proximity of the injured centres. Hemianopsia itself, a symptom that seems curious and strange to the unscientific mind, is only explicable by the crossing of the fibres of the optic nerve at the chiasma; like all the details of cerebral paralyses it is the clinical expression of an anatomical fact.

Since there cannot be more than one authentic cerebral anatomy, and since that one is expressed in the clinical characteristics of cerebral paralyses, it is evidently impossible for that anatomy to explain the distinctive traits of hysterical paralyses. For this reason we should not draw conclusions about cerebral anatomy based upon the symptomatology of these paralyses.

We must certainly turn our attention to the nature of the lesion to find this difficult explanation. In organic paralyses the nature of the lesion plays a secondary part, it is rather the extent and localization of it that, under the given conditions of the structure of the nervous system, produce the characteristics of organic paralysis we have mentioned above. What can be the nature of the lesion in hysterical paralysis which alone dominates the situation, independent of localization, of extent, and of the anatomy of the nervous system?

Charcot constantly taught us that it is a cortical lesion, but one of a purely dynamic or functional kind.

It is easy to understand the negative side of this proposition. It is equivalent to affirming that no appreciable tissue changes will be found *post mortem*; but regarded from a positive stand-point, it is far from being devoid of ambiguity. After all, what is a dynamic lesion? I am sure that many who read the works of Charcot think that dynamic lesion is indeed a lesion, but a lesion of which no trace is found after death, like œdema, anæmia, active hyperæmia. But the latter, although they do not necessarily persist after death, are true organic lesions, however insignificant and transitory. Paralyses produced by lesions of this type partake, necessarily, of all the characteristics of organic paralyses. Œdema and anæmia could no more produce the dissociation and intensity of an hysterical paralysis than could hæmorrhage and softening. The only difference would be that a paralysis produced by œdema, by vascular constriction etc., would be less lasting than a paralysis caused by the destruction of nervous tissue. All the other conditions are common to both, and the anatomy of the nervous system will determine the characteristics of a paralysis in a case of transitory anæmia no less than in a case of permanent anæmia.

I do not think that these remarks are wholly uncalled-for. Reading 'there must be an hysterical lesion' in a given centre (the same centre an organic lesion of which would produce the corresponding organic syndrome) and recollecting that it is customary to localize the dynamic hysterical lesion in the same way as the organic lesion, we are led to believe that there lurks behind the expression 'dynamic lesion' the idea of a lesion like oedema and anæmia, which are in fact transitory organic affections. I maintain on the contrary that the lesion in hysterical paralyses must be entirely independent of the anatomy of the nervous system, since *hysteria behaves in its paralyses and other manifestations as if anatomy were non-existent, or as if it had no knowledge of it.*

Indeed, a good number of the features of hysterical paralyses justify this statement. Hysteria is ignorant of the distribution of the nerves and for this reason does not simulate the periphero-spinal or projection paralyses; it is not acquainted with the optic chiasma and consequently does not produce a hemianopsia. It regards the organs according to the common popular meaning of their names: the leg is the leg up to its insertion into the hip, the arm is the upper extremity as mapped out by our clothing. It would see no reason for combining a facial paralysis to a brachial one. An hysterical patient who loses the power of speech has no motive for forgetting the meaning of language, since motor aphasia and word-deafness are not related in the popular mind. On this point I must agree completely with the views expressed by Janet in the latest numbers of the *Archives de Neurologie;* hysterical paralyses demonstrate their truth just as well as anæsthesias and psychic symptoms do.

IV

I shall now try finally to suggest what might be the lesion that causes hysterical paralyses. I do not claim that I shall demonstrate what it actually is; it is merely a matter of pointing out a line of thought that may lead to a concept not in contradiction with the features of hysterical paralysis, in so far as this differs from organic cerebral paralysis.

I will take the word 'functional or dynamic lesion' in its proper sense: 'alteration in function or mechanism', alteration in a functional attribute. Such an alteration, for example, would be a diminution in excitability or in a physiological quality which in the normal state remains constant or varies within fixed limits.

But it will be said that a functional alteration is only an organic one considered from a different aspect. Let us suppose that nervous tissue is in a state of transitory anæmia, its excitability will be diminished by that circumstance; it is not possible by this means to avoid considering organic lesions.

I will try to show that a functional alteration may exist without an accompanying organic lesion, at least without a lesion capable of detection even by means of the most delicate methods. In other words, I will give an appropriate example of a primary functional change; to do so, I only ask permission to pass over into the field of psychology, which cannot be ignored in dealing with hysteria.

With Janet I maintain that it is the common, popular idea of the organs and of the body in general that is at work in hysterical paralyses as well as in anæsthesias, etc. This idea is based, not upon a profound knowledge of neuro-anatomy, but upon our tactile and, above all, our visual perceptions. If it determines the characteristics of hysterical paralysis the latter must prove to be ignorant and independent of any idea of the anatomy of the nervous system. The lesion of hysterical paralysis will be an alteration of the concept, of the idea 'arm', for example. But what kind of alteration in regard to the concept is capable of producing a paralysis?

Psychologically considered, the paralysis of the arm is embodied in the fact that the concept 'arm' cannot enter into association with those other ideas that make up the ego, of which the body of the individual is an important part. The lesion, then, would consist in the abolition of the accessibility of the concept 'arm' in association. The arm acts as if it did not exist in the interplay of associations. Of course, if the physical conditions corresponding with the concept 'arm' are profoundly changed then the concept will also be lost, but I must show that it may be inaccessible without being destroyed and without its physical substratum (the nervous tissue of the corresponding cortical area) being damaged.

I will commence with examples taken from ordinary life. A comic story is told of a loyal subject who would no longer wash his hand because his sovereign had touched it. The relation of this hand to the idea 'king' seems to be so important for the psychic life of this person that he refused to let it enter into other relations. We obey the same impulse when we break the glass in which we have drunk the health of a newly-married couple. Ancient savage tribes, in burning the horse, the weapons, and even the wives of a deceased chief together with his body, followed a similar idea that no one should touch them after him. The motive for all these acts is clear. The affective value which attaches to the first association is reluctant to let the object enter into a new association with another object and consequently renders the idea inaccessible to association.

If we now pass on to the field of the psychology of concepts we find that this is not a simple comparison but an almost identical situation. If the concept 'arm' is attached to an association of great affective value it will be inaccessible to the free play of other associations. The arm will be paralysed in proportion to the persistence of that affective value or to the diminution in the latter effected by suitable psychic measures. This is the solution of the problem that we have raised; for in every case of hysterical paralysis we find that the paralysed organ or the abolished function is engaged in a subconscious association endowed with great affective value, and it may be demonstrated that the arm becomes free as soon as this affective value is removed. The concept 'arm' exists, then, in the physical substratum; but it is not accessible to conscious associations and volition because its entire associative affinity, so to speak, is saturated by a subconscious association with the recollection of the event, of the trauma, that produced the paralysis.

Charcot was the first to teach us that we must turn to psychology for the explanation of the hysterical neurosis. Breuer and I have followed his example in a preliminary paper.[1] In this paper we show that the permanent symptoms of so-called non-traumatic hysteria (the stigmata excepted) may be explained

[1] See No. II of this volume, above, p. 24.

by the same mechanism that Charcot recognized in traumatic paralyses. But we also give the reasons why these symptoms persist and why they can be cured by a special form of hypnotic psychotherapy. Every occurrence, every psychic impression is supplied with a certain affective value (*Affektbetrag*), of which the ego rids itself either by means of a motor reaction or by a process of mental association. If the person cannot or will not free himself of this excess, the memory of the impression acquires the importance of a trauma and becomes the cause of the permanent symptoms of hysteria. When the impression remains subconscious its elimination is impossible. We have called this theory: *Das Abreagieren der Reizzuwächse* (the abreaction of an accumulation of stimuli).

To sum up, I think that it is quite in harmony with our general conception of hysteria, formed from the teachings of Charcot, to state that the lesion in hysterical paralyses consists of nothing but the inaccessibility of the concept of the organ or function to the associations of the conscious ego; that this purely functional change (the concept itself being intact) is caused by the fixation of that concept in subconscious association with the memory of the trauma; and that this concept cannot become free or accessible as long as the affective value of the psychic trauma has not been eliminated by an adequate motor reaction or a conscious psychic process. Even if this mechanism does not take place, if a direct auto-suggestive idea is always necessary in an hysterical paralysis, as in the traumatic cases of Charcot, we have succeeded in showing what the nature of the lesion, or rather of the change, in hysterial paralysis may be, so as to explain the differences between it and organic cerebral paralysis.

IV

THE DEFENCE NEURO-PSYCHOSES[1]

An endeavour to provide a psychological theory of acquired hysteria, many phobias and obsessions, and certain hallucinatory psychoses.

(1894)

After a close study of several patients suffering from phobias and obsessions a tentative explanation of these symptoms forced itself upon me; and as it later enabled me successfully to divine the origin of similar pathological ideas in other cases, I consider it worthy of publication and of further tests. Along with this 'psychological theory of phobias and obsessions', observation of these patients has resulted in a contribution to the theory of hysteria, or rather an alteration in it, which appears to account for an important characteristic common both to hysteria and to the neuroses mentioned above. Further, I had opportunities of gaining some insight into the psychological mechanism of a form of disease that is undoubtedly of mental origin, and then found that the tentative point of view I had adopted established an intelligible connection between these psychoses and the two neuroses mentioned. At the end of this essay I shall bring forward an hypothesis which I have employed in all three cases.

I

Let me begin with the alteration that in my view we are called upon to make in the theory of the hysterical neurosis.

---

[1] First published in the *Neurologisches Zentralblatt*, 1894, Nos. 10 and 11. [Translated by John Rickman.]

Since the publication of the fine work carried out by P. Janet, J. Breuer and others, it may be taken as generally acknowledged that the syndrome of hysteria, in so far as it permits of understanding up to the present, justifies the concept of a splitting of consciousness, with the formation of separate psychical groups; opinions are less definite, however, concerning the origin of this splitting of consciousness and the part which this character plays in the structure of the hysterical neurosis.

According to Janet's theory[1] the splitting of consciousness is a primary feature of the hysterical change. It is dependent on an inborn weakness in the capacity for psychical synthesis, on the narrowness of the 'field of consciousness' (*champ du conscience*) which in the form of a psychic stigma is evidence of the degeneration of hysterical persons.

In contradistinction to Janet's view, which seems to me to admit of many and various objections, we have that advocated by J. Breuer in our joint publication[2]. According to Breuer, the 'foundation and condition' of hysteria is the occurrence of peculiar dream-like states of consciousness with diminished capacity for association, for which he suggests the name 'hypnoid states'. The splitting of consciousness is then secondary and acquired; it occurs because the ideas which emerge in hypnoid states are cut off from associative connection with the remaining contents of consciousness.

I can now bring forward evidence of two other more extreme forms of hysteria in which it is impossible to regard the splitting of consciousness as primary in Janet's sense. In the first of these forms I repeat-

[1] *Etat mental des hystériques*, Paris, 1893 and 1894. — Quelques définitions récentes de l'hystérie, *Archives de Neurologie*, 1893, XXXV—XXXVI.

[2] See No. II of this volume, above, p. 24.

edly succeeded in demonstrating that the splitting of the contents of consciousness is the consequence of a voluntary act on the part of the patient; that is to say, it is instituted by an effort of will, the motive of which is discoverable. By this I do not of course mean that the patient intends to produce a splitting of his consciousness; the patient's aim is a different one, but instead of attaining its end it produces a splitting of consciousness.

In the third form of hysteria, as shown by the mental analysis of intelligent patients, the splitting of consciousness plays an insignificant part, or perhaps none at all. These are the cases in which all that had happened was that the reaction to traumatic stimuli had failed to occur, so that they are accordingly dissolved and cured by 'abreaction'[1]—they are the pure 'retention' hysterias.

In connection with what I have to say about phobias and obsessions I shall here deal only with the second form of hysteria, which for reasons that will soon be evident I shall designate as *defence hysteria*, and distinguish by this name from *hypnoid* and *retention hysteria*. I may also provisionally represent my cases of defence hysteria as cases of 'acquired hysteria', because there was in them no question either of grave hereditary taint or of individual atrophic degeneration.

These patients whom I analysed had enjoyed good mental health up to the time at which an intolerable idea presented itself within the content of their ideational life; that is to say, until their ego was confronted by an experience, an idea, a feeling, arousing an affect so painful that the person resolved to forget it, since he had no confidence in his power

[1] See No. II of this volume, above, p. 24.

to resolve the incompatibility between the unbearable idea and his ego by the processes of thought.

Such unbearable ideas develop in women chiefly in connection with sexual experiences and sensations, and the patients can recollect with the most satisfactory minuteness their efforts at defence—their resolution to 'push the thing out', not to think of it, to suppress it. I will give from my experience some examples which I could easily multiply: A young girl who disapproved of herself because while nursing her sick father she had let her mind dwell on the thought of a young man who had made a slight erotic impression on her; a governess who had fallen in love with her employer and had resolved to thrust this affection from her mind because it appeared to her incompatible with her pride; and so on.[1]

I do not of course assert that an effort of will to thrust such things out of the mind is a pathological act, nor am I able to say whether and in what manner intentional forgetting is successful in people who remain healthy, although subject to similar mental impressions. I only know that this kind of 'forgetting' did not succeed with the patients whom I analysed, but led to various pathological reactions, giving rise either to hysteria, or to an obsession, or to an hallucinatory psychosis. The ability to bring about by an effort of will one of these states, which are all of them associated with splitting of consciousness, is to be regarded as the manifestation of a pathological disposition—which, however, is not necessarily identical with personal or hereditary 'degeneration'.

In regard to the intermediate processes between the patient's effort of will and the onset of the neurotic symptom, I have formed an opinion which may be

---

[1] These examples are more fully described in *Studien über Hysterie*, Breuer and Freud. 1895.

expressed in the customary psychological abstractions somewhat as follows: The task which the ego undertakes in defence—of treating the unbearable idea as '*non arrivée*'—is absolutely insoluble; both the memory-trace and the affect attached to the idea are there once and for all, and it is no longer possible to extirpate them. But it amounts to an approximate fulfilment of this task if the ego succeeds in transforming a strong idea into a weak one, in depriving it of its affect—the quantity of excitation with which the idea is charged. The weak idea will then make practically no demands on the work of association; the quantity of excitation, however, which is then detached from the idea, must be utilized in another direction.

Up to this point the processes are the same in hysteria and in phobias and obsessions; from now onwards their ways diverge. In hysteria the unbearable idea is rendered innocuous by the quantity of excitation attached to it being transmuted into some bodily form of expression, a process for which I should like to propose the name of *conversion*.

The conversion may be either total or partial, and it proceeds along the line of the motor or sensory innervation that is more or less intimately related to the traumatic experience. Thus the ego succeeds in resolving the incompatibility within itself; but instead it has burdened itself with a memory-symbol, which dwells in consciousness, like a sort of parasite, either in the form of a persistent motor innervation or else as a constantly recurring hallucinatory sensation, and remains until a reversion takes place in the opposite direction. The memory-trace of the repressed idea is not, however, annihilated by this process; on the contrary, from now onwards it forms the nucleus of a secondary psychical group.

I will only add a few more words to this conception of the psycho-physical processes in hysteria. When once such a nucleus of an hysterical splitting has been formed owing to a 'traumatic' factor it will be developed by the influence of other factors (which might be called 'auxiliary traumatic' factors) as soon as an impression of a similar kind, subsequently experienced, succeeds in breaking through the barriers erected by the will, in furnishing the weakened idea with fresh affect and in re-establishing for a time an associative connection between the two psychical groups—until a further conversion creates a defence against it. The distribution of excitation thus brought about in hysteria proves as a rule an unstable one; the excitation which is directed into a wrong channel (into somatic innervation) now and then finds its way back to the idea from which it was detached, and then compels the subject either to undertake the work of associative absorption or else to discharge it by the way of hysterical attacks—a conclusion which is supported by the familiar opposition between the hysterical attack and chronic symptoms. Breuer's cathartic method achieves its results by deliberately effecting such a re-transmutation of the excitation from the somatic into the mental field, in order then to enforce a resolution of the opposed elements by a process of thought and a discharge of the excitation in speech.

The conclusion that the splitting of consciousness in acquired hysteria is based on an act of will also explains with surprising simplicity the remarkable fact that hypnosis regularly widens the narrowed consciousness of the hysteric and makes the psychical group which has been split off accessible. Indeed, we know it to be a peculiarity of all sleep-like conditions that they abrogate that distribution of excitation upon which the 'will' of the conscious personality depends.

Thus we can see that the characteristic factor in hysteria is not to be found in the splitting of consciousness but in the *capacity for conversion*, and we may assume that the psycho-physical capacity to transmute such large quantities of excitation into somatic innervation is an important element of the disposition to hysteria, which in other respects is still unknown.

This capacity does not in itself preclude mental health and leads to hysteria only where there is some mental incompatibility or an accumulation of excitation. With this new turn in the theory Breuer and I approach Oppenheim's[1] and Strümpell's[2] well-known definition of hysteria, and recede from Janet[3] who assigns too great importance to the splitting of consciousness as a characteristic of hysteria. The presentation here given may claim to have rendered the relation between conversion and the hysterical splitting of consciousness intelligible.

II

If the capacity for conversion does not exist in a person predisposed to hysteria and yet the separation of its affect from an unbearable idea is nevertheless

---

[1] Oppenheim: Hysteria is an intensified expression of emotion. The 'expression of emotion', however, represents that quantity of the psychical excitation which normally undergoes conversion.

[2] Strümpell: In hysteria the disturbance lies in the psycho-physical sphere, where body and mind have their connection with each other.

[3] In the second edition of his ingenious paper, '*Quelques definitions, etc.*', Janet has himself dealt with the objection that splitting of consciousness occurs also in the psychoses and in psychasthenia, so-called, but in my judgement he has not solved the difficulty satisfactorily. It is essentially this objection that has forced him to regard hysteria as a form of degeneration. He cannot, however, adequately distinguish the hysterical splitting of consciousness from the psychotic and other such forms by any characterization.

undertaken as a defence against the latter, then this affect must persist in the psychical sphere. Thus weakened, the idea remains present in consciousness, detached from all associations; but its affect, now freed from it, attaches itself to other ideas which are not in themselves unbearable, but which through this 'false connection' grow to be obsessions. This is shortly the psychological theory of obsessions and phobias which I mentioned to start with.

I will now enumerate the various elements necessary to the structure of this theory that admit of direct proof, and then describe those that I have myself supplied. Apart from the final result of the process, that is, the obsession, it is possible in the first place to demonstrate the ultimate source of the affect which is now falsely attached to some other idea. In all the cases I have analysed it was in the sexual life that a painful affect—of precisely the same quality as that attaching to the obsession—had originated. On theoretical grounds it is not impossible that this affect may at times arise in other spheres; I have merely to state that hitherto I have not discovered any other origin of it. Incidentally, it is easy to see that it is precisely in regard to the sexual life that unbearable ideas most frequently arise.

Further, we have the most unequivocal utterances on the part of patients in proof of the effort of will, the attempt at defence, upon which the theory lays emphasis; and in at least a number of cases the patients themselves will inform us of the fact that the phobia or obsession first made its appearance after this effort of will had apparently succeeded in its aim. 'Once something very disagreeable happened to me, and I did my utmost to thrust it out of my mind, to think no more about it. Finally I succeeded, but then I got this, which since then I have never been rid of.' With these words a patient confirmed the chief points of the theory I have developed here.

Not all those who suffer from obsessions are themselves so clear about the origin of them. As a rule, when one draws these patients' attention to the original idea of a sexual nature, the answer is, 'It can't come from that; indeed, I thought very little about that. For a moment I was scared, but I turned my mind to something else and since then it hasn't troubled me.' In this frequent objection we have a proof that the obsession represents a substitute or surrogate for the unbearable sexual idea, and has taken its place in consciousness.

Between the patient's effort of will which successfully represses the intolerable sexual idea, and the appearance of the obsessional idea, which though having little intensity in itself is now endowed with incomprehensibly strong affect, there lies a gap which the theory here developed aims at filling in. The detachment of the sexual idea from its affect and the connection of the latter with another idea, suited to it but not intolerable, are processes which occur outside consciousness—they may be presumed but they cannot be proved by any clinical-psychological analysis. Perhaps it would be more correct to say: These processes are not of a psychical nature at all, but are physical processes the psychical consequences of which are so represented as if what is expressed by the words 'detachment of the idea from its affect and false connection of the latter' had really happened.

Alongside the cases which show the unbearable sexual idea followed subsequently by the obsession, there is another series in which obsessions and painful sexual ideas are present simultaneously. We cannot very well call the latter 'sexual obsessions', for *one* essential feature of obsessions is missing from them;

they are fully justified, whereas the painfulness of the ordinary obsession constitutes a problem for both physician and patient. So far as I have been able to see in cases of this kind, it appears that in them a perpetual defence is going on against sexual ideas continually arising anew; that is, we are here concerned with an operation that has not yet been completed.

As long as they are conscious of the sexual origin of their obsessions, the patients often keep them concealed. When they complain about them, they as a rule express their astonishment that they are subject to the affect in question—that they feel anxious, or that they have such and such an impulse, and so on. To the experienced physician this affect appears, on the contrary, to be justified and comprehensible; he only finds it surprising that an affect of that kind should be associated with an inappropriate idea. The affect of the obsession appears to him, in other words, to be *dislocated* or *transposed*, and if he is proceeding on the assumptions here laid down he can in a great number of cases attempt its re-translation into the sexual.

Any idea which is either suited by nature to be associated with an affect of this quality or else bears a certain relation to the unbearable idea—in consequence of which it appears practicable to employ it as a surrogate for the latter—may be made use of in secondary connection with the detached affect. Thus for example, an unattached anxiety, the sexual origin of which the patient is unable to recall, will seize upon the common primary phobias of mankind in regard to animals, thunderstorms, darkness and the like, or upon things which are manifestly associated with the sexual in some way or other, such as urination, defæcation, defilement and contagion generally.

The ego gains considerably less advantage by choosing the method of *transposition* of affect as a measure of defence than it does by the hysterical conversion of psychical excitation into somatic innervation. The affect which the ego had to endure remains unchanged and undiminished, just as before—the only difference being that the unbearable idea is suppressed and cut off from recollection. The repressed ideas then form again the nucleus of a second psychical group, which, as it seems to me, is accessible even without the aid of hypnosis. If in phobias and obsessions the striking symptoms which in hysteria accompany the formation of an independent psychical group fail to appear, this is probably because in the former the whole transformation takes place within the psychical sphere—the relation between psychical excitation and somatic innervation has undergone no change.

To illustrate what has been said concerning obsessions I will give a few examples, which are probably typical:

1. A young girl suffered from obsessive reproaches. If she read in the papers about counterfeiting coinage the thought occurred to her that she also had forged coins; if an unknown criminal had committed a murder she asked herself anxiously whether she had not done the deed. At the same time she was quite conscious of the absurdity of these obsessive reproaches. This sense of guilt gained for a time such an influence over her that her critical faculty was stifled, so that she accused herself to her relations and her physician of having really committed all these crimes (psychosis through simple intensification —overwhelming-psychosis—*Überwältigungspsychose*). A close examination then revealed the source in which her sense of guilt arose: Accidentally stimulated by

a voluptuous sensation, she had allowed herself to be led astray by a friend into masturbation and had practised it for years, with full knowledge of her wrong-doing and accompanied by most intense self-reproaches, which as usual were of no avail. An excessive indulgence after attending a ball had evoked the intensification leading to the psychosis. After a few months of treatment and close watching the patient was cured.

2. Another young girl had suffered from the dread of being forced to pass water and wet herself ever since the time when an impulse of this kind had really obliged her to leave a concert during a performance. This phobia had gradually made her completely unable to enjoy herself or to go into society. She only felt well if there was a closet near at hand to which she could have access without arousing attention. Any organic complaint justifying this lack of confidence in her control of the bladder was excluded; at home under quiet conditions and at night the urgency did not arise. A penetrating enquiry showed that the urgency had appeared for the first time in the following circumstances: A gentleman to whom she was not indifferent had been sitting not far from her at the concert; she began to think about him and to imagine how she would sit beside him as his wife. During this erotic reverie she had that bodily sensation which is to be compared with erection in men and which in her case—I do not know if it is always so—ended with a slight desire to micturate. She became greatly frightened by the sexual sensation, to which she was otherwise quite accustomed, because she had resolved within herself to overcome her affection for this man as well as for all others, and the next moment the affect transferred itself to the accompanying desire to

micturate and compelled her to leave the hall after a very painful struggle. In her life she was so prudish that she positively shuddered at anything sexual and could not even contemplate the thought of marrying; on the other hand, she was sexually so hyperæsthetic that during every erotic reverie, which she willingly indulged in, that pleasurable sensation appeared. The erection was always accompanied by the desire to micturate which, up to the time of the scene at the concert, had made no impression on her. Treatment led to a nearly complete mastery of the phobia.

3. A young woman who in five years of married life had had only one child complained to me of an obsessive impulse to throw herself from the window or balcony, and also of the fear of stabbing her child which seized her at the sight of a sharp knife. She confessed that marital relations seldom occurred, and only with precautions against conception; but she added that this was no privation to her as she was not of a sensual nature. I ventured to tell her that at the sight of a man she had erotic ideas and that she had therefore lost confidence in herself and regarded herself as a depraved person, capable of anything. The re-translation of the obsession into the sexual was successful; in tears she confessed at once to her long-concealed misery in her marriage and later on related in addition some painful thoughts of an unchanged sexual nature, such as the often-recurring sensation of something forcing itself under her skirts.

I have turned experiences of this kind to therapeutic advantage by re-directing the attention of patients with phobias and obsessions, in spite of all their protestations, back to the repressed sexual ideas and, where feasible, in blocking the source whence they arose. I naturally cannot assert that *all* phobias and obsessions arise in the manner here described; for, first, my experience of them embraces only a limited number as compared with the relative frequency of these neuroses, and secondly, I myself know that these 'psychasthenic' symptoms, as Janet terms them, are not all to be estimated alike.[1] There are, for example, pure hysterical phobias. I believe, however, that the mechanism of transposition of affect will be found to exist in the great majority of phobias and obsessions; and I would therefore urge that these neuroses, which are as often found in an isolated form as combined with hysteria or neurasthenia, should not be loosely classified together with ordinary neurasthenia, in which there is absoltely no ground for assuming a psychical mechanism of the principal symptoms.

III

In both the cases described above defence against an unbearable idea was effected by detachment of its affect from it; the idea itself remained in consciousness, although weakened and isolated. Now there exists a very much more energetic and successful kind of defence, which takes the following form: the ego rejects the unbearable idea together with its associated affect and behaves as if the idea had never occurred to the person at all. But, as soon as this process has been successfully carried through, the person in question will have developed a psychosis, and his state can only be described as one of 'hallu-

[1] The group ot typical phobias, of which agoraphobia is a model, cannot be traced back to the psychical mechanism mentioned above; on the contrary, the mechanism of agoraphobia differs from that of true obsessions, and of the phobias derived from them, in *one* decisive particular—there is here no repressed idea from which the affect of anxiety would be detached. The anxiety of these phobias has another origin.

cinatory confusion'. A single example will serve to illustrate this.

A young girl gave her first impulsive affection to a man and firmly believed in the return of her love. As a matter of fact she was mistaken; the young man had another motive for visiting the house. Disappointments were not spared her; first of all she defended herself against her experiences by means of hysterical conversion, thus preserving her belief that he would one day come and seek her hand; but at the same time she felt unhappy and ill on account of incomplete conversion and of the perpetual experience of fresh painful impressions. Finally on a certain day, the day of a family festival, she waited for him in a state of intense excitement. The day wore on without his coming; after all the trains by which he could arrive had gone by, her condition passed into one of hallucinatory confusion. He *is come*, she hears his voice in the garden, hastens downstairs in her night-dress to receive him. From that time she lived for two months in a happy dream, of which the content was that he is there, ever by her side, everything is as it was a little while ago (before the time of the disappointment against which she had so strenuously defended herself). The hysteria and the depression of spirits were both overcome; nothing of the latter period of doubt and suffering was alluded to during her illness; she was happy as long as she was left undisturbed, and only raved when some circumstance of her surroundings prevented her from carrying out the logical promptings of her blissful dream. This psychosis, which at the time of its occurrence had been unintelligible, was explained ten years later with the aid of an hypnotic analysis.

The fact to which I now wish to call attention is that the content of such an hallucinatory psychosis consists precisely in the accentuation of the very idea which was first threatened by the experience occasioning the outbreak of the illness. One is therefore justified in saying that the ego has averted the unbearable idea by a flight into psychosis; and the process by which this result is obtained again withdraws itself out of range of self-perception as well as of psychological-clinical analysis. It is to be regarded as the expression of a high degree of pathological predisposition and may perhaps be described somewhat as follows: The ego has broken away from the unbearable idea; but, the latter being inseparably bound up with a part of reality, in so far as the ego achieves this result it has also cut itself loose from reality, totally or in part. In my opinion, this is the condition under which certain ideas acquire hallucinatory vividness, and consequently when this form of defence is successfully carried through the person finds himself in a state of hallucinatory confusion.

I have very few analyses of psychoses of this kind at my disposal; but I think we must here be concerned with a type of psychical illness that is very frequently developed, for in no insane asylum are analogous examples wanting—for instance, the mother who, falling ill after the loss of her baby, is to be seen incessantly rocking a log of wood in her arms, or the jilted bride arrayed in all her finery who has for years been awaiting her betrothed.

It is perhaps not superfluous to point out that the three modes of defence here described, together with the three forms of illness to which they lead, may all be combined in the same person. The simultaneous appearance of phobias and hysterical symptoms, observed so often in practice, is one of those factors which render it difficult to distinguish hysteria in a clear-cut manner from other neuroses, and make it necessary to set up the category of 'mixed neuroses'. To be sure, hallucinatory confusion is not often compatible with a continuance of hysteria, nor of obsessions, as a rule. On the other hand, it is not rare for a defence psychosis to break out episodically in the course of an hysterical or mixed neurosis.

I should like finally to dwell for a moment on the hypothesis which I have made use of in the exposition of the defence neuroses. I mean the conception that among the psychic functions there is something which should be differentiated (an amount of affect, a sum of excitation), something having all the attributes of a quantity—although we possess no means of measuring it—a something which is capable of increase, decrease, displacement and discharge, and which extends itself over the memory-traces of an idea like an electric charge over the surface of the body. We can apply this hypothesis, which by the way already underlies our theory of 'abreaction',[1] in the same sense as the physicist employs the conception of a fluid electric current. For the present it is justified by its utility in correlating and explaining diverse psychical conditions.

[1] See No. II of this volume, above, p. 24.

V

THE JUSTIFICATION FOR DETACHING FROM NEURASTHENIA A PARTICULAR SYNDROME: THE ANXIETY-NEUROSIS[1]

(1894)

It is difficult to say anything of general validity concerning neurasthenia so long as we allow this name to cover all that Beard included under the term. In my opinion, nothing but gain to neuropathology can result if we make an attempt to distinguish from neurasthenia proper all those neurotic disturbances of which the symptoms, on the one hand, are more closely related to one another than to the typical symptoms of neurasthenia (headache, spinal irritation, and dyspepsia with flatulence and constipation) and, on the other hand, show in their ætiology and their mechanism essential differences from typical neurasthenia. If we accept this plan we shall soon obtain a more or less uniform picture of neurasthenia; and shall then be in a position to differentiate more sharply than had hitherto been possible between neurasthenia proper and various kinds of pseudo-neurasthenia, such as the clinical picture of the organically determined nasal reflex neurosis, the nervous disorders of the cachexias and arterio-sclerosis, the early stages of general paralysis of the insance and of the psychoses. Further, it will be possible—as Möbius proposed—to eliminate many of the nervous conditions of the hereditarily degen-

---

[1] First published in the *Neurologisches Zentralblatt,* 1895, Nr. 2. [Translated by John Rickman.]

erate; and we shall also find good reason to include under melancholia many neuroses (especially intermittent and periodic types) which are to-day called neurasthenia. But the most decisive change of all will be introduced if we decide to distinguish from neurasthenia the syndrome I here propose to describe, which fulfils with unusual completeness the conditions set forth above. The symptoms of this syndrome are clinically much more closely related to one another than to those of neurasthenia proper (that is, they frequently appear together and replace each other during the course of the illness), while the ætiology and mechanism of this neurosis are essentially different from what remains of true neurasthenia after this subtraction has been made from it.

I call this syndrome 'Anxiety-Neurosis', because all its component elements can be grouped round the central symptom of 'morbid anxiety' and because individually they each have a definite connection with this. I believed that this conception of the symptoms of the anxiety-neurosis had originated with myself until an interesting paper by E. Hecker[1] came into my hands, in which I found the same idea expounded with the most satisfying clearness and completeness. Although Hecker recognizes certain symptoms as equivalents or incomplete manifestations of an anxiety-attack, he does not separate them from neurasthenia as I propose to do; this is evidently due to his not having taken into account the difference in the ætiological conditions of the two forms of disease. When this last difference between them is fully recognized, we

---

[1] E. Hecker: Über larvierte und abortive Angstzustände bei Neurasthenie. *Zentralblatt für Nervenheilkunde*, Dec. 1893. Morbid anxiety is actually quoted as one of the principal symptoms of neurasthenia in a paper by Kaan: Der neurasthenische Angstaffekt bei Zwangsvorstellungen und der primordiale Grübelzwang. Wien, 1893.

have no longer any motive for designating anxiety symptoms by the same term as those of neurasthenia proper; for the purpose served by giving a name, however arbitrary it may be in other respects, is above all that of enabling us more easily to form generalizations.

I. CLINICAL SYMPTOMATOLOGY OF ANXIETY-NEUROSIS

What I call 'anxiety-neurosis' manifests itself in a partial and in a complete form, and may be met with either as an isolated state or combined with other neuroses. The cases which are more or less complete and at the same time isolated are naturally those which in particular give support to the idea that anxiety-neurosis is a clinical entity. In other cases where there is a complex of symptoms corresponding to a mixed neurosis, we have to distinguish and separate from it those symptoms which belong neither to neurasthenia nor to hysteria and so on, but to anxiety-neurosis.

The clinical picture of anxiety-neurosis comprises the following symptoms:

1. *General irritability*. This is a common nervous symptom and as such belongs to many nervous conditions. I include it here because it invariably appears with anxiety-neurosis and is important theoretically. An increase of irritability always signifies an accumulation of excitation or an inability to tolerate such an accumulation, that is, an absolute or a relative accumulation of excitation. One form of expression of this increase of irritability —auditory hyperæsthesia—seems to me worthy of special mention; this undue sensitiveness to noise is undoubtedly explicable on the basis of the close inborn connection between auditory impressions and fright. Auditory hyperæsthesia is frequently a cause

of sleeplessness, more than one form of which belongs to the anxiety-neurosis.

2. *Anxious expectation.* I cannot better describe the condition I have in mind than by this name and by appending a few examples. A woman who suffers from anxious expectation will imagine every time her husband coughs, when he has a cold, that he is going to have influenzal pneumonia, and will at once see his funeral in her mind's eye. If when she is coming towards the house she sees two people standing by her front door, she cannot avoid the thought that one of her children has fallen out of the window; if the bell rings, then someone is bringing news of a death, and so on; whereas on all these occasions there is no particular ground for exaggerating a mere possibility.

Anxious expectation of course fades off imperceptibly into normal anxiousness. It comprises all that is covered by the word 'nervousness'—apprehensiveness, the tendency to look on the dark side of things; but at every opportunity it exceeds the limits of this plausible form of nervousness and is frequently recognized by the patient himself as a kind of compulsion. For one form of anxious expectation—that relating to one's own health—we may reserve the old term *hypochondria.* Hypochondria does not always coincide with a high degree of anxious expectation; in general it requires as a preliminary condition the presence of paræsthesias and disagreeable bodily sensations, and therefore hypochondria is the form favoured by true neurasthenics when they fall victims to anxiety-neurosis, as they often do.

The tendency to *pangs of conscience,* scrupulousness and pedantry may be a further expression of anxious expectation, a tendency which is especially frequent among morally sensitive people and likewise ranges from the normal to an exaggeration known as *folie du doute*.

Anxious expectation is the nuclear symptom of this neurosis; it clearly reveals, too, something of the theory of it. We may perhaps say that there is here *a quantum of anxiety in a free-floating condition*, which in any state of expectation controls the selection of ideas, and is ever ready to attach itself to any suitable ideational content.

3. This is not the only way in which apprehensiveness—which is not usually present in consciousness but is ever lying in wait—can express itself. It can, on the contrary, erupt suddenly into consciousness without being called forth by any train of thought, and thus bring about an *anxiety-attack*. An anxiety-attack of this kind either consists of a feeling of anxiety alone without any associated idea, or associated with the nearest interpretation, such as sudden death, a stroke, or approaching insanity; or else the feeling of anxiety is combined with paræsthesias (similar to the hysterical aura); or finally, together with the feeling of anxiety there is an accompanying disturbance of any one or more of the bodily functions, such as respiration, heart's action, vasomotor innervation, or glandular activity. The patient lays stress on one or other of these symptoms, and complains of 'heart-spasms', 'difficulty in breathing', 'drenching sweats', 'ravenous hunger' and the like; and in his description the feeling of anxiety frequently recedes into the background or is described quite vaguely as a 'feeling of illness', of 'distress , and so on.

4. It is interesting, and important diagnostically, that the degree to which these elements are combined in anxiety-attacks varies extraordinarily, and that almost every accompanying symptom can alone

constitute the attack just as well as the anxiety itself can. There are consequently *rudimentary anxiety-attacks* and *equivalents of an anxiety-attack* (all probably having the same meaning), showing a manifold and hitherto little appreciated variety of forms. A closer study of these larval anxiety-states (Hecker) and their diagnostic differentiation from other attacks should soon become a necessary piece of work in neuropathology.

I will here append a list including only those types of anxiety-attack known to me:

a. Attacks accompanied by disturbances of the *heart's action*, such as palpitation, either with transitory arhythmia, or with tachycardia of longer duration that may end in grave weakness of the heart, the differentiation from organic morbus cordis never being easy; or pseudo-angina pectoris—diagnostically a delicate problem!

b. Attacks accompanied by disturbances of *respiration*, several forms of nervous dyspnœa, attacks similar to asthma, and the like. I would emphasize that even these attacks are not always accompanied by recognizable anxiety.

c. Attacks of *sweating*, often nocturnal.

d. Attacks of *tremor* and *shuddering*, which are only too easily confounded with hysteria.

e. Attacks of *ravenous hunger*, often accompanied by giddiness.

f. Attacks of sudden *diarrhœa*.

g. Attacks of locomotor *vertigo*.

h. Attacks of so-called *congestion*, practically embracing all that has been called vasomotor neurasthenia.

i. Attacks of *parœsthesias* (but these seldom occur without anxiety or some similar feeling of distress).

5. *Awakening in fright* (the *pavor nocturnus* of adults), which is usually combined with morbid anxiety, dyspnœa, sweating and the like, is very frequently nothing but a variety of the anxiety attack. This disturbance conditions a second type of sleeplessness which also lies within the compass of anxiety-neurosis.—I have no doubt in my own mind that the *pavor nocturnus* of children also includes a type which belongs to anxiety-neurosis. The hysterical tinge, i. e. the coupling of morbid anxiety with the reproduction of some appropriate experience of dream, gives the *pavor nocturnus* of children the appearance of being something distinct; but it also appears in a pure form without dream or recurring hallucination.

6. *Vertigo* takes a prominent place in the group of symptoms of the anxiety-neurosis. Its mildest form is better described as giddiness; and its graver manifestations, 'attacks of vertigo' (with or without anxiety), constitute one of the most momentous symptoms of this disease. The dizziness of the anxiety-neurosis is neither rotatory nor is it confined to particular planes or directions as is Menière's vertigo. It belongs to the class of locomotor or coordinatory dizziness, as do the cases of oculo-motor paralysis; it consists of a specific discomfort accompanied by the feeling that the ground is rocking, the legs giving way, that one can't keep upright because one's legs are as heavy as lead and are shaking and wobbling. This dizziness never leads to a fall. I venture, however, to assert that a profound fainting fit may supervene in the place of an attack of vertigo of this kind. Other swoon-like conditions in anxiety-neurosis appear to result from cardiac collapse.

An attack of vertigo is not seldom accompanied by the worst kind of morbid anxiety, and is frequently attended by cardiac and respiratory disturbances. According to my observations the vertigo produced by heights, mountains and precipices also frequently belongs to the anxiety-neurosis; further, I do not know whether one would not be justified in recognizing alongside this the existence of a vertigo of gastric origin.

7. On the basis of chronic apprehensiveness (anxious expectation) on the one hand, and a tendency to attacks of vertigo with anxiety on the other, two groups of typical phobias develop, the first relating to common physiological dangers, the other to locomotion. To the first group belongs the fear of snakes, thunderstorms, darkness, vermin, and so on, as well as the typical moral over-sensitiveness, and the forms of '*folie du doute*'; the available anxiety is here used simply to exaggerate the aversions which are implanted instinctively in everyone. Usually, however, a phobia with obsessive strength arises only when, added to such an instinctive aversion, a reminiscence of an experience in which the anxiety could come to expression supervenes—for example, after the patient has actually experienced a thunderstorm in the open air. To attempt to explain such cases as mere continuations of strong impressions would be incorrect; what makes these experiences significant and their retention in memory of long duration is indeed simply the anxiety, which both originally and subsequently thus found a means of expression. In other words, such impressions remain potent only in cases where 'anxious expectation' is present.

The other group includes *agoraphobia* with all its accessory forms, collectively characterized by their relation to movement. We frequently find a precursory attack of vertigo as the foundation of the phobia; but I do not believe that one can postulate this every time. Occasionally we see that after a first attack of giddiness without anxiety locomotion still continues possible without hindrance, although henceforth constantly accompanied by the sensation of giddiness; but that under certain conditions, such as being alone, in narrow streets and so on, locomotion becomes impossible when once anxiety has become combined with an attack of vertigo.

The relation of these phobias to those of the obsessional neurosis, the mechanisms of which I have discussed in an earlier paper[1] in this Journal, is of the following kind: the correspondence between them is that in both an idea becomes obsessive in consequence of its being connected with an unattached affect. The mechanism of *transposition of affect* holds good therefore for both kinds of phobia; but in the phobias of the anxiety-neurosis (1) this affect is always the same, always that of anxiety; (2) it does not originate in a repressed idea, proves not reducible further by psychological analysis, and is also not amenable to psychotherapy. The mechanism of substitution does not therefore hold good for the phobias of the anxiety-neurosis.

Both kinds of phobias (or obsessional ideas) frequently appear side by side, although the atypical phobias which are based on obsessional ideas need not necessarily develop on the basis of an anxiety-neurosis. A very frequent, apparently complicated mechanism makes its appearance when the content of an originally simple phobia of the anxiety-neurosis type is replaced by another idea, the substitution being then subsequently added to the phobia. The 'protective measures' originally directed towards combating the phobia are the ideas most frequently

[1] See No. IV of this volume, above, p. 59.

employed as substitutions. Thus, for example, 'brooding mania' arises from the patient's effort to disprove that he is crazy, as his hypochondriacal phobia maintains: the hesitations and doubts, and still more the repetitions, of *folie du doute*, arise from a justifiable doubt about his own powers of correct reasoning, since he is aware of the persistent disturbance of the obsessional idea; and so on. We can therefore assert that many syndromes of the obsessional neurosis, such as *folie du doute* and the like, are also clinically, though not conceptually, to be reckoned as belonging to the anxiety-neurosis.[1]

8. Digestive processes are subject to only a few disturbances in anxiety-neurosis, but these are characteristic. Sensations such as nausea and biliousness are not at all rare, and the symptom of ravenous hunger can, by itself or in combination with others (congestions), constitute a rudimentary anxiety-attack; as a chronic condition analogous to anxious expectation we find a tendency to diarrhœa which has given rise to the queerest diagnostic mistakes. If I am not mistaken, it is this diarrhœa to which Möbius[2] has recently called attention in a short paper. I conjecture further that Peyer's reflex diarrhœa, which he derives from the disorders of the prostate,[3] is nothing but this diarrhœa of anxiety-neurosis. The deception of a reflex relationship comes about because the same factors which are active in the origin of such prostatic affections also come into play in the ætiology of anxiety-neurosis.

The behaviour of the gastro-intestinal tract in anxiety-neurosis presents a sharp contrast to the influence of neurasthenia on those functions. Mixed

[1] See No. VII of this volume, p. 128.

[2] Möbius: *Neuropathologische Beiträge*, Heft 2, 1894.

[3] Peyer: Die nervösen Affektionen des Darmes. *Wiener Klinik*, January, 1893.

cases often show the well-known 'alternation of diarrhœa and constipation'. The urgent need to micturate that occurs in the anxiety-neurosis is analogous to this diarrhœa.

9. The *parœsthesias* which may accompany attacks of vertigo or anxiety are interesting in that they (as also the sensations of the hysterical aura) become associated in a definite sequence; but I find that, in contrast to those of hysteria, these associated sensations are atypical and changing. A further similarity to hysteria ensues because a kind of *conversion*[1], which may otherwise easily be overlooked, to bodily sensations takes place in anxiety-neurosis, e. g. a conversion which takes effect in rheumatic muscles. Quite a number of rheumatic persons, so-called, who moreover are demonstrable as such, in reality suffer from anxiety-neurosis. Along with this increased sensitiveness to pain I have observed in a series of cases of anxiety-neurosis a tendency to *hallucinations* which could not be explained as hysterical.

10. Several of the symptoms mentioned which accompany or take the place of an anxiety-attack appear also in a chronic form. They are then still less easy to recognize, since the accompanying anxious sensation is less clearly recognizable than in anxiety-attacks. This is particularly true of diarrhœa, vertigo, paræsthesias. Just as an attack of vertigo may be replaced by a fainting-fit, so may chronic giddiness be replaced by a constant feeling of sinking to the ground, exhaustion, etc.

II. THE INCIDENCE AND ÆTIOLOGY OF ANXIETY-NEUROSIS

In many cases of anxiety-neurosis no ætiology is recognizable at all. It is remarkable that in such

[1] See No. IV of this volume, above, p. 59.

cases evidence of a grave hereditary taint is seldom difficult to establish.

But where there are grounds for regarding the neurosis as an acquired one, careful enquiry to that end reveals a series of injurious conditions (*noxiæ*) and influences within the sexual life as important factors in the ætiology. At first sight these appear to be very various in their nature but they soon disclose their common character, which explains the fact that they always have the same effect on the nervous system; further, they are either present alone or together with other 'ordinary' injurious factors, which latter may be regarded as having a contributory effect. As this sexual ætiology of the anxiety-neurosis is so very commonly demonstrable I feel justified *for the purpose of this short paper* in disregarding cases with a doubtful or a different ætiology.

In setting forth in greater detail the ætiological conditions under which anxiety-neurosis makes its appearance it will be advisable to treat of men and women separately. Anxiety-neurosis appears in female persons—disregarding for the moment their predisposition—in the following cases:

a. as *virginal anxiety or anxiety in adolescents.* A number of unambiguous observations has shown me that anxiety-neurosis can be evoked in maturing girls by their first meeting with the sexual problem, that is, by any more or less sudden revelation of what had hitherto been hidden, for example, seeing the sexual act, or hearing or reading something of that nature; in these cases anxiety-neurosis is typically combined with hysteria;

b. as *anxiety in the newly-married.* Young married women who remain anæsthetic during the first acts of intercourse often fall ill of an anxiety-neurosis which again disappears as soon as the anæsthesia gives way to normal sensitivity. Since the majority of young women remain healthy during a temporary anæsthesia of this kind, there are conditions necessary to the outbreak of this anxiety, which I will mention later;

c. as anxiety in women whose husbands suffer from ejaculatio præcox or from impaired potency; and

d. whose husbands practise coitus interruptus or reservatus. These cases belong together, for on analysing a large number of examples it is easy to convince oneself that they depend simply on whether the wife obtains satisfaction in coitus or not. The latter case provides the condition for the genesis of an anxiety-neurosis. On the other hand, the wife is saved from neurosis if the husband who is afflicted with ejaculatio præcox can immediately repeat the congress with a better result. Congressus reservatus by means of condoms is not injurious to the wife if she is very quickly roused and the husband very potent; if not, this kind of contraception is no less injurious than the others. Coitus interruptus is almost always harmful; though only for the wife when the husband practises it regardlessly, that is to say, when he interrupts coitus as soon as *he* is near to ejaculation without troubling himself about the stage of his wife's excitement. If on the other hand the husband waits for his wife's satisfaction then the coitus will be equivalent to the normal for her—but the husband will become a sufferer from anxiety-neurosis. I have collected and analysed a great number of observations which have provided the material for these conclusions;

e. as *anxiety in widows and voluntarily abstinent persons,* often found in typical combination with obsessional ideas;

f. as anxiety in the *climacteric* during the last great increase of sexual need.

Cases *c.*, *d.*, and *e.* embrace the conditions under which anxiety-neurosis in the female sex most frequently arises and is least dependent on hereditary predisposition. On the basis of these cases of anxiety-neurosis—curable, acquired cases—I shall try to prove that the injurious sexual condition (*noxia*) discovered in them really represents the ætiological factor of this neurosis. Before doing so, however, I will go on to discuss the sexual conditions for anxiety-neurosis in men. I propose to set up the following groups, which all have their analogies among women:

a. anxiety of the voluntarily *abstinent*, frequently combined with *defence* symptoms (obsessional ideas, hysteria). The motives which are decisive for intentional abstinence bring it about that a number of hereditarily-disposed or eccentric persons, etc. belong to this category;

b. anxiety in men during *frustrated excitement* (during an engagement to marry), in persons who (from fear of the consequences of sexual intercourse) content themselves with handling or gazing at the woman. This group of conditions (which by the way applies equally to the other sex: engagement, relationships involving sexual forbearance) furnishes the purest cases of the neurosis;

c. anxiety in men who practise coitus interruptus. As has been said already, coitus interruptus is harmful to the woman when it is practised without regard to her satisfaction; but it becomes harmful to the man if, in order to provide satisfaction for the woman, he voluntarily controls coitus and delays the ejaculation. It thus becomes intelligible that as a rule only *one* partner of a married couple practising coitus interruptus falls ill. Incidentally, coitus interruptus but rarely leads to a pure anxiety-neurosis in men; there usually results a combination of it with neurasthenia;

d. anxiety in *ageing men.* There are men who have a climacteric like women and who develop anxiety- neurosis at the time of their waning potency and increased libido.

Finally I must add two other cases which are valid for both sexes:

e. The neurasthenics who after practising masturbation fall victims to anxiety-neurosis as soon as they desist from their form of sexual gratification. These persons have rendered themselves particularly incapable of tolerating abstinence.

I observe here that in order to understand the anxiety-neurosis it is important to realize that any pronounced manifestation of it occurs only among men who are still potent and among women who are not anæsthetic. Among neurasthenics whose potency has already been seriously diminished by masturbation, the anxiety-neurosis resulting from abstinence is of a very meagre character and confines itself as a rule to hypochondria and mild chronic dizziness. The majority of women are to be regarded as 'potent'; a really impotent, i. e. really anæsthetic, woman is likewise only mildly affected by anxiety-neurosis and tolerates the injurious sexual conditions described surprisingly well.

How far beyond this we may be justified in postulating a constant relation between particular ætiological factors and particular symptoms in the complex of anxiety-neurosis, I do not yet wish to express any opinion.

f. The last of the ætiological conditions I have to bring forward appears at first sight not to be of a sexual nature at all. Anxiety-neurosis also arises (in both sexes) as a result of the factor of over-work or exhausting exertion, for example, nights of watching, sick-nursing, or even after severe illness.

The principal objection to my proposition of a sexual ætiology for the anxiety-neurosis will probably run as follows: abnormal conditions in the sexual life of the kind mentioned are found so very frequently that they must be forthcoming wherever one looks for them. Their presence in the cases of anxiety-neurosis quoted does not therefore prove that the ætiology of this neurosis is to be found in them. The number of people, moreover, who practise coitus interruptus, etc., is incomparably greater than the number of those afflicted with anxiety-neurosis and the great majority of the former tolerate this unhealthy condition quite well.

To this I have to reply that we should certainly not be right in expecting to find in the neuroses an ætiological factor of *rare* occurrence, seeing how very great their frequency admittedly is, especially that of anxiety-neurosis; also that it actually fulfils a postulate of pathology if in an ætiological enquiry the ætiological factor is proved to be more frequent than its effect, since for the latter other conditions are also required (disposition, summation of specific ætiological factors, reinforcement by other 'ordinary' injurious factors); and further, that detailed exploration of suitable cases of anxiety-neurosis proves beyond question the importance of the sexual factor. I will here confine myself to the ætiological factor of coitus interruptus only and to adducing certain observations which confirm it.

1. So long as an anxiety-neurosis in young married women is not yet established, but only appears

sporadically and disappears again spontaneously, it is possible to demonstrate that every such wave of the neurosis is traceable to a coitus lacking in satisfaction. Two days after this experience, or in persons of little resistance, on the next day, an attack of anxiety or vertigo regularly appears, bringing in its train the other symptoms of the neurosis, which all again disappear together with the attack if marital relations occur sufficiently seldom. A chance absence from home on the part of the husband, or a holiday in the mountains necessitating the separation of the couple, have a good effect; the gynæcological treatment that is usually resorted to in the first instance is beneficial because marital relations are broken off while it lasts. Strange to say, however, the success of local treatment is but transitory—and even in the mountains the neurosis reappears as soon as the husband in his turn arrives; and so forth. When a physician who understands this ætiology advises a patient in whom the neurosis is not yet established to substitute normal relations for coitus interruptus a *therapeutic* test of the statements made here is supplied. The anxiety is removed and does not return again without a fresh cause of a similar nature.

2. In the history of many cases of anxiety-neurosis both among men and women we find a striking fluctuation in the intensity of the clinical symptoms, and even in the appearance and disappearance of the whole condition. One year, they will say, was pretty good, the next was frightful; on one occasion the improvement coincided with a certain treatment which however on the next attack turned out quite useless; and so on. Now if we enquire into the number and sequence of the children and compare this record with the history of the neurosis a simple

solution results—the periods of improvement and well-being coincide with the wife's pregnancies, during which of course the need for contraception was no longer present. The treatment that had been so beneficial to the man, however, regardless of whether it was at Pfarrer Kneipp's or at a hydro-therapeutic sanatorium, was the one after which his wife had become pregnant.

3. From the anamnesis of patients we frequently find that the symptoms of anxiety-neurosis have at some definite time supplanted the symptoms of some other neurosis, for instance, neurasthenia, and have taken their place. In such a case it can quite regularly be proved that, shortly before the change in the clinical picture, a corresponding change had taken place from one to another of the various kinds of unhealthy sexual conditions possible.

Observations of this kind can be supplemented to any extent at pleasure, positively compelling the physician to acknowledge a sexual ætiology for a certain category of cases; other cases, however, which would otherwise remain quite unintelligible, can at least be understood without difficulty and classified by employing the sexual ætiology as a key to them. These are those very numerous cases in which we find everything that is also present in the previous category—the clinical symptoms of anxiety-neurosis on the one hand, and the specific factor of coitus interruptus on the other—but where something else has interposed itself as well, namely, a long interval between the ætiology we assume and its effect, and perhaps also ætiological factors of a non-sexual nature too. Take, for example, a man who has a heart-attack after receiving news of his father's death and from that time onwards suffers from anxiety-neurosis. The case is not clear, for the man was not nervous before this event; the death of the father who was well advanced in years did not occur under any special circumstances, and one must admit that the normal, expected decease of an aged father is not an experience which usually causes illness in a healthy adult. Perhaps the ætiological analysis will be clearer if I add that this man had for eleven years practised coitus interruptus and always with regard for his wife's satisfaction. The clinical symptoms at least are identical with those that appear in other persons after an unhealthy condition of the same sexual nature lasting for a short period and without the interpolation of another trauma. Other cases must be estimated similarly, that of a woman in whom anxiety-neurosis broke out after the loss of a child, or that of a student whose studies preparatory to his qualifying examination were interrupted by an anxiety-neurosis. I do not find that the effect in these cases is explained by the ostensible ætiology. One is not necessarily 'over-worked' by close study, and a healthy mother usually reacts only with normal grief to the loss of a child. More particularly, too, I should expect that the student would develop cephalasthenia through over-work, and the mother in our example hysteria. That they both develop an anxiety-neurosis induces me to lay emphasis on the fact that the mother had lived for eight years in marital coitus interruptus, and that the student had for three years had a passionate love-relationship with a 'respectable' girl whom he dared not allow to conceive.

These considerations lead to the conclusion that the specific sexual *noxia* contained in coitus interruptus at least disposes the person concerned to acquire it in those cases where it is not in itself enough to induce anxiety-neurosis. The neurosis then breaks out as soon as the influence of another ordinary injurious factor is added to the latent effect of the specific factor; the former can *reinforce the specific factor quantitatively but cannot replace it qualitatively*. The specific factor always remains decisive for the form taken by the neurosis. I hope to be able to prove this statement in regard to the ætiology of the neuroses also on a wider scale.

Some few pages back I mentioned an assumption which is not improbable in itself—namely, that a *noxia* such as coitus interruptus attains its effect by *summation*. According to the disposition of the person concerned and the other burdens on his nervous system, a longer or shorter time will be required before the effect of this summation becomes evident. Those persons who tolerate coitus interruptus apparently without harmful results are in reality becoming thereby disposed to the disorder of anxiety-neurosis, which may break out either at any time spontaneously or after an ordinary and otherwise insufficient trauma; just as the chronic alcoholic will in the end develop a cirrhosis or other illness as an effect of summation, or under the influence of a fever will go down with a delirium.

III. ATTEMPTS TO FORMULATE A THEORY OF THE ANXIETY-NEUROSIS

The following considerations can only claim the value of a preliminary tentative attempt at a theory; criticism of them should not affect the reader's acceptance of the *facts* set forth above. Moreover, this 'Theory of Anxiety-Neurosis' represents only a fragment of a more comprehensive presentation of the neuroses which increases the difficulty of assessing its value.

The material already brought forward in regard to the anxiety-neurosis has provided a few openings for some insight into its mechanism. In the first place it was surmised that we are here dealing with an accumulation of excitation; secondly, there was the exceedingly important fact that the anxiety, which underlies all the clinical symptoms of this neurosis, *is not derived from any psychical source.* A psychical origin would be present, for example, if we found as the basis of an anxiety-neurosis a single or repeated shock, justified by the circumstances, which had subsequently become the source of the readiness to anxiety. But this is not what we find; an hysteria or a traumatic neurosis may develop as a result of a single shock—an anxiety-neurosis never. Since among the causes of anxiety-neurosis coitus interruptus forces itself so much into the foreground, I thought at first that the source of the continual anxiety might lie in the fear, revived with every act, that the method might miscarry and be followed by conception. But I have found that this state of mind either in man or woman during coitus interruptus is irrelevant for the genesis of anxiety-neurosis; that women who at bottom are indifferent to the consequences of a possible conception are just as liable to the neurosis as those who shudder at the possibility, and that all depends on which of the partners forfeits satisfaction in this method of intercourse.

A further indication is furnished by the observation, not before mentioned, that in whole groups of cases anxiety-neurosis is accompanied by a very noticeable abatement of sexual libido,[1] i. e. of *psychical desire*; so that, on being told that their sufferings result from 'insufficient satisfaction', patients

[1] [This term is here used in its original sense of conscious sexual feeling; it was only later employed by the author as a technical term in his theory of mental dynamics.—Ed.]

regularly answer that that is impossible, because all their need for it has now disappeared. From all these data: that an accumulation of excitation is involved; that the anxiety which probably represents this accumulated excitation is of somatic origin, so that it is somatic excitation which is accumulated; further, that the somatic excitation is of a sexual nature and that a decline in the psychical share in the sexual process goes along with it—all these data prepare our minds for the statement that *the mechanism of anxiety-neurosis is to be sought in the deflection of somatic sexual excitation from the psychical field, and in an abnormal use of it, due to this deflection.*

This conception of the mechanism of anxiety-neurosis becomes clearer if we accept the following view of the sexual process, which relates primarily to men. In the sexually mature male organism somatic sexual excitation is produced—probably continuously—and periodically acts as a psychical stimulus. In order to define this idea more clearly, let us interpolate that this somatic sexual excitation takes the form of pressure on the walls of the vesiculæ seminales which are lined with nerve-endings; this visceral excitation will then actually develop continuously, but only when it reaches a certain height will it be sufficient to overcome the resistance in the paths of conduction to the cerebral cortex and express itself as a psychical stimulus. Thereupon the constellation of sexual ideas existing in the mind becomes charged with energy and a psychical state of libidinous tension comes into existence, bringing with it the impulse to relieve this tension. The necessary psychical relief can only be effected by what I shall describe as a *specific* or *adequate activity*. For the male sexual impulse this adequate activity consists in a complicated spinal reflex act resulting in the relief of the tension at these nerve-endings and in all the preparatory psychical processes necessary to induce this reflex. Nothing but the adequate activity would be effective; for, once it has reached the required level, the somatic sexual excitation is continuously transmuted into psychical excitation; the activity which will free the nerve-endings from burdensome pressure and so abolish the whole of the somatic excitation present, thus allowing the subcortical tracts to re-establish their resistance, must absolutely be carried into operation.

I will refrain from describing more complicated forms of the sexual process in this manner. I will only add the statement that in essentials this formula is applicable also to women, notwithstanding the confusion introduced into the problem by all the artificial arresting and stunting that the female sexual impulse undergoes. In women also we must postulate a somatic sexual excitation, and a condition in which this excitation becomes a psychical stimulus, evoking libido and the impulse to a specific activity to which sensual pleasure is attached. Where women are concerned, however, we cannot state what is the process analogous to the relief of tension in the vesiculæ seminales.

The ætiology of neurasthenia proper as well as of anxiety-neurosis can now be brought within the compass of this conception of the sexual process. Neurasthenia arises whenever a less adequate relief (activity) takes the place of the adequate one, thus, when masturbation or spontaneous emission replaces normal coitus under the most favourable conditions; while anxiety-neurosis is produced by all those factors which prevent the somatic sexual excitation from being assimilated psychically. The clinical symptoms of anxiety-neurosis appear when the somatic sexual excitation that is deflected from the mind is expended subcortically in quite inadequate reactions.

I shall now try to test the ætiological conditions of anxiety-neurosis given above, in order to see whether they show the common character I have ascribed to them. The first ætiological factor in men that I mentioned is voluntary abstinence. Abstinence consists in foregoing the specific activity which otherwise follows upon libido. Privation of this kind can have two consequences, namely, that the somatic excitation becomes augmented by accumulation, and secondly, that it is then dissipated along other paths, through which it may find its discharge more easily than along the path to the mind. Libido will therefore subside again and the excitation will express itself instead subcortically as anxiety. In cases where libido does not subside or where the somatic excitation is expended by a short cut in emissions, or where it actually becomes exhausted in consequence of being restrained, anything else may arise, but not anxiety-neurosis. Abstinence leads to anxiety-neurosis in the way described. Abstinence is also the agent in the second ætiological group, that of frustrated excitement. The third case, that of coitus reservatus with regard for the woman, acts by disturbing the psychical state of preparedness for the sexual process, in that it adds to the task of dealing with the sexual affect another, a deflecting, psychical task. In consequence of this psychical deflection libido also gradually subsides, the further developments being then the same as in abstinence. Anxiety in ageing men (the male climacteric) requires another explanation. There is no reduction in libido here; but, just as during the climacteric in women, such an increase in the production of somatic excitation occurs that the psyche proves relatively unable to master it.

There is no greater difficulty in bringing the ætiological conditions in women within the scope of our theory than in the case of men. Virginal anxiety is a particularly clear example; the constellations of ideas to which the somatic sexual excitation should become attached are not yet sufficiently developed. In anæsthetic newly-married women anxiety only appears when the first acts of intercourse arouse a sufficient quantity of somatic excitation. When local indications of the state of excitement (such as spontaneous local sensations, desire to micturate and the like) are lacking, then anxiety is also absent. In cases where intercourse involves ejaculatio præcox or coitus interruptus, the explanation is similar to that given for men—libido gradually declines from the psychically unsatisfying act, while the excitation called forth by the act is expended subcortically. An *estrangement* between the somatic and the psychical in the course taken by sexual excitation is established sooner and is more difficult to remove in women than in men. In widowhood and in voluntary abstinence, as also in the climacteric, the process is the same in women as in men; although in abstinence there must also be the additional factor of an intentional repression of sexual ideas which the abstinent woman battling with desire must frequently resolve upon, and similarly, at the time of the menopause, the detestation with which the ageing woman regards the unduly increased libido must come into operation.

The two last ætiological conditions enumerated also seem to fall into line without difficulty.

The tendency to anxiety in masturbators who

have become neurasthenic is explained by the fact that these persons very easily pass into a condition of 'abstinence' after they have for so long been accustomed immediately to discharge every access of somatic excitation, however small, although not in a normal manner. Finally, the last case, in which anxiety-neurosis arises from serious illness, overwork, exhausting sick-nursing, etc., may be brought into relation with the mode of action of coitus interruptus and then find a simple interpretation: by reason of the deflection of interest the mind is no longer capable of mastering the somatic sexual excitation, a task which is continuously incumbent on it. We know to what a low level libido can sink under these conditions; and we have here an excellent example of a *neurosis which has, it is true, no sexual ætiology, but nevertheless shows a sexual mechanism.*

The theory here developed shows the symptoms of anxiety-neurosis to be in some measure *surrogates* for the specific activity which should follow upon sexual excitation, but has not done so. In further corroboration of this I may point out that even in normal coitus the excitation expresses itself also in accelerated breathing, palpitations, sweating, congestion and so on. In the corresponding anxiety-attacks of our neurosis we see the dyspnœa, palpitations, etc. of coitus in an isolated and exaggerated form.

The question may now be asked: Why does the nervous system under such conditions—of psychical incapacity to master sexual excitation—take on the particular affective state of anxiety? The reply may be indicated somewhat as follows: The psyche develops the affect of anxiety when it feels itself incapable of dealing (by an adequate reaction) with a task (danger) approaching it externally; it develops the neurosis of anxiety when it feels itself unequal to the task of mastering (sexual) excitation arising endogenously. That is to say, *it acts as if it had projected this excitation into the outer world.* The affect and the neurosis corresponding to it stand in a close relation to each other; the first is the reaction to an exogenous, the second to an analogous, endogenous, excitation. The affect is a state which passes rapidly, the neurosis is a chronic state; because an exogenous excitation acts like a single shock, an endogenous one like a constant pressure. *The nervous system reacts to an internal source of excitation with a neurosis, just as it reacts to an analogous external one with a corresponding affect.*

IV. RELATION TO OTHER NEUROSES

There are still a few words to be said concerning the relation of anxiety-neurosis to the other neuroses in respect of its incidence and its inner connections with them.

The purest cases of anxiety-neurosis are as a rule the most developed. These cases are found among young and sexually potent persons; they show a uniform ætiology and no very long duration.

More frequently, however, anxiety symptoms occur contemporaneously and in combination with those of neurasthenia, hysteria, obsessions and melancholia. If because of this clinical confusion we are to refrain from distinguishing anxiety-neurosis as a self-contained unity, then to be logical we should have in addition to renounce the distinction between hysteria and neurasthenia which has been acquired so laboriously.

For the analysis of 'mixed neuroses' I can advocate the following important formula: *Wherever a mixed neurosis exists a combination of several specific ætiologies may be discovered.*

The number of ætiological factors which conditions a mixed neurosis may occur quite fortuitously; for instance, if a fresh injurious factor adds its effect to those already existing, e. g. a woman who had always been hysterical begins at a certain point in her married life to experience coitus reservatus and then acquires anxiety-neurosis in addition to her hysteria; a man who had previously been in the habit of masturbating, and had become neurasthenic, becomes engaged to be married and is sexually roused during the intimacy with his fiancée, and then acquires anxiety-neurosis in addition to his neurasthenia.

In other cases the number of ætiological factors is no accident; on the contrary, some one of them has brought another into activity; for example, a woman whose husband practises coitus reservatus without regard to her satisfaction finds herself compelled to relieve by masturbation the distressing excitation aroused by the act, as a result of which she develops an anxiety-neurosis, but not in a pure form, showing at the same time symptoms of neurasthenia; another woman in the same injurious situation will have to battle with lewd thoughts and visions, against which she struggles to defend herself, and will in this way develop obsessional ideas as well as the anxiety-neurosis as a result of coitus interruptus; lastly, a third woman's husband will lose his attraction for her in consequence of coitus interruptus and she will develop an affection for another man which she carefully keeps secret, as a result of which we find a mixture of anxiety-neurosis and hysteria.

In a third category of mixed neuroses the interrelation of the symptoms is even closer, in that the very same ætiological determinant regularly and simultaneously evokes both neuroses. Thus for example, the sudden sexual revelation which is active in cases of virginal anxiety always gives rise to hysteria as well as anxiety-neurosis; cases of voluntary abstinence are for the most part from the beginning united with true obsessional ideas; coitus interruptus never seems to me to be able to provoke a pure anxiety-neurosis in men, but always a combination of it with neurasthenia; and so on.

It follows from these considerations that the ætiological conditions for the incidence of the neuroses must be distinguished more clearly from their specific ætiological factors. The former, for example, coitus interruptus, masturbation and abstinence, are still capable of various interpretations; each one of them can produce many neuroses; only the ætiological factors into which they can be resolved, such as *inadequate relief*, *psychical inadequacy*, *defence by substitution*, have an unequivocal and specific relation to the ætiology of the individual great neuroses.

* * *

In its essence anxiety-neurosis presents the most interesting similarities to and differences from the other great neuroses, particularly neurasthenia and hysteria. It shares with neurasthenia its main characteristic: the source of the excitation, the inciting factor in the disturbance, is somatic in nature, whereas in hysteria and the obsessional neurosis it is psychical in nature. In other respects we see rather a kind of antithesis between the symptoms of neurasthenia and those of anxiety-neurosis which may be summed up in the words: impoverishment or accumulation of excitation respectively. This antithesis does not prevent the two neuroses from being combined with one another, but is nevertheless clearly demonstrated by the fact that the most extreme forms of both neuroses are also the purest.

In symptomatology anxiety-neurosis and hysteria have many points in common, which need to be better appreciated. The appearance of symptoms either in a chronic form or as attacks, the paræsthesias grouped like auræ, the hyperæsthesias and points of pressure which are found in certain surrogates of the anxiety-attack (dyspnœa and heart-attacks), the exacerbation (through conversion) of pains perhaps having an organic basis—these and other common features even permit the conjecture that much of what we attribute to hysteria may with more justification be laid at the door of anxiety-neurosis. If we go into the mechanism of the two neuroses so far as it has been possible to discover it up to the present, aspects come to light which suggest that anxiety-neurosis is actually the somatic counterpart of hysteria. In each of them there is an accumulation of excitation—which perhaps accounts for the similarity of the symptoms already described; in each of them there is a *psychical inadequacy as a consequence of which abnormal somatic processes come about.* In each of them there occurs a deflection of excitation to the somatic field instead of psychical assimilation of it; the difference is merely this, that in anxiety-neurosis the excitation (in the displacement of which the neurosis expresses itself) is purely somatic (the somatic sexual excitation), whereas in hysteria it is purely psychical (evoked by conflict). Little wonder then that hysteria and anxiety-neurosis are regularly combined with one another, as in 'virginal anxiety' or 'sexual hysteria', and that hysteria simply borrows a number of its symptoms from the anxiety-neurosis. These intimate relations between anxiety-neurosis and hysteria provide a new argument for demanding the distinction of anxiety-neurosis from neurasthenia; for if this distinction is not admitted then neither are we justified in maintaining the distinction between neurasthenia and hysteria which was so laboriously come by and is so indispensable for the theory of the neuroses.

VI

A REPLY TO CRITICISMS ON THE ANXIETY-NEUROSIS[1]

(1895)

In No. 2 of Mendel's *Neurologisches Zentralblatt* 1895, I published a short paper in which I ventured an attempt to distinguish a series of nervous states from neurasthenia and give them independence under the name of 'Anxiety-Neurosis'.[2] I was led to do so by finding a constant combination of certain clinical and ætiological characters, which may always decide us to make such distinctions. I found, as E. Hecker[3] had done before me, that the neurotic symptoms in question could all be united under the head of 'pertaining to the expression of *anxiety*'; and I was able to add from my study of the ætiology of the neuroses that these component parts of the complex 'anxiety-neurosis' show special ætiological conditions which are almost the opposite of the ætiology of neurasthenia. My observations had shown me that in the ætiology of the neuroses (at least of the acquired and acquirable forms) sexual factors play a predominant part, hitherto far too little appreciated; so that the assertion: 'the ætiology of the neuroses lies in sexuality', with all its necessary inexactness *per excessum et defectum*, nevertheless comes nearer to the truth than the other doctrines ruling at the present time. A further

[1] First published in the *Wiener Klinische Rundschau*, 1895. [Translated by John Rickman.]

[2] See No. V of this volume, above, p. 76.

[3] E. Hecker: Über larvierte und abortive Angstzustände bei Neurasthenie, *Zentralblatt für Nervenheilkunde*, Dec., 1893.

statement to which experience forced me was to the effect that the various sexual noxiæ were not to be found indifferently in the ætiology of all neuroses, but that there were evidently special relationships of particular noxiæ to particular neuroses. I thought I could assume, therefore, that I had discovered the specific causes of the different neuroses. I then sought to comprehend in a short formula the peculiarity of the sexual noxiæ which constitute the ætiology of anxiety-neurosis, and arrived at the statement, dependent on my idea of the sexual process (see pp. 98—9): Anxiety-neurosis is produced by anything which withholds somatic sexual tension from the psychical and interferes with its elaboration within the psychical field. If we refer to the concrete circumstances in which this factor expresses itself, we come to the conclusion that voluntary or involuntary abstinence, sexual intercourse with incomplete gratification, coitus interruptus, the deflection of psychical interest from sexuality and so on, are the specific ætiological factors of the states I have called anxiety-neurosis.

When I published the paper mentioned above, I in no way deceived myself about its power to arouse conviction. In the first place I knew that I had only given a scanty, incomplete presentation—one that was even in parts difficult to comprehend; it was perhaps just sufficient to arouse the reader's expectation. I had besides adduced hardly any examples and quoted no statistics; the technique of collecting the case-histories was not touched on; no provision was made to avoid misunderstandings; other objections than the most obvious ones were not considered; and concerning the theory itself, only the main theme was brought into prominence and its limitations were disregarded. Accordingly, everyone was justified in forming his own judgement upon the conclusiveness of the whole proposition. I had to look forward, moreover, to yet another source of disagreement. I know very well that I have advanced nothing new by suggesting the 'sexual ætiology' of the neuroses, that undercurrents in medical literature acknowledging these facts have never been absent, and that the official medicine of the schools has actually been aware of them also. But the last has behaved, however, as if it knew nothing about it, making no use of its knowledge, and deducing nothing from it. Such conduct must surely have a deep-rooted cause, originating perhaps in a kind of aversion from looking into sexual matters, or in a reaction against older attempts at explanation which were regarded as outworn. At all events, anyone who ventures to make something credible to others who could without any trouble have discovered it for themselves, must be prepared to meet with opposition.

With such a state of affairs it would perhaps have been more expedient not to answer critical objections until I had expressed myself in greater detail upon the complicated theme itself and had made myself more intelligible. Nevertheless I cannot resist the motives which induce me immediately to join issue with a recent criticism of my theory of anxiety-neurosis. I do this because the writer, L. Löwenfeld (Munich), the author of *Pathologie und Therapie der Neurasthenie und Hysterie,* is one whose judgement probably has great weight with the medical public, and because of a mistaken conception which Löwenfeld imputes to me; and also because I wish at once to combat the idea that my theory is to be overthrown so very easily by the first casual and impromptu objections.

Löwenfeld correctly discovers at a glance the essence of my work to be my assertion that anxiety symptoms are due to a specific and uniform ætiology of a sexual nature. If this cannot be established as a fact then the principal reason for distinguishing an independent anxiety-neurosis from neurasthenia also falls to the ground. There remains, however, one difficulty to which I called attention—namely, that anxiety symptoms have manifest relations also to hysteria; so that the decision as Löwenfeld would have it brings the distinction between hysteria and neurasthenia to grief; though this difficulty is obviated by reference to heredity as the common cause of all the neuroses, a point which will be discussed later.

Now by what arguments does Löwenfeld support the case against my theory?

1. I have emphasized as a point essential for comprehension of the anxiety-neurosis that the anxiety of that condition does not admit of a psychic derivation, that is, that the anxious expectation which constitutes the nucleus of the neurosis cannot be acquired through a single or repeated affect of fright which is justified psychically. Fright, as I have pointed out, may result in hysteria or a traumatic neurosis, but not in an anxiety-neurosis. It is easy to see that this negation is simply the obverse of my assertion (with a positive content): the anxiety of my neurosis represents a somatic sexual tension deflected from the psychical field where it would otherwise have made itself felt as libido.

Against this, Löwenfeld lays stress on the fact that in a series of cases 'anxiety states appear immediately or shortly after a mental shock (fright alone, or accidents accompanied by fright) and that these circumstances make the co-operation of sexual noxiæ of the kind mentioned at least most improbable.' He gives in brief, as a particularly pregnant example, one observation of a patient out of many. This example relates to a woman aged thirty, married for four years, of tainted stock, who had undergone a first difficult confinement a year before. A few weeks after it her husband had an attack of illness which frightened her exceedingly and in her excitement she ran about the cold room in her chemise. From that time onward she was ill, first with anxiety and palpitations in the evenings, later with attacks of convulsive trembling, and in further sequence phobias and the like—the picture of a fully-developed anxiety-neurosis. 'Here', concludes Löwenfeld, 'the anxiety states are manifestly of psychic origin consequent on a single shock.'

I do not doubt that my honoured critic can produce many similar cases; I myself can supply a long series of analogous examples. Anyone who had not seen such very common cases of the outbreak of anxiety-neurosis following upon a mental shock could not regard himself as qualified to discuss the question of anxiety-neurosis. I will only observe in this connection that neither shock nor anxious expectation is necessarily always demonstrable in the ætiology of such cases; any other emotion will serve as well. If I hurriedly call to mind a few cases from recollection there occurs to me that of a man of forty-five who first had an anxiety-attack (with cardiac collapse) on receiving the news of the death of his aged father: from that time onwards a complete and typical anxiety-neurosis with agoraphobia developed; further, a young man who fell a victim to the same neurosis on account of the disagreements between his young wife and his mother, and developed the agoraphobia afresh after every domestic quarrel;

a student who was rather an idler and had his first anxiety-attacks during a period of hard cramming under the spur of paternal displeasure; a woman, herself childless, who fell ill in consequence of anxiety concerning the health of her small niece, and so on. As to the facts themselves which Löwenfeld employs against me there cannot be the slightest doubt.

It is otherwise with their interpretation! Are we then without further ceremony to accept the *post hoc ergo propter hoc* conclusion and save ourselves all critical consideration of the raw material? Surely we are acquainted with examples enough in which the final exciting factor cannot keep up its reputation as *causa efficiens* in the face of critical analysis? Take the relation between trauma and gout, as an example. The rôle of a trauma in provoking an attack of gout in the injured limb is probably not different from the part it plays in the ætiology of tabes and general paralysis of the insane; only in the case of gout everyone would see that it is absurd to say the trauma has 'caused' the gout, instead of provoked it. It should make us cautious when we meet with ætiological factors of such a kind—ordinary factors, I should like to call them—in the ætiology of the most varied forms of illness. Emotion, such as fright, is also an ordinary factor of this kind; fright can evoke chorea, apoplexy, paralysis agitans and what not, just as well as an anxiety-neurosis. Now I should certainly not continue to argue along these lines, that because of their prevalence the ordinary factors do not satisfy our requirements, and therefore there must be specific causes besides; it would beg the question at issue. But I am justified in concluding as follows: If a single specific cause can be proved in the ætiology of all or almost all cases of anxiety-neurosis, then our view will not necessarily be erroneous because the outbreak of illness only occurs under the influence of some one or other ordinary factor, such as emotion.

So it was in my cases of anxiety-neurosis. The man who fell ill—inexplicably—after receiving the news of his father's death (I make this interpolated comment because this death was not unexpected and did not occur in unusual or tragic circumstances) had for eleven years practised coitus interruptus with his wife whom he usually endeavoured to satisfy; the young man who could not tolerate the quarrels between his wife and his mother had practised withdrawal with his young wife from the beginning, in order to save them the burden of offspring; the student who developed anxiety-neurosis through overwork, instead of cerebrasthenia as we should expect, had for three years had a relationship with a girl whom he dared not let become pregnant; the woman who had no children herself and fell ill of anxiety-neurosis owing to the illness of a niece was married to an impotent man and had never been sexually gratified; and so on. Not all these cases are equally clear nor prove my theory with equal force; but if I add them to the very considerable series of cases in which the ætiology shows nothing but the specific factor, they conform without a dissentient note to the theory I have put forward and make it possible for us to extend our ætiological comprehension beyond the boundaries which have existed hitherto.

If anyone wishes to prove to me that I have unduly neglected the significance of ordinary ætiological factors in the foregoing discussion, he must confront me with observations in which my specific factor is lacking, that is, with cases in which, although the *vita sexualis* is (more or less) normal, anxiety-neurosis breaks out after a mental shock. Now let us see whether Löwenfeld's case fulfils this condition. My worthy opponent has manifestly not clearly recognized this necessity in his own mind, otherwise he would not have left us so completely in the dark concerning the *vita sexualis* of his patient. I will leave on one side the fact that the case of the lady of thirty is obviously complicated by an hysteria, about the psychical origin of which I should be the last to have any doubt; I naturally admit without protest the presence of an anxiety-neurosis alongside this hysteria. But before I make use of a case as evidence either for or against my theory of the sexual ætiology of the neuroses I must study the sexual conduct of the patient more thoroughly than Löwenfeld has done here. I should not be contented with the conclusion that, because the lady had the mental shock shortly after a confinement, coitus interruptus had probably played no part during the previous year and that therefore no sexual noxiæ had arisen here. I know of cases of women who become pregnant year after year and develop anxiety-neurosis because—*incredibile dictu*—all sexual relations ceased after pregnancy had set in; so that in spite of having many children they might have lived all the years of their married life in sexual privation. It is known to every physician that women do conceive from men whose potency is very feeble and who are not able to give them satisfaction; and finally there are many women who are afflicted with a congenital anxiety-neurosis, that is to say, are endowed with a *vita sexualis* (or develop it without demonstrable external provocation) of the kind usually acquired by coitus interruptus and similar noxiæ—a consideration which upholders of the ætiology of heredity ought to take into account. In a number of these women we are able eventually to discover a past history of a hysterical illness in their youth, which has affected the *vita sexualis* ever since or has established a deflection of sexual tension away from the psychical field. Women with this kind of sexuality are incapable of real satisfaction, even in normal coitus, and develop anxiety-neurosis either spontaneously or after further effective factors have supervened. Which of all these factors mentioned could have contributed to Löwenfeld's case I do not know; but I repeat that this case is evidence against me only if the lady who responded to a single fright with an anxiety-neurosis had previously enjoyed a normal *vita sexualis*.

It is impossible to pursue ætiological research by means of the anamnesis of patients if we accept the patient's account as he gives it or are satisfied with what he volunteers. If syphilidologists allowed themselves to depend upon the declarations of their patients, when endeavouring to trace an initial infection of the genitalia back to an act of sexual intercourse, they would have to attribute an imposing number of chancres to a chill in persons who protest their virginity, and gynæcologists would have little difficulty in confirming the miracle of parthenogenesis among their unmarried clients. I hope that some day the idea will gain admittance that neuropathologists too may be subject to similar ætiological prejudices in the work of collecting the case-histories of the great neuroses.

2. Löwenfeld further says that he has repeatedly seen anxiety-states appear and disappear where a change in the sexual life had certainly not taken place, but where there were other factors in play.

I too have had exactly the same experience, but I was not misled by it. I too have brought anxiety-attacks to an end by psychical treatment, improvement of the patient's general condition and so on. I have naturally not concluded from this that lack of treatment was the cause of anxiety-attacks. Not that I would credit Löwenfeld with a conclusion of this kind, to be sure; my joking remark is only intended to show that the state of affairs may easily be so complicated as to nullify his objection completely. I have not found any difficulty in harmonizing the fact brought forward here with the theory of a specific ætiology of anxiety-neurosis. It will readily be granted that ætiological factors exist which, in order to become effective, must act with a certain intensity (or quantity) and over a certain length of time, which therefore *summate*; the effects of alcohol are a standard example of illness produced by summation. Accordingly we must reckon with a space of time in which the specific ætiology is at work, but during which its effects are not yet manifest. During such a period the person is not yet ill, but he is disposed to a particular illness—in this case to anxiety-neurosis—and as soon as the 'ordinary' noxia supervenes it can excite the outbreak of the neurosis just as well as a further increase in operation of the specific noxia. We can also express this as follows: It is not sufficient for the specific ætiological factor to exist; a certain measure of it must also be reached, and in attaining this measure a degree of the specific noxia can be made up by an amount of 'ordinary' injurious factors. If the last is again eliminated, the level of the specific ætiological factor falls below the threshold; the symptoms recede again. The entire therapy of the neuroses rests upon the fact that the total load upon the nervous system, to which the latter is succumbing, can be reduced below this level by very various influences on the combination of ætiological factors. No conclusions can be drawn from this state of things in regard to the presence or absence of a specific ætiology.

These considerations are surely indisputable and assured. Anyone who does not think them sufficient may permit the following argument to weigh with him. According to the views of Löwenfeld and many others the ætiology of anxiety states lies in heredity. Now heredity can certainly not be altered; if anxiety-neurosis is curable by treatment we (and Löwenfeld too) ought to conclude that heredity cannot account for its ætiology.

For the rest, I might have been spared defending myself against both of Löwenfeld's objections if my worthy opponent had bestowed greater attention upon my paper itself. Both objections are anticipated in it and answered (p. 92 ff.); I could only repeat here what I said there; I have even purposely analysed the same cases of illness afresh. Further, the ætiological formulæ upon which I had previously laid weight are contained in the text of my former paper. I will repeat them once again here. I maintain that: *There exists a specific ætiological factor for the anxiety-neurosis which in taking effect can be reinforced quantitatively by 'ordinary' injurious factors but cannot be replaced by them qualitatively*. Further: *This specific factor determines more than anything the type of neurosis; whether a neurotic illness occurs at all depends on the total load on the nervous system (in relation to its capacity to carry the load)*. As a rule neuroses are *overdetermined;* that is to say, several factors in their ætiology operate together.

3. I shall have less trouble in refuting Löwenfeld's next comments because on the one hand they have little to do with my theory and on the other because they call attention to difficulties which I acknowledge. Löwenfeld says: 'The Freudian theory is totally insufficient to explain the appearance and non-appearance of individual anxiety-attacks. If anxiety states, i. e. the clinical symptoms of anxiety-neurosis, occurred solely through subcortical accumulation of somatic sexual excitation and through abnormal expenditure of the same, then everyone subject to anxiety states would have an attack from time to time so long as no alteration took place in his sexual life, just as the epileptic has his attack of *grand et petit mal;* but this, as every-day experience shows, is by no means so. Anxiety-attacks occur for the most part only on definite occasions. If the patient avoids these or knows how to paralyse their influence by means of any precaution, then he remains exempt from anxiety-attacks, whether he habitually practises coitus interruptus or abstinence or enjoys a normal *vita sexualis.*'

Now there is a great deal to be said about this. In the first place Löwenfeld forces my theory to a conclusion which is not inherent in it. That the process must be the same with an accumulation of somatic sexual excitation as with an accumulation of the stimuli resulting in an epileptic convulsion is a far too detailed proposition, for which I have given no occasion; and it is not the sole one which offers itself. I need only assume that the nervous system possesses the power to master a certain amount of somatic sexual excitation even when this is deflected from its purpose, and that disturbances then occur only if the *quantum* of this excitation suddenly undergoes an increase—and Löwenfeld's claim would be quashed. I have not ventured to extend my theory far in that direction; chiefly because I did not expect to find reliable support on the way. I will merely indicate that we should not conceive the production of sexual tension to be independent of its expenditure; that in normal sexual life this production, when stimulated by the sexual object, takes a form essentially different from that which it has in psychic repose, and so on.

It must be admitted that the conditions here are in all probability different from those obtaining in the tendency to epileptic convulsion, and that they are not yet wholly correlated with the theory of an accumulation of somatic sexual excitation.

To Löwenfeld's further assertion—that anxiety-attacks only appear under certain conditions and fail to appear when these are avoided, whatever the *vita sexualis* of those concerned—we may urge in contradiction that Löwenfeld manifestly has in mind only the anxiety of *phobias*, as is shown by the examples appended to the part of his essay which I have quoted. He says not a word concerning spontaneous anxiety-attacks, taking the form of dizziness, palpitation, dyspnœa, trembling, sweating, etc. My theory, however, seems quite equal to explaining the appearance and non-appearance of these anxiety-attacks. The semblance of periodicity in the onset of anxiety states may be found in a great number of such cases of anxiety-neurosis, similar to that observed in epilepsy, only that here the mechanism of this periodicity is more perspicuous. On closer examination we find with great regularity an exciting sexual occurrence (that is, one capable of releasing somatic sexual excitation), recurring at definite and often quite constant intervals of time, to which the anxiety-attack is related. In abstinent women this part is played by menstrual excitation, and in both men and women by recurrent nocturnal pollutions and above all by sexual intercourse itself (injurious when it is incomplete), which transfers its own periodicity to the anxiety-attacks resulting from it. If anxiety-attacks occur apart from the usual periodicity, it is usually possible to trace them back to an occasional cause of more rare and irregular incidence, to a single sexual experience, something read, a visual impression, or the like. The interval I referred to varies from a few hours up to two days: it is the same as that which in other persons is followed by the well-known sexual migraine, due to the same causes, which has an undoubted connection with the symptom-complex of anxiety-neurosis.

Besides these there are plenty of cases in which a single anxiety state is provoked by an ordinary factor, i. e. by excitement of any kind. The same mechanism of displacement thus holds good for the ætiology of a single anxiety-attack as for the causation of a whole neurosis. That the anxiety of phobias answers to different conditions is not very remarkable; phobias have a more complicated structure than purely somatic anxiety-attacks. In them the anxiety is connected with a definite ideational or conceptional content, and the chief condition for the development of this anxiety comes into being when this psychical content is aroused. The anxiety is then 'released', just as, for example, sexual tension is released by the awakening of libidinous ideas; this process, however, is not yet clearly eludicated in its relation to the theory of anxiety-neurosis.

I see no reason why I should try to conceal the gaps and weaknesses in my theory. The main point in the problem of phobias seems to me that *phobias do not occur at all when the vita sexualis is normal*, that is, when the specific determinant is absent; by this specific determinant we mean a disturbance of the *vita sexualis* by deflection of the somatic away from the psychical field. However obscure otherwise the mechanism of phobias may be, my theory is only to be gainsaid by evidence of phobias occurring together with a normal *vita sexualis*, or even together with some disturbance of it that is not specific.

4. I now pass on to a remark made by my esteemed critic which I cannot leave uncontradicted. I had written in my essay on anxiety-neurosis (loc. cit. p. 86):

'In many cases of anxiety-neurosis no ætiology is recognizable at all. It is remarkable that in such cases evidence of a grave hereditary taint is seldom difficult to establish. But where there are grounds for regarding the neurosis as an acquired one, careful enquiry directed to that end reveals a series of injurious conditions (noxiæ) and influences within the sexual life as important factors in the ætiology . . .' Löwenfeld quotes this paragraph and adds the following comment: 'According to this Freud always appears to regard a neurosis as "acquired" whenever exciting causes are discoverable.'

If this meaning is readily conveyed by my text then the latter gives a very distorted expression of my thoughts. Let me point out that in the preceding paragraphs I have shown myself far stricter than Löwenfeld in assessing the importance of exciting causes. If I myself were to explain the meaning of my statement I should do so by adding to it, after the conditional: '*But where we have ground for regarding the neurosis as acquired*', the phrase: '*because the evidence* (mentioned in the previous sentence) *of hereditary taint is not forthcoming.*' The meaning is: I hold a case to be acquired in which heredity is not demonstrable. I behave in this respect just as everyone else does, perhaps with the slight difference that others will also explain a case as conditioned by heredity where no heredity exists, so that they overlook the entire category of acquired neuroses. But this difference runs in my favour. I admit however that I am myself to blame for this misunderstanding on account of the way I expressed myself in the first sentence: 'an ætiology cannot be found at all.' I shall also certainly be told that I have created useless trouble for myself by searching for specific causes of the neuroses. It will be said that the real ætiology of anxiety-neurosis, as of the neuroses in general, is already known to be that of heredity, and two real causes cannot exist side by side. Am I prepared to deny the ætiological rôle of heredity? If not, all other ætiologies must be equally valid or equally invalid—merely exciting causes.

I do not share this view concerning the ætiological rôle of heredity and, since on my short paper on anxiety-neurosis I have dealt less with this theme than with any other, I shall try to some extent to make good this omission and to efface the impression that in the composition of my paper I had not given equal consideration to all the inter-related problems.

I think we can effect a presentation of the probably very complicated ætiological conditions which exist in the pathology of the neuroses, if we establish the following ætiological concepts:

(*a*) *Predisposition*, (*b*) *Specific Cause*, (*c*) *Contributory Cause* and, as a term not equivalent to the former (*d*) *Exciting* or *Releasing Cause*.

In order to satisfy all posibilities let us assume that we are dealing with ætiological factors capable of quantitative alterations, and consequently of increase or decrease.

If we may use the conception of a compound ætiological formula which must be fulfilled if the effect is to take place, then we may designate as exciting or releasing cause that which last makes its appearance in the formula, so that it immediately precedes the manifestation of the effect. It is this temporal element alone which constitutes the essence of an incitement; each of the other factors can in individual cases play the part of an incitement, and this part can even alternate within this same ætiological conglomeration.

The factors which are to be described as predisposition are those in whose absence the effect would never come about; but which, however, are incapable of alone bringing about the effect, no matter to what degree they may be present. For the specific cause is lacking.

The *specific cause* is one which is never absent when the effect actually takes place, and which also suffices, in the required quantity or intensity, to bring about the effect, provided that the predisposition is present as well.

As *contributory causes* we may comprehend such factors as are not necessarily present every time nor able in any degree to produce the effect alone, but which co-operate with the predisposition and the specific ætiological cause to make up the ætiological formula.

The peculiar position of the contributory or auxiliary causes seems clear; but how are we to distinguish between predisposition and specific causes, since both are indispensable and no one of them alone is sufficient as a cause?

In these circumstances the following considerations would seem to make a decision possible. Among the 'indispensable causes' we find several which are also present in the ætiological formulæ of many other conditions beside anxiety-neurosis, thus showing that they have no particular relation to individual disorders; *one* of these causes, however, stands out with special prominence, in that it is found in no other or in very few ætiological formulæ, and this has a claim to be called the *specific* cause of the disease in question. Further, predisposing factors and specific causes are particularly clearly distinguished in cases where the former have the quality of long duration and little alteration in their condition, whereas the specific cause corresponds to a factor which has recently come into action.

I will attempt to give an example of this complete ætiological scheme:

Effect: Phthisis pulmonum.

Predisposition: For the most part an hereditary disposition of the organs concerned.

Specific Cause: Koch's bacillus.

Contributory Causes: Everything that lowers resistance; emotion as well as infections or colds.

The scheme for the ætiology of anxiety-neurosis seems to me to run similarly, thus:

Predisposition: Heredity.

Specific Cause: A sexual factor in the sense of a deflection of sexual tension from the psychical field.

Contributory Causes: All 'ordinary' injurious factors: emotion, fright, as well as physical exhaustion through illness or over-exertion.

If I go into this ætiological formula for the anxiety-neurosis in greater detail I can add the following remarks: Whether a special personal disposition (which need not necessarily be ascribed to heredity) is unconditionally required in anxiety-neurosis or whether every normal person can develop that neurosis if there should be a quantitative increase of the specific factor, I am not able to decide with certainty, but I incline strongly to the latter view. —Hereditary disposition is the most important determinant of anxiety-neurosis, but not an *indispensable* one, since it is lacking in a series of border-line cases.—The specific sexual factor is in the very great majority of cases to be demonstrated with certainty; in a series of cases (congenital) it is not distinguishable from the hereditary determinant, but comes to expression with it; that is to say, these persons are endowed with a peculiarity of the *vita sexualis* as a stigma (being psychically unequal to the task of mastering somatic sexual tension), which in other cases must be acquired before the patient can fall ill of this neurosis. In another series of border-line cases the specific factor is contained in a contributory one, for example, if the psychical inadequacy mentioned above comes about in consequence of exhaustion, etc. All these cases fall into shifting series, not discrete categories; through all of them, however, runs one common factor—the same behaviour in regard to sexual tension, and for most of them the distinction between predisposition, specific and contributory causes is valid, in conformity with the completion of the ætiological formula given above.

When I consult my experience for the purpose I cannot find that an antithetic relation exists between hereditary disposition and the specific sexual factor in anxiety-neurosis. On the contrary, the two ætiological factors reinforce and complement each other. The sexual factor is *as a rule* effective only with those persons who are also endowed with an hereditary taint; heredity alone is not usually able to produce an anxiety-neurosis, but waits for the incidence of a sufficient quantity of the specific sexual noxia. The existence of an hereditary factor does not spare us therefore the search for a specific factor, upon which, incidentally, all therapeutic interest also depends. For where are we to begin therapeutically with an hereditary ætiology? It has always been present in the patient and will continue in him until his end is come. Taken by itself it cannot explain either the episodic outbreak of a neurosis or the cessation of one through treatment. It is nothing but a condition of the neurosis—an incalculably important one, it is true; but one that is nevertheless overestimated, to the disadvantage of therapy and theoretical comprehension. One has only to think, by way of contrast, of the cases of familial nervous diseases (chorea chronica, Thomsen's disease and so on) in which heredity unites in itself all the ætiological determinants.

In conclusion I desire to repeat the few statements in which I am accustomed, as a first approximation to the truth, to express the inter-relation of the different ætiological factors:

1. Whether a neurotic illness *occurs at all* depends upon a quantitative factor, upon the total load on the nervous system in relation to its capacity for resistance. Anything which can keep this factor below a certain threshold, or bring it back below it, is effective therapeutically, since the ætiological formula is thus kept unfulfilled.

What is meant by 'total load' or 'capacity for resistance' could be explained in greater detail on the basis of certain hypotheses concerning nerve function.

2. To what *extent* the neurosis develops depends in the first place on the measure of hereditary taint. Heredity acts like a multiplier introduced into the circuit, which increases the deflection of the needle many times.

3. But what *form* the neurosis takes—the direction of deflection—is determined only by the specific ætiological factor arising in the sexual life.

I hope that on the whole, although I am myself conscious of the many still unsolved difficulties of the subject, my theory of anxiety-neurosis will prove more fruitful for the elucidation of the neuroses than Löwenfeld's attempt to account for the same facts by reference to 'a combination of neurasthenic and hysterical symptoms in the form of attacks'.

VII

OBSESSIONS AND PHOBIAS: THEIR PSYCHICAL MECHANISMS AND THEIR ÆTIOLOGY[1]

(1895)

I shall begin by challenging two assertions often found repeated with regard to the syndromes: obsessions and phobias. I must state, first, that they should not be included under neurasthenia proper, since the patients afflicted with these symptoms are often neurasthenics, but as often not; and secondly, that we are not justified in regarding them as the effect of mental degeneration, because they are found in persons no more degenerate than the majority of neurotics in general, because at times they improve, and indeed at times we even succeed in curing them.[2]

Obsessions and phobias are separate neuroses, with a special mechanism and ætiology which I have succeeded in demonstrating in a certain number of cases, and which, I hope, will prove similar in a large number of new cases.

As regards classification of the subject, I propose to exclude a group of intense obsessions which are nothing but memories, unaltered images of important experiences. As an example, I will cite Pascal's obsession: he always thought he saw an abyss on

---

[1] First published in the *Revue Neurologique*, 1895, t. III. [Translated by M. Meyer.]

[2] I am very glad to find that the authors of the most recent work on this subject express opinions very similar to mine. Cf. Gélineau, *Des peurs maladives ou phobies*, 1894, and Hack Tuke, On Imperative Ideas, *Brain*, 1894.

his left hand 'after he had nearly been thrown into the Seine in his coach'. These obsessions and phobias, which might be called *traumatic*, are allied to the symptoms of hysteria.

Apart from this group we must distinguish: (*a*) obsessions proper; (*b*) phobias. The essential difference between them is the following:

Two components are found in every obsession: (1) an idea that forces itself upon the patient; (2) an associated emotional state. Now in the group of phobias this emotional state is always one of 'morbid anxiety', while in true obsessions other emotional states, such as doubt, remorse, anger, may occur in the same capacity as fear does in the phobias. I will first attempt to explain the remarkable psychological mechanism of true obsessions, a mechanism quite different from that of the phobias.

I

In many true obsessions it is quite plain that the emotional state is the chief element, since this state persists unchanged while the idea associated with it varies. The girl in Case 1 quoted below, for example, felt remorse in some degree for all sorts of reasons—for having stolen, for having ill-treated her sisters, for having counterfeited money, etc. Persons who doubt have many doubts at the same time or consecutively. In them it is the emotional state which remains constant; the idea changes. In other cases the idea, too, seems fixed, as in Case 4, the girl who persecuted servants in the household with an incomprehensible hatred, constantly changing the individual object, however.

Now a careful psychological analysis of these cases shows that the emotional state, as such, is always justified. Case 1, the girl who suffered from remorse, had good reasons for it; the women in Case 3 who doubted their resistance against temptation knew very well why. The girl in Case 4, who detested servants, was justified in complaining, etc. Only, and it is in these two characteristics that the pathological sign lies, (1) the emotional state persists continually, and (2) the associated idea is no longer the appropriate original one, ætiologically related to the obsession, but is one which replaces it, a substitute for it.

The proof of this is the fact that we can always find in the previous history of the patient, at the beginning of the obsession, the original idea that has been replaced. The replaced ideas all have common attributes; they correspond to really painful experiences in his sexual life which the person is striving to forget. He succeeds merely in replacing the irreconcilable idea by another ill-adapted to the emotional state, which for its part remains unchanged. It is this incongruity between the emotional state and the associated idea that accounts for the absurdity so characteristic of obsessions. I will now bring forward my observations and conclude with a tentative theory and explanation.

Case 1. A girl reproached herself for things which she knew were absurd, for having stolen, for having counterfeited money, for having dabbled in magic, etc. according to whatever she had been reading during the day.

Reinstatement of the replaced idea. She reproached herself with the onanism she had been practising secretly without being able to renounce it. She was cured by careful surveillance which prevented her masturbating.

Case 2. A young man, a medical student, suffered from an analogous obsession. He reproached himself for all sorts of immoral acts: for having killed his cousin, for having violated his sister, for having set fire to a house, etc. He got to the point of having to turn round in the street to see if he had not killed the last passer-by.

Reinstatement. He had been much affected by reading in a quasi-medical book that onanism, to which he was addicted, destroyed one's morale.

Case 3. Several women complained of an impulsion to throw themselves out of the window, to cut their children with knives, scissors, etc.

Reinstatement. Typical temptation-obsessions.—They were women who, not being at all satisfied in marriage, had to struggle against the desires and voluptuous ideas that haunted them in the presence of men.

Case 4. A girl who was perfectly sane and very intelligent displayed an uncontrollable hatred against servants in the household. It had been provoked by an impertinent servant, and had been transferred from servant to servant, to a degree that rendered housekeeping impossible. The feeling was a mixture of hate and disgust. As a reason for it she stated that the vulgarity of these girls sullied her idea of love.

Reinstatement. This girl had accidentally been witness of an amorous scene in which her mother had taken part. She had hidden her face, had stopped up her ears, and had done her utmost to forget it, as it disgusted her and made her feel quite unable to remain with her mother whom she loved tenderly. She succeeded in her efforts; but her anger at the person who had profaned her idea of love continued to exist within her, and this emotional state soon linked itself to the image of a person who could be a substitute for her mother.

Case 5. A young girl had become almost completely isolated on account of an obsessive fear of incontinence of urine. She could no longer leave her room or receive visitors without having urinated a number of times. When at home or entirely alone the fear did not trouble her.

Reinstatement. It was an obsession of temptation or mistrust. She did not mistrust her bladder, but her resistance against amorous inclinations. The origin of the obsession shows this well. She had once in a theatre, at the sight of a man who pleased her, felt an amorous desire, accompanied (as spontaneous pollutions in women always are) by the desire to urinate. She was obliged to leave the theatre, and from that moment on she was a prey to the fear of reproducing the same sensation, but the desire to urinate had replaced the amorous one. She was completely cured.

Although the cases enumerated show varying degrees of complexity, they have the following in common: the original (intolerable) idea has been replaced by another idea, the substituted idea. In the cases which I now append the original idea has also been replaced, but not by another idea; it has been replaced by acts or impulses which originally served as measures of relief or as *protective* procedures, and are now incongruously associated with an emotional state that does not fit them, but that has persisted in its original form and was also originally justified.

Case 6. Obsession of arithmomania.—A woman became obliged to count the boards in the floor, the steps in the staircase, etc.—acts which she performed in a state of ridiculous distress.

Reinstatement. She had begun the counting in order to turn her mind from obsessive ideas of temptation. She had succeeded in so doing, but the impulse to count had replaced the original obsession.

Case 7. Obsessive brooding and speculating.—A woman suffered from attacks of this obsession that ceased only when she was ill, and then gave place to hypochondriacal fears. The theme of her worry was always a part or function of her body, for example, respiration: Why must I breathe? What if I try not to breathe? etc.

Reinstatement. At the very beginning she had suffered from the fear of becoming insane, a hypochondriacal phobia common enough among women who are not satisfied by their husbands, as she was not. To assure herself that she was not going mad, that she still possessed her mental faculties, she had begun to catechize herself and busy herself with serious problems. This quieted her at first, but with time the habit of speculation replaced the phobia. For more than fifteen years periods of fear (pathophobia) and of obsessive speculating had alternated in her.

Case 8. Folie du doute. Doubting mania.—Several cases showed the typical symptoms of this obsession but were explained very simply. These persons had suffered or were still suffering from various obsessions, and the knowledge that the obsessions had disturbed all their acts and had many a time interrupted their train of thought provoked a legitimate doubt about the reliability of their memory. The confidence of each one of us would be shaken, and we should all of us have to re-read a letter or repeat a calculation if our attention had been distracted several times during the performance. Doubt is a quite logical result when obsessions are present.

Case 9. Folie du doute (Hesitation).—The girl in Case 4 had become extremely slow in performing all ordinary everyday actions, particularly in her toilet. She took hours to tie her shoe-laces or to clean her finger-nails. As an explanation she stated that she could not make her toilet while obsessive ideas occupied her, nor immediately after. As a result, she had become accustomed to wait a definite period after each return of the obsessive idea.

Case 10. Folie du doute. Fear of paper.—A young woman had suffered scruples after having written a letter; at the same time she collected all the pieces of paper she saw, which she explained by confessing to a love which she had formerly refused to admit. As she was constantly repeating her lover's name, she was seized with a fear that the name might have slipped off the end of her pen, that she might have written it upon some bit of paper in a pensive moment.[1]

Case 11. Mysophobia.—A woman who washed her hands constantly and touched door-handles only with her elbow.

Reinstatement. The case of Lady Macbeth. The washing was symbolic, designed to replace by physical purity the moral purity which she regretted having lost. She tormented herself with remorse for conjugal infidelity, the memory of which she had resolved to banish from her mind. She also washed her genitalia.

As regards the theory and explanation of this substitution, I will content myself with answering three questions that arise here.

1. How does this substitution come about?

It seems to be the expression of a special mental disposition. At least, a 'similar heredity' is often enough found in obsessional cases, as in hysteria. Thus the patient in my second case related to me

[1] Cf. the popular German song:
Auf jedes weiße Blatt Papier möcht' ich es schreiben:
Dein ist mein Herz und soll es ewig, ewig bleiben.

that his father had suffered from similar symptoms. He once introduced me to a second cousin who had obsessions and convulsive tic, and to his sister's daughter, aged eleven, who already showed obsessions (probably of remorse).

2. What is the motive for this substitution?

I think it may be regarded as a defensive reaction (*Abwehr*) of the ego against the intolerable idea. Among my patients several remember a deliberate effort to banish the idea or the painful recollection of the voice of conscience. (See Cases 3, 4, 11.) In other cases the repugnance is banished by an unconscious process that has left no trace in the patients' memory.

3. Why does the emotional state that is attached to the obsessive idea persist instead of vanishing like other conditions of the ego?

This question may be answered by applying to it the theory of the genesis of hysterical symptoms developed by Breuer and myself.[1] I will here only remark that by the very fact of the substitution the disappearance of the emotional state is rendered impossible.

II

In addition to these two groups of true obsessions there is the class of 'phobias', which must now be considered. I have already mentioned the great difference between obsessions and phobias: that in the latter the emotion is always one of anxiety, fear. I might add that obsessions are varied and more individualized, phobias are more uniform and typical. But this distinction is not all-important.

Among the phobias two groups may be differentiated, according to the nature of the object feared:

[1] See. No. II of this volume, p. 24.

(1) common phobias, an exaggerated fear of all those things that everyone detests or fears to some extent: such as night, solitude, death, illness, dangers in general, snakes, etc.; (2) specific phobias, the fear of special circumstances that inspire no fear in the normal man; for example, agoraphobia and the other phobias of locomotion. It is interesting to note that these phobias have not the obsessive feature that characterizes true obsessions and the common phobias. The emotional state appears in them only under special conditions which the patient carefully avoids.

The mechanism of phobias is entirely different from that of obsessions. Substitution is no longer the predominant feature in the former; psychological analysis reveals no intolerable replaced idea in them. Nothing is ever found but the *anxiety state* which, by a sort of selection, brings up all the ideas adapted to become the subject of the phobia. In the case of agoraphobia, etc., we often find the recollection of a state of *panic*; and what the patient actually fears is a repetition of such an attack under those special conditions in which he believes he cannot escape it.

The fear of this emotional state, which underlies all phobias, is not derived from any memory whatever; we must ask what the source of this overpowering nervous state can be.

I hope to be able to demonstrate, on another occasion, that there is some reason for distinguishing a special neurosis, the anxiety-neurosis,[1] of which the chief symptom is this emotional state. I shall then enumerate its various symptoms and lay stress on those which differentiate this neurosis from neurasthenia, with which it is now confounded. Phobias,

[1] See No. V of this volume, p. 76.

then, are a part of the anxiety-neurosis, and are almost always accompanied by other symptoms belonging to it.

The anxiety-neurosis has a sexual origin too, as far as I can see, but it does not attach itself to ideas taken from sexual life; properly speaking, it has no psychical mechanism. Its specific cause is the accumulation of sexual tension, produced by abstinence or by frustrated sexual excitation (using the term as a general formula for the effects of coitus reservatus, of relative impotence in the husband, of excitation without satisfaction in engaged couples, of enforced abstinence, etc.).

It is under such conditions, extremely frequent in modern civilized society, especially among women, that anxiety-neurosis develops; phobias are a psychical manifestation of it.

In conclusion I will state that combinations of a phobia and an obsession proper may co-exist, and that indeed this is a very frequent occurrence. We may find that a phobia had developed at the beginning of the disease as a symptom of anxiety-neurosis. The thought-content of the phobia accompanying the state of fear may be replaced by another idea or perhaps by a *protective procedure* that lessens the fear. Case 7 (obsessive speculating) presents a neat example of this group, a phobia coupled with a true obsession evolved by substitution.

VIII

HEREDITY AND THE ÆTIOLOGY OF THE NEUROSES[1]

(1896)

I am addressing the pupils of J. M. Charcot especially to bring to their attention some objections to the theory concerning the ætiology of the neuroses which was passed on to us by our master.

The part ascribed to neurotic heredity in this theory is well known. It is the only true and indispensable cause of nervous disease; other ætiological factors may aspire only to the title of precipitating causes. Thus the master himself and his pupils, Guinon, Gilles de la Tourette, Janet and others, have promulgated this doctrine for the major neurosis, hysteria; I believe that the same opinion is held in France and to some extent everywhere for the other neuroses, although it has not been laid down quite so solemnly and decidedly for conditions analogous to hysteria.

For a long time I have entertained suspicions in this matter, but I had to wait to find corroborating facts in my daily medical experience. My objections are now of two kinds, arguments based upon facts and arguments of a more speculative order. I will begin with the former, arranging them according to the importance that I ascribe to them.

I. (*a*) Sometimes diseases which are often enough foreign to the sphere of neuropathology and which do not necessarily depend upon disease of the nerv-

[1] First published in the *Revue Neurologique*, 1896, t. IV [Translated by M. Meyer.]

ous system have been considered nervous and indicative of neuropathic heredity. Thus, true facial neuralgias and many headaches have been considered nervous which are caused rather by post-infectious pathological changes and by suppuration in the nasal sinuses. I am convinced that these patients would profit if we were more often to leave the treatment of these conditions to rhinologists.

(*b*) All nervous diseases found in the patient's family, without reference to their frequency or their gravity, have been accepted as justifying the accusation of nervous hereditary taint. Does not this point of view seem to imply a sharp distinction between families that are free from any nervous predisposition and families that are subject to it without limit or restriction? And do not the facts speak rather in favour of the opposite opinion, namely, that there are transitions and degrees of nervous predisposition and that no family escapes it entirely?

(*c*) Our opinion as to the ætiological rôle of heredity in nervous disease must assuredly be the result of an impartial statistical study and not of a *petitio principii*. Until this study has been made, the existence of acquired neuropathies should be considered as probable as that of hereditary neuropathies. But if the existence of neuropathies acquired by persons not predisposed to them is possible, it can no longer be denied that some of the nervous diseases found among the relatives of our patients may have such an origin. They can then no longer be called upon as conclusive proofs of the hereditary predisposition that is imputed to the patient by virtue of his family history, for a retrospective diagnosis of the diseases of ancestors or of absent members of the family is only very rarely successful.

(*d*) Those who are adherents of the view of Fournier and of Erb, concerning the part played by syphilis in the causation of tabes dorsalis and in progressive paralysis, have learned that powerful ætiological factors must be recognized the presence of which is indispensable in the pathogenesis of certain diseases that heredity alone could not cause. Charcot remained to the end, however, as I learned through a private letter from him, strictly opposed to Fournier's theory, which, nevertheless, gains ground day by day.

(*e*) There is no doubt that certain neuropathies may develop in a man who was perfectly sound and of untainted family. One observes this every day in Beard's neurasthenia; if neurasthenia were limited to predisposed people, it would never have gained the importance and prevalence with which we are familiar.

(*f*) In nervous pathology there is a so-called similar and a so-called dissimilar heredity. No fault will be found with the former concept; it is even very remarkable that in the affections that depend upon similar heredity (Thomsen's disease, Friedreich's disease, Huntington's chorea, the myopathies, etc.), no trace of any accessory ætiological factor is ever found. But the much more important concept of dissimilar heredity has gaps that must be filled out to arrive at a satisfactory solution of the ætiological problems. They consist of the fact that members of the same family prove to be afflicted with the most varied forms of nervous disease, functional and organic, without our being able to discover a law that determines the substitution of one disease for another or the order in which they follow one another in successive generations. There are in these families, beside the affected members, persons who remain sound. The theory of dissimilar heredity tells us neither why one person carried the same hereditary taint without succumbing to it, nor why another selects, among the diseases that constitute the great family of neuropathies, one particular nervous affection instead of another, hysteria instead of epilepsy, insanity, etc. Since there is no such thing as chance in the pathogenesis of nervous disease any more than elsewhere, it must be admitted that it is not heredity that controls the choice of a neuropathy developing in a member of a predisposed family, and that there is ground for suspecting the existence of other ætiological factors of a less incomprehensible nature which deserve to rank as the specific ætiology of any such nervous disease. Without the existence of this special ætiological factor heredity would have been powerless; it would have lent itself to the production of a different neuropathy if the specific ætiology in a given case had been replaced by any other.

II. These specific, determining causes of neuropathy have been too little investigated, for the vision of physicians has been dazzled by the imposing prospect of the hereditary factor in ætiology. Nevertheless, they are well worth making the object of careful study; although their pathogenic power may be in general only auxiliary to that of heredity, great practical interest centres on the understanding of this specific ætiology. It affords a point of attack for our therapeutic efforts, while hereditary predisposition, predetermined for the patient from birth, frustrates all our efforts by the strength of its position.

I have been engaged for years in a study of the ætiology of the major neuroses (functional nervous states analogous to hysteria), and in what follows I shall report the result of these studies. In order to avoid all possible misunderstanding, I shall begin by making two observations on the nosography of the neuroses and on their ætiology in general.

I had to start my work with an innovation in nosography. I have found reason to place the obsessional neurosis upon the same footing as hysteria, as an independent and autonomous disease, although the majority of authors classify obsessions among the syndromes comprising mental degeneration or else confound them with neurasthenia. I have learned, by examining their mental mechanism, that these disorders are much more closely allied to hysteria than one would have believed.

Hysteria and the obsessional neurosis form the first group of the major neuroses that I studied. The second contains Beard's neurasthenia, which I split up into two functional conditions differentiated both ætiologically and symptomatologically: neurasthenia proper and anxiety-neurosis—a term, by the way, which does not altogether please me. I have given detailed reasons for this differentiation, which I consider necessary, in a paper published in 1895.[1]

As for the ætiology of the neuroses, I think we should recognize that the various ætiological factors, differing in their importance and in the way in which they are related to the effect they produce, may be arranged theoretically in three classes: (1) *Conditions* that are indispensable for the production of the disease in question, but which are of a universal nature and occur as well in the ætiology of many other diseases. (2) *Concurrent causes* that share with the conditions in group (1) the characteristic of entering into the causation of other diseases as well as into that of the disease in question, but which

[1] See No. V of this volume, above, p. 76.

are not indispensable for the production of the latter disease. (3) *Specific causes* just as indispensable as the first conditions but appearing only in the ætiology of the disease for which they are specific.

Now, in the pathogenesis of the major neuroses heredity plays the part of a *condition*, potent in all cases and even indispensable in the majority of them. It cannot do without the assistance of the specific causes; but the importance of hereditary predisposition is demonstrated by the fact that the same specific causes operating on a sound person would produce no manifest pathological effect, while its presence in a predisposed person will precipitate a neurosis, the development of which will in intensity and extent be proportional to the degree of hereditary predisposition.

The action of heredity is comparable to that of a multiplier in an electric circuit, which increases the visible deviation of the needle but which cannot determine its direction.

There is another point to be noted in the relations between the hereditary condition and the specific causes of the neuroses. Experience shows, as might have been anticipated, that among the problems of ætiology that of the quantitative relationship of the ætiological factors to one another should not be neglected. But one would not have guessed the fact which seems to follow from my observations, that heredity and the specific causes may replace one another quantitatively, that the same pathological effect will be produced by the co-existence of a very grave specific ætiology and a moderate degree of predisposition as by that of a severe neuropathic heredity with a slight specific factor. So that it is merely a quite possible extreme in this series when one finds cases of neurosis in which a tangible degree of hereditary predisposition is looked for in vain, provided that this deficiency is compensated for by a powerful specific factor.

As *concurrent or accessory causes* all those 'ordinary' factors found elsewhere may be mentioned: mental excitement, physical exhaustion, acute illness, intoxication, traumatic accidents, intellectual overwork, etc. I would maintain that none of them, not even the last, enters regularly or necessarily into the ætiology of neuroses, well knowing that the enunciation of this opinion is in direct opposition to a theory regarded as universal and incontestable. Since Beard declared neurasthenia to be the product of our modern civilization he has found only believers; but it is impossible for me to accept this opinion. A painstaking study of the neuroses has taught me that the specific ætiology of the neuroses has escaped Beard's attention.

I do not wish to underestimate the ætiological importance of these every-day factors. They are very varied, of frequent occurrence, and most often blamed by the patient; they are more manifest than the specific causes, which are either concealed or not understood. They often fulfil the function of precipitating causes bringing the hitherto latent neurosis to the surface; and a practical interest attaches to them, since consideration of these ordinary causes may furnish a basis for a therapy that does not aim at a radical cure, but contents itself with reducing the disease to its previous latent state.

But a constant and intimate relation between a given ordinary cause and a given nervous affection cannot be established; mental excitement, for example, is found as often in the ætiology of hysteria, of obsessions, of neurasthenia, as in that of epilepsy, Parkinson's disease, diabetes, and numerous others.

The ordinary concurrent causes can also replace the specific ætiology quantitatively, but can never completely supplant it. There are numbers of cases in which hereditary predisposition and the specific factor constitute the entire ætiology, the ordinary causes being absent. In other cases the indispensable ætiological factors are not strong enough in themselves to precipitate the neurosis and a state of apparent good health may be maintained for a long time, a state that is really one of neurotic predisposition. It requires only the added effect of an ordinary cause to make the neurosis become manifest. It must be noted, however, that in such circumstances the nature of the supervening ordinary factor, whether it be excitement, trauma, infectious disease, or any other, is entirely a matter of indifference; the pathological result does not vary in accordance with it, and the nature of the neurosis will always be determined by the pre-existing specific cause.

What then are the *specific causes* that produce neuroses? Is there only one or are there several? And can a constant ætiological relationship be established between a given cause and a given neurosis so that each major neurosis may be referred to a particular ætiology?

Supported by a painstaking investigation of the facts, I wish to affirm that this hypothesis agrees well with the truth, that each of the major neuroses mentioned has as its immediate cause a special disturbance of the nervous economy, and that these pathological functional changes *betray, as their common source, the sexual life of the person concerned, either a disturbance of his present sexual life or important events in his past life.*

This is, strictly speaking, not a new, unheard-of proposition. It has always been admitted that sexual disturbances were among the causes of nervousness, but they were grouped together on a level with other precipitating causes as subordinate to heredity; their ætiological importance was restricted to a limited number of the cases studied. Physicians had even acquired the habit of not looking for them if the patient did not himself accuse them. The distinctive characteristic of my point of view lies in my raising the sexual factors to the rank of specific causes, in my recognizing their influence in all cases of neurosis, and finally in my finding a constant parallelism, proof of a special ætiological relationship, between the nature of the sexual factor and the kind of neurosis.

I am quite sure that this theory will provoke a storm of contradiction from my fellow physicians. But this is not a fitting occasion to present the data and observations that have imposed my conviction on me, nor to explain the strict meaning of the somewhat vague term 'disturbances of nervous economy'. This will be done, I hope as thoroughly as possible, in a work that I am preparing on the subject. In this paper I shall confine myself to the presentation of my results.

Pure neurasthenia, which after it has been differentiated from anxiety-neurosis presents a monotonous clinical picture (exhaustion, sense of pressure on the head, flatulent dyspepsia, constipation, spinal paræsthesias, sexual weakness, etc.), admits of only two specific ætiological factors, excessive onanism and spontaneous emissions.

The prolonged and intense effect of this pernicious form of sexual satisfaction alone suffices to produce neurasthenia, or else it stamps the subject with the specific neurasthenic habitus which later is made manifest under the influence of a chance accessory cause. I have also met persons who showed the signs of a neurasthenic constitution, but in whom I did not succeed in demonstrating the ætiology just mentioned; I was able at least to prove, however, that in these patients the sexual function had never developed to a normal degree. They seemed to be endowed by heredity with a sexual organization analogous to that which arises in the neurasthenic as a result of onanism.

The anxiety-neurosis, the clinical picture of which is much richer (irritability, states of anxious expectation, phobias, more or less severe panics, fear, vertigo, trembling, sweats, congestion, dyspnœa, tachycardia, etc.; chronic diarrhœa, chronic locomotor vertigo, hyperæsthesia, insomnia, etc.)[1] is easily shown to be the specific result of various disturbances of sexual life, all having a common trait. Forced abstinence, frustrated sexual excitement (not gratified by sexual intercourse), incomplete or interrupted coitus (not attaining gratification), sexual efforts that exceed the psychical capacity of the person, etc., all these factors, all too common in modern life, seem to unite in disturbing the equilibrium of psychical and somatic functions in sexual activity, and in hindering the psychical co-operation necessary to relieve the nervous economy from sexual tension.

These considerations, which contain perhaps the nucleus of a theoretical explanation of the functional mechanism of the neurosis in question, arouse the suspicion that a complete and really scientific demonstration of the matter is not at the moment possible, and that the problem of the physiology of the sexual life will first have to be approached from a new angle.

[1] For the symptomatology and ætiology of the anxiety-neurosis see my paper cited above, No. V of this volume, p. 76.

I will conclude by stating that the presence of hereditary predisposition is not indispensable in the pathogenesis of neurasthenia and of the anxiety-neurosis. This is the result of daily observation; if the hereditary factor is present, however, the development of the neurosis will be strongly influenced thereby.

In the second class of major neuroses, hysteria and the obsessional neurosis, the solution of the ætiological problem is surprisingly simple and uniform. I owe my conclusions to the use of the new psycho-analytic[1] method, the probing procedure of J. Breuer, a method that is somewhat subtle but irreplaceable, so fruitful has it proved to be in explaining obscure unconscious mental processes. By means of this method, which cannot be explained here,[2] hysterical symptoms are traced to their origin, which invariably proves to be an experience in the person's sexual life well adapted to produce a painful emotional reaction. Going back into the patient's life step by step, guided always by the structural connection between symptoms, memories, and associations, I finally came to the starting-point of the pathological process; and I had to realize that the same factor was at the bottom of all the cases subjected to analysis, namely, the effect of an agent that must be accepted as the specific cause of hysteria.

It is indeed a memory connected with the person's sexual life, but one that presents two extremely important features. The event, the unconscious image of which the patient has retained, is a premature sexual experience with actual stimulation of the genitalia, the result of sexual abuse practised by

[1] [The first use of this term by the author to designate his technique.—Ed.]

[2] See J. Breuer and Sigmund Freud. *Studien über Hysterie.* 1895.

another person, and the period of life in which this fateful event occurs is early childhood, up to the age of eight to ten, before the child has attained sexual maturity.

A passive sexual experience before puberty: this is the specific ætiology of hysteria.

I will at once supplement these conclusions by some detailed facts and some explanatory remarks, so as to combat the doubt that I anticipate. I have been able to analyse thirteen cases of hysteria completely. Three of this number were true combinations of hysteria with an obsessional neurosis (I do not say hysteria with obsessions). The experience mentioned above was not lacking in a single case; it was present either as a brutal attempt committed by an adult or as a less sudden and less repugnant seduction, having however the same result. In seven cases out of the thirteen we were dealing with a liaison between children, sexual relations between a little girl and a boy slightly older, generally her brother who had himself been the victim of an earlier seduction. These liaisons were sometimes continued for years, up to puberty, the boy repeating upon the little girl without alteration those practices that he had himself experienced at the hands of a servant or governess; because of this origin they were often of a disgusting kind. In some cases there had been both assaults and an infantile liaison or repeated brutal abuse.

The date of the premature experience was variable: in two cases it went back to the second year (?) of the child; in my observations the age of predilection was the fourth or fifth year. It may be a matter of chance, but I have the impression from them that a passive sexual experience occurring after the age of eight or ten can no longer be the foundation of a neurosis.

How can one be convinced of the truth of these confessions made in analysis and said to be memories preserved since early childhood, and how can we protect ourselves against the inclination to fabricate and the facility for invention ascribed to hysterics? I would charge myself with blameworthy credulity if I did not offer more convincing proofs. But the fact is that patients never relate these histories spontaneously, and never suddenly offer, in the course of the treatment, the complete recollection of such a scene to the physician. The mental image of the premature sexual experience is recalled only when most energetic pressure is exerted by the analytic procedure, against strong resistance; so that the recollection has to be extracted bit by bit from the patients, and while it comes back into consciousness they fall prey to emotions difficult to simulate.

If we remain uninfluenced by the patient's behaviour and are able to follow impartially, in detail, the psycho-analysis of a case of hysteria, we are finally convinced ourselves.

The premature experience in question has left a permanent imprint upon the history of the case, being represented in it by a mass of symptoms and peculiar features that permit of no other explanation; the delicate but firm inter-relationship of the structural elements of the neurosis compel us to accept this view; the therapeutic result is retarded if we do not go so deep as this; no other choice exists then except that of rejecting or believing the whole matter.

Is it to be believed that a premature sexual experience of this kind, undergone by a person whose sex is scarcely differentiated, may become the starting-point of a permanent mental abnormality like hysteria? And further, how would such a view harmonize with our present conception of the psychical mechanism of that neurosis? A satisfactory reply can be given to the first question: it is just because the subject is a child that premature sexual stimulation produces little or no effect at the time, but a mental impression of it is retained. Later, at puberty, when the sexual organs have developed a degree of activity immeasurably greater than that of childhood, this unconscious mental impression is somehow or other reawakened. Owing to the changes produced by puberty the memory will exercise a power which was entirely lacking when the experience itself took place; *the memory will produce the same result as if it were an actual event.* We have, so to speak, *the subsequent effect of a sexual trauma.*

As far as I know, the reawakening of a sexual recollection after puberty, the event itself having occurred at a time antedating this period, affords the only psychological conjunction in which the effect of a memory surpasses that of the event itself. But it is an abnormal constellation, which attacks the mind at a weak point and necessarily produces a pathological result.

I believe that this inverse relation between the psychical effect of the recollection and that of the event contains the reason why the memory has remained unconscious.

We thus approach a very complex psychical problem, one which, however, if duly appreciated promises to throw a flood of light some day upon the most intricate problems of mental life.

The ideas set forth here, based upon the results of psycho-analysis, namely, that the memory of a premature sexual experience is always found as the specific cause of hysteria, do not agree with Janet's psychological theory of the neurosis, nor with any other; but they harmonize perfectly with my own hypotheses, described elsewhere, on the 'defence neuroses'.

All events occurring after puberty to which an influence on the development of hysteria and the formation of its symptoms must be ascribed are only concurrent causes, '*agents provocateurs*' in the words of Charcot, to whom neuropathic heredity occupied the position that I claim for premature sexual experiences. These accessory factors are not subject to the strict rules that govern the specific causes; analysis demonstrates beyond question that they produce a pathological effect in hysteria only by virtue of their ability to awaken the unconscious mental impression of the infantile experience. It is also because of their connection with the original pathogenic impression and by its magnetism, so to speak, that the memory of them becomes unconscious in turn, and is able to assist the growth of a mental process withdrawn from the influence of conscious processes.

The obsessional neurosis arises from a specific cause closely analogous to that of hysteria. A premature sexual experience, which has occurred before puberty and the memory of which becomes active during or after that period, is also found here and the same observations and arguments made in reference to hysteria apply to cases of this neurosis (six cases, three pure forms). There is only one difference that seems of capital importance. At the base of the ætiology of hysteria we found a passive sexual experience undergone with indifference or with a slight degree of disgust or fright. In the obsessional neurosis we are concerned, on the other hand, with an experience that was pleasurable, with a sexual aggression inspired by desire (in the case of the boy) or with a pleasurable participation in sexual acts (in the case of the little girl). The obsessive ideas, whose inner meaning is made recognizable by analysis, reduced, so to speak, to their simplest form, are nothing but reproaches that the patient makes to himself because of that premature sexual pleasure, but reproaches disguised by an unconscious psychical work of transformation and substitution.

The very fact that this sexual aggression occurs at such a tender age seems to betray the effect of a previous seduction, which would result in precocity of sexual desire. Analysis has confirmed this suspicion in the cases I have treated. In this way an interesting fact always present in these obsessional cases is explained, namely, the regular way in which the clinical picture is complicated by a certain number of purely hysterical symptoms.

The importance of the active sexual attitude as a cause of obsessions, and that of the passive attitude in the pathogenesis of hysteria, seems to give the reason of hysteria's close association with the female sex and of the preference of the male for the obsessional neurosis. One sometimes comes across a pair of neurotics who had a liaison in early childhood, the man suffering from obsessions, the woman from hysteria; if we are dealing with brother and sister we may mistake for the result of heredity what is really derived from premature sexual experience.

There are, unquestionably, pure and isolated cases of hysteria and obsessional neurosis, independent of neurasthenia and anxiety-neurosis, but they are not the rule. More frequently, the psychoneurosis appears as accessory to the neurasthenic neuroses, having been provoked by the latter and following their decline. This happens because the specific causes of the latter, current disturbances of the sexual life, act at the same time as accessory causes of the psychoneuroses, the specific cause of which, the memory of an early sexual experience, they re-awaken and revive.

As for neurotic heredity, I am far from being able to estimate accurately its influence in the ætiology of the neuroses. I admit that its presence is indispensable in serious cases; I doubt whether it is a *sine qua non* in mild cases, but I am convinced that neurotic heredity alone cannot cause a psychoneurosis if the specific ætiology of the latter, premature sexual stimulation, be lacking. I even believe that the question which of the two neuroses, hysteria or obsessional neurosis, will develop in a given case is determined not by heredity but by the particular nature of the early sexual experience in childhood.

IX

FURTHER REMARKS ON THE DEFENCE NEURO-PSYCHOSES[1]

(1896)

In a short paper[2] published in 1894 I included hysteria, obsessions and certain cases of acute hallucinatory confusion under one heading as 'Defence Neuro-Psychoses'. I did this because one point of view showed itself as applying in common to all these affections: their symptoms arise through the psychical mechanism of (unconscious) defence, that is, through an attempt to repress an intolerable idea which was in painful opposition to the patient's ego. In a book since published by Dr. J. Breuer and myself (*Studien über Hysterie*) I have been able by quoting clinical observations to elucidate and illustrate what is meant by this psychical process of 'defence' or 'repression'. Information may also be found in it concerning the toilsome but completely reliable method of psycho-analysis which I use in making these investigations and by which at the same time the investigations serve a therapeutic purpose.

My experiences in the last two years of work have strengthened me in my surmise that defence is the nucleus of the psychic mechanism of the neuroses under discussion and have also made it possible for me to give this psychological theory a clinical basis. To my own surprise I came unexpectedly upon a

---

[1] First published in the *Neurologisches Zentralblatt*, Oct., 1896, No. 10. [Translated by John Rickman.]

[2] See No. IV of this volume, above, p. 59.

few simple but narrowly definable solutions of the problems contained in the neuroses and in the following paper I will give a short preliminary account of them. I cannot in this kind of communication bring forward the evidence on which my statements are based, but I hope to fulfil this obligation in a more detailed presentation.

I. THE 'SPECIFIC' ÆTIOLOGY OF HYSTERIA

In earlier publications Breuer and I have already expressed the opinion that the symptoms of hysteria can be understood only by tracing them back to 'traumatic' experiences and that these psychical traumas are related to the patient's sexual life. What I have to add here, as a uniform result of my analysis of thirteen cases of hysteria, concerns on the one hand the nature of these sexual traumas, and on the other hand the period of life in which they occur. The occurrence at any time of life of an experience in some way touching on the sexual life, which then becomes pathogenic on account of the generation and suppression of a painful affect, does not suffice to bring about a hysteria. *These sexual traumas must on the contrary occur in early childhood (before puberty) and they must consist in actual excitation of the genital organs (coitus-like processes).*

I have found this specific determinant of hysteria —*sexual passivity in the pre-sexual period*—present in all the cases of hysteria analysed (including two men). I need here only allude to the great reduction in the importance of the factor of hereditary disposition which is effected by thus establishing accidental ætiological factors as a necessary condition; moreover, we are also thus provided with a clue to the reason for the much greater frequency of hysteria in the female sex, which even in childhood is more likely to provoke sexual assaults.

The more obvious objections to this theory will probably be the following: that sexual assaults on small children occur too frequently for them to be of great ætiological importance when they can be confirmed; or else that such experiences must remain ineffective for the very reason that they happen to a sexually undeveloped person; further, that one must guard against instigating patients to ostensible reminiscences of this kind by a cross-examination and guard against believing the romances which they themselves invent. In reply to the latter objections we may ask the favour that on this obscure topic no one should pass too certain a judgement before he has himself practised the only method which can throw light upon it—psycho-analysis, the method of making conscious what was previously unconscious.[1] The essential element in the first-mentioned objections is disposed of when we remember that it is not the experience itself which acts traumatically, but the memory of it when this is re-animated after the subject has entered upon sexual maturity.

My thirteen cases of hysteria were all of them severe; all of them had symptoms of many years duration, a few after long and fruitless treatment in institutions. The infantile traumas which analysis discovered in these severe cases must without exception be described as grave sexual injuries; some of them were absolutely appalling. Most prominent among the people who were guilty of these abuses with all their serious consequences were nursemaids,

[1] I myself am inclined to think that the tales of outrage which hysterics so frequently relate may be obsessive fictions which arise in the memory-trace of the trauma that occurred in childhood.

governesses, or domestic servants, to whose care children are all too thoughtlessly abandoned, and teachers and tutors appear regrettably often; in seven of the thirteen cases, however, the assaults were perpetrated by innocent childish assailants, mostly brothers, who had for years carried on some kind of sexual relation with somewhat younger sisters. The course of events was probably in all cases similar to that which we were able to follow with certainty in some individual cases—namely, the boy was first misused by a person of the female sex, by which his libido was prematurely awakened and then a few years later he committed a sexual aggression reproducing exactly the procedure to which he himself had been subjected.

I must exclude active masturbation from the list of sexual noxiæ occurring in early childhood that are pathogenic for hysteria. Although indeed it may be very frequently found in cases of hysteria, this is due to the circumstance that masturbation is much more often the consequence of abuse or seduction than is generally supposed. It is by no means rare for both of the young couple to fall ill of a defence neurosis at a later date, the brother with obsessions, the sister with hysteria, which naturally gives the appearance of a familial neurotic disposition. This pseudo-heredity, however, is explained now and then in surprising ways; on one occasion I was able to observe a brother, sister and a somewhat older male cousin who were all ill. I learnt from the analysis which I undertook with the brother that he suffered from self-reproaches for being the cause of his sister's illness; he had been seduced by his cousin, who in his turn—as was known in the family—had himself been the victim of his nursemaid.

I cannot say for certain up to what age-limit sexual injury falls within the ætiology of hysteria; but I doubt whether sexual passivity after the eighth to tenth year can evoke repression in the absence of previous experiences of the same kind. The lower limit extends as far as memory itself, that is, therefore, to the tender age of from one and a half to two years! (Two cases.) In a number of my cases the sexual trauma (or series of traumas) occurred in the third or fourth year. I should not myself give credence to these singular revelations if they had not been proved worthy of belief by the part they played in the subsequent development of the neurosis. In every case a number of morbid symptoms, habits, and phobias is only to be accounted for by going back to these experiences of childhood, and the logical structure of the neurotic manifestations makes it impossible to reject these faithfully preserved memories which emerge from among the experiences of childhood. It would, indeed, be quite useless to question an hysteric outside analysis about these traumas in childhood; their traces are never to be found in conscious memory, only in the symptoms of illness.

All the experiences and excitements which in the period of life after puberty prepare the way for or occasion the outbreak of hysteria can be proved to act only because they awaken the memory-trace of those traumas in childhood; this memory-trace does not become conscious but leads to a liberation of the affect and to repression. In close accord with this view of the part played by the traumas occurring in later life is the circumstance that they are not subject to the strict conditions governing the traumas of childhood, but may vary in intensity and quality from actual sexual assaults to mere sexual overtures, witnessing sexual acts by others, or being told about sexual matters.[1]

In my first paper on the defence neuroses it was left unexplained how the efforts of previously healthy persons to forget some traumatic experience of this kind could have the result of really producing the repression intended and of thereby opening the door to a defence neurosis. It could not lie in the nature of the experiences, because other people remain well in spite of similar incitements to illness. Hysteria could not therefore be fully explained as the effect of the trauma; one had to acknowledge that the disposition to hysterical reaction had already existed before the trauma.

Now the subsequent effect of an infantile sexual trauma can fill the place either totally or partially of this indefinite hysterical disposition. 'Repression' of the memory of a painful sexual experience in maturer years is possible only for those people in whom this experience can re-activate the memory-trace of an infantile trauma.[2]

---

[1] In a paper on the Anxiety-Neurosis (see No. V of this volume, p. 87) I mentioned that 'anxiety-neurosis can be evoked in maturing girls by their first meeting with the sexual problem; in these cases it is typically combined with hysteria'. I now know that the occasion on which such 'virginal anxiety' breaks out in young girls does not indeed represent their *first* encounter with sexuality; but that an experience of a sexually passive nature had previously occurred in their childhood, the memory of which is awakened by the 'first encounter'.

[2] A psychological theory of repression should also throw light on the question why it is only ideas with a sexual content that can be repressed. The following hints may assist us: The formation of ideas with a sexual content produces, as is well-known, excitation-processes in the genital organs similar to sexual experience itself. We may suppose that this somatic excitation transposes itself into the psychical sphere. As a rule this kind of effect is much stronger during actual experiences than during the recollection of them. But if the sexual experience occurs at a time of sexual immaturity and the memory of it is aroused during or after maturity, then the exciting effect of the recollection will be very much stronger than that of the experience itself; because in the meantime puberty has

Obsessional ideas likewise presuppose a sexual experience in childhood (different in nature from that in hysteria). The ætiology of the two defence neuro-psychoses now presents the following relation to the ætiology of the two simple neuroses—neurasthenia and anxiety-neurosis. The latter are direct results of the sexual noxiæ themselves, as I have shown in a paper on the anxiety-neurosis (1895);[1] the two defence neuroses are the indirect consequences of sexual noxiæ occurring before the onset of sexual maturity, that is, consequences of the psychical memory-traces of these noxiæ. The current causes which produce neurasthenia and anxiety-neurosis frequently play at the same time the part of inciting causes in the defence neuroses; on the other hand, the specific causes of the defence neuroses—the traumas of childhood—can at the same time lay the foundations of a neurasthenia which will develop later. Finally, it not infrequently happens that a neurasthenia or anxiety-neurosis is maintained, not by the current sexual noxiæ, but only by the continuous effect of the memory of the childhood-traumas.

II. THE NATURE AND MECHANISM OF THE OBSESSIONAL NEUROSIS

In the ætiology of the obsessional neurosis sexual experiences in early childhood play the same part

increased to an incomparable degree the capacity of the sexual apparatus for response. An inverted relation of this kind between real experience and memory appears to be the psychological condition of repression. Through the delay in the maturing of the sexual functions in comparison with that of the psychical functions, sexual life affords a unique possibility for this inversion of relative effectiveness. *The traumas of childhood act subsequently as fresh experiences —then, however, unconsciously.* I must postpone psychological discussions of wider range until another time. Let me say, however, that the period of 'sexual maturity' here referred to does not coincide with puberty, but comes earlier (eighth to tenth year).

[1] See No. V of this volume, above, p. 76.

as in hysteria; it is here, however, no longer a question of sexual passivity, but rather of aggressive acts performed with pleasure and of pleasurable participation in sexual acts—of sexual activity, therefore. This difference in the ætiological conditions explains why the obsessional neurosis appears to favour the male sex.

In all my cases of obsessional neurosis I have, moreover, found a *substratum of hysterical symptoms* which can be traced back to a scene of sexual passivity of earlier date than the pleasurable activity. I surmise that this coincidence is a regular one and that early sexual aggressivity always implies a previous experience of seduction. Nevertheless, I can as yet give no complete presentation of the ætiology of the obsessional neurosis; I simply have the impression that the decision whether hysteria or obsessional neurosis will arise on the basis of the infantile traumas depends on *temporal* factors in the development of the libido.

The nature of the obsessional neurosis permits of description in a simple formula:—*Obsessions are always reproaches re-emerging in a transmuted form under repression—reproaches which invariably relate to a sexual deed performed with pleasure in childhood.* To illustrate this statement it will be necessary to give a description of the typical course of an obsessional neurosis.

In the first period, that of childish immorality, occur the experiences containing the germ of the neurosis which develops later; first of all in very early childhood the experiences of sexual seduction that make subsequent repression possible, then the deeds of sexual aggression against the opposite sex which appear later as acts to which self-reproach becomes attached.

This period is brought to a close by the onset of sexual 'maturity', often itself premature. No self-reproach becomes connected with the memories of those pleasurable activities, and the relation with the initial passive experience makes it possible to repress them and substitute for them a *primary defence-symptom*—often only after conscious and remembered efforts. Conscientiousness, shame and self-distrust are the kind of symptoms which introduce the third period, that of apparent health, or better, that of *successful defence*.

The next period, that of illness, is distinguished by the *return of the repressed memories*, i. e. by failure of the defence; it is doubtful whether the awakening of these memories usually occurs accidentally or spontaneously or as a kind of by-product in consequence of current sexual disturbances. The reanimated memories and the self-reproach which is built up on them, however, never appear in consciousness unchanged. The obsessional idea and the obsessive affects which appear in consciousness and take the place of the pathogenic memory in conscious life are *compromise-formations* between the repressed and the repressing ideas.

In order to describe clearly and with probable accuracy the processes of repression, the return of the repressed, and the formation of pathological compromise-ideas, one must resolve upon quite definite concepts in regard to the substratum underlying mental processes and consciousness. So long as one avoids this one must be content with the following rather figurative remarks: There are two forms of the obsessional neurosis, according to whether the memory-content alone of the deed which evokes reproach has forced itself into consciousness, or whether the affect of reproach attaching to it is also present. To the first class belong the typical cases of obsessional ideas, in which the patient's attention is directed to the content, an indefinite affect of discomfort merely being felt, whereas the affect of self-reproach would alone be suited to the content of the obsessional idea. The content of the obsessive act in childhood is changed in a twofold manner before it emerges as an obsessional idea: first, something present is substituted for something past, secondly, something sexual is replaced by something analogous but not sexual. Both these alterations are the effect of the tendency to repression, still in operation—a tendency which we should ascribe to the 'ego'. The influence of the reanimated pathogenic memory is shown by the fact that the content of the obsessional idea is still partly identical with what is repressed, or is derived from it by means of a logical train of thought. If one reconstructs by means of the psycho-analytic method the development of a single obsessional idea one finds that two different trains of thought have been stirred by a recent impression; the one which proceeds *via* the repressed memory proves to be as correctly and logically formed as the other, although it is incapable of becoming conscious and is insusceptible of correction. If the results of the two psychical operations do not harmonize what happens is not a logical reconciliation of the contradiction between the two, but instead, alongside the normal thought-process, there appears in consciousness, as a compromise between the resistance and the pathological thought-process, an apparently absurd obsessional idea. If both trains of thought point to the same end they reinforce each other, so that we find a normally developed thought-process now behaving psychically like an obsessional idea. *Wherever a neurotic com-*

pulsion makes its appearance in psychical life it arises in repression. Obsessional ideas have, so to say, a forced currency psychically, not on account of their intrinsic value, but on account of the source from which they arise or which has furnished a contribution to their value.

The second form of obsessional neurosis comes about if what has compelled representation for itself in conscious mental life is not the repressed memory-content but the self-reproaches that are likewise repressed. The affect of reproach can with the aid of some psychical reinforcement transmute itself into any other unpleasant affect; when this has happened there is nothing to hinder the substituted affect any longer from becoming conscious. Thus *self-reproach* (for having performed a sexual deed in childhood) can easily transform itself into *shame* (lest another person should come to hear about it), into *hypochondriacal anxiety* (lest some bodily injury should result from the action which evoked the self-reproach), into *dread of the community* (fear of punishment by the world at large for the lapse), into *religious anxiety*, into *delusions of reference* (dread of betraying the deed), into *dread of temptation* (justified mistrust in the personal strength of moral resistance), and so on. Together with this the memory of the deed which evokes reproach may either be represented in consciousness too, or be completely withheld—a fact which renders exact diagnosis much more difficult. Many cases which on superficial examination would be regarded as ordinary (neurasthenic) hypochondria belong to this group of obsessional affects; so-called 'periodic neurasthenia' or 'periodic melancholia' in particular appears to be reducible with unexpected frequency to obsessional affects and obsessional ideas—a recognition that is therapeutically by no means unimportant.

In addition to these compromise-symptoms, which signify the return of the repressed and consequently a collapse of the defence originally aimed at, the obsessional neurosis forms a series of further symptoms quite different in origin. The ego seeks to ward off those derivatives of the original repressed memory and in this struggle for defence creates symptoms which may be grouped together as '*secondary defence*' symptoms. These are all '*protective measures*' which had already performed good service in the struggle with the obsessional ideas and affects. If these aids to defence are really successful in once more repressing the symptoms due to the return of the repressed which have been forced upon the ego, then the compulsion is transferred to the protective measures themselves and creates a third form of 'obsessional neurosis'—that of *obsessive actions*. These are never primary, never anything but defensive; they never contain anything of an aggression; psychical analysis of them shows that—in spite of all their oddity—they are to be fully explained by tracing them back to the obsessive memory which they are combating.

To take one example only: an eleven-year-old boy had instituted the following obsessive ceremonial before going to bed. He did not sleep until he had told his mother in the minutest detail all the events of the day; there must be no scraps of paper or other rubbish on the carpet of the bedroom; the bed must be pushed right up to the wall; three chairs must stand by it and the pillows must lie in a particular way. In order to get to sleep he himself must first kick out a certain number of times with both legs and then lie on his side.—This was explained in the following manner: years before a servant-girl who had to put the handsome boy to bed took the opportunity of lying upon him and abusing him sexually. Later on when this memory was awakened by a recent experience, it manifested itself in consciousness in the form of a compulsion to perform the ceremonial described; its meaning was easily guessed and was established point by point by means of psycho-analysis: the chairs by the bedside and pushing the bed against the wall—so that no one could later come near the bed; the pillows arranged in a certain way—so that they should be arranged differently from the way they were on that evening; kicking the legs—pushing away the person lying on him; sleeping on his side—because in the scene he lay on his back; the circumstantial confession to his mother—because he had concealed from her this and other sexual experiences in obedience to his seductress; finally, keeping clean the floor of his bedroom—because this was the principal reproach that he had previously had to endure from his mother.

Secondary defence against obsessional ideas may be brought about by an enforced diversion on to other thoughts, in content as different as possible; therefore when this succeeds *obsessive speculating* results and the thoughts are regularly occupied with abstract, transcendental topics, because the repressed ideas were always of a sensual kind. Or else the patient tries to master each particular idea by logic and by appeals to his conscious memory; this leads to *obsessive thinking*, the *compulsion to test everything*, and to *folie du doute*. The patient's preference for perception over memory in making these tests first leads him, and later compels him, to amass and preserve all objects with which he comes into contact. Secondary defence against the obsessional affects calls into being a still wider series of protective measures, which may be transformed into obsessive acts. These may be grouped according to their tendencies: *penitential* measures (burdensome ceremonials, the observation of numbers) *precautionary* measures (all kinds of phobias, superstitions, pedantry, exaggeration of the primary symptom of conscientiousness), *dread of betrayal* (collecting paper, misanthropia), *hebetude* (dipsomania). Among these obsessive actions and impulses the phobias play the greatest part in circumscribing the patient's life.

There are cases in which one can observe the way in which the compulsion transfers itself from the idea or from the affect on to the defensive measure; others in which the compulsion oscillates periodically between the symptom due to the return of the repressed and the symptom of secondary defence; and still other cases in which no obsessional idea is formed at all, but in which the repressed memory is replaced forthwith by the apparently primary defensive measure. The stage which is otherwise attained only after a defensive battle and which concludes the development of an obsessional neurosis is here reached in one leap. Severe cases of this disease end in the obsessive ceremonial becoming firmly established, in a general *folie du doute*, or in an eccentric way of life conditioned by phobias.

That the obsessional idea and all its derivatives find no credence is probably due to the fact that the defence-symptom of *conscientiousness* is formed at the onset of repression, and that this symptom has a similar obsessional value. The certainty that a moral life has been lived throughout the whole period of successful defence makes it impossible to give credence to the self-reproach involved in the obsessional idea. Only transitorily, upon the appearance of a new obsessional idea or now and then in a condition of melancholic exhaustion of the ego, do the morbid symptoms of the return of the repressed compel belief. The 'compulsion' of the psychical productions here described has in general nothing to do with belief in them and is also not to be confounded with that factor which one designates as the 'strength' or 'intensity' of an idea. Its essential character is rather its insolubility through conscious psychical activity, and this character undergoes no change whether the idea to which the compulsion adheres is strongly or weakly, more or less intensely, 'suffused', 'endowed with cathexis', and so on.

The cause of this invulnerability of the obsessional idea or its derivatives, however, is only its connection with the repressed memory of early childhood; for if it is possible to succeed in making this connection conscious—and psycho-therapeutic methods appear to be already competent to do so—we find that at the same time the compulsion is removed.

III. ANALYSIS OF A CASE OF CHRONIC PARANOIA

For a long time I have entertained the suspicion that paranoia, or groups of cases belonging to it, is also a defence-psychosis; that is to say, that it results from the repression of painful memories, as do hysteria and obsessions, and that the form of the symptoms is determined by the content of the repressed memory. A special path or mechanism of repression, however, must be peculiar to paranoia; just as in hysteria the repression is effectively established by means of *conversion* into bodily innervation, and in the obsessional neurosis by means of *substitution* (displacement along certain associated channels). I observed several cases which favoured this view, but had found none which proved it until I had the opportunity some months ago through the kindness of Dr. J. Breuer of undertaking psycho-analytic treatment of an intelligent woman, aged thirty-two, in whose case the diagnosis of chronic paranoia was undeniable. I am already here reporting a few of the points which it was possible to obtain light upon in the course of this piece of work, because I have no opportunity of studying paranoia except in very isolated cases, and because I consider it possible that these observations may induce a psychiatrist more favourably situated than I to bring the factor of 'defence' into its rightful place in the discussion, now so brisk, on the nature and psychical mechanism of paranoia. On the basis of a single observation I should naturally not think of going further than some such conclusion as this: this case is a defence-psychosis and in the category of paranoia there are probably others like it.

Frau P., thirty-two years of age, three years married and the mother of a two-year-old child, was born of parents who were not nervous; her brother and sister I knew, however, to be also neurotic. It is doubtful whether she was not temporarily depressed and confused in her judgement in her twenties; in later years she was healthy and active until six months after the birth of her child when she showed the first symptoms of her present illness. She became uncommunicative and distrustful, showed a disinclination to meet her husband's family and complained that the neighbours in the small town where she lived had changed towards her and were now rude and disagreeable. By degrees these complaints increased in intensity, though not in definiteness: people had something against her, although she had no notion what it could be; there was not the slightest doubt that everyone—relations and friends—had ceased to respect her, and that they did all sorts of things to wound her; she racked her brains to find the reason for this, but could not discover it. Somewhat later she complained that she was being watched, that people read her thoughts, that they knew everything that went on in her house. One afternoon she suddenly got the idea that people watched her undressing at night. From that time onwards she employed the most complicated precautions when undressing, slipping into bed in the dark and undressing under the bedclothes. Since she cut herself off from the world, ate little, and was very depressed, she was sent in the summer of 1895 to a hydrotherapeutic institution. There new symptoms appeared and those she already had became exacerbated. In the previous spring when alone one day with a housemaid she had suddenly had a sensation in her genitals and the idea came into her mind that the girl had just then had an improper thought. This sensation became more frequent in the summer and was almost continuous, her genitals felt 'as if there was a heavy hand there'. Then she began to see images which horrified her—hallucinations of naked females, in particular an uncovered vulva with hair; occasionally male genitals as well. The vision of the hairy vulva and the physical sensation in the genital organs usually occurred simultaneously. These images were very tormenting to her, for they recurred regularly whenever she was in the company of a woman, and she supposed that she was seeing the woman in a state of most unseemly nakedness and that at the same moment the woman was having the same vision of her (!). Simultaneously with these visual hallucinations, which after their first appearance in the institution disappeared again for several months, voices which she did not recognize and which she could not explain began to pester her; when she was in the street they said, 'That is Frau P. There she goes! Where's she going?' Some one commented on her every movement and action, occasionally she heard threats and reproaches. All these symptoms became worse if she was among several people or even when she was in the street; she therefore refused to go out and then declared that eating disgusted her, so that her condition became rapidly worse.

I gathered this from her when she came to Vienna in the winter of 1895 to be treated by me. I have described the case circumstantially in order to demonstrate that we are really dealing here with a quite frequent type of chronic paranoia; the details of the symptoms and of her conduct which will be adduced later will also support this conclusion. At the time she concealed from me any delusions concerning the meaning of the hallucinations or perhaps they had really not yet been formed; her intelligence was unimpaired; the only unusual thing I was informed of was that she had repeatedly made appointments with her brother, who lived in the neighbourhood, in order to tell him something important but had never actually told him anything. She never spoke about her hallucinations and towards the end said practically nothing about the grievances and persecutions which she suffered from.

What I have to report about this patient concerns the ætiology of the case and the mechanism of her hallucinations. I discovered the ætiology while I was applying Breuer's method, exactly as in a case of hysteria, for the investigation and removal of the hallucinations. I started from the assumption that there must be in this case of paranoia unconscious thoughts and repressed memories, as there were in the two other defence neuroses which were known to me—unconscious thoughts and repressed memories which might be brought to consciousness as in the other cases by overcoming a certain resistance. The patient at once confirmed my expectation by behaving under analysis exactly like, for example, an hysteric; in a state of attention under the pressure of my hand[1] thoughts came into her mind which she did not remember ever to have had, which at first she did not understand and which were quite contrary to her expectations. The presence of significant unconscious ideas was thus demonstrated in a case of paranoia too, and I had hopes of tracing back the compulsion of the paranoia also to repression. The only peculiar thing was that the thoughts arising in the unconscious were usually heard inwardly or hallucinated in the same way as she had heard the voices.

About the origin of the visual hallucinations or at least of the vivid images I gathered the following: The vision of the female genitals came almost always in connection with the organic sensation in her own genitals; but the latter was much more constant and very often occurred without the vision.

The first of these images had appeared in the hydrotherapeutic establishment a few hours after she had actually seen a number of women naked in the bathing-room, and proved therefore to be a simple reproduction of a real impression. It was to be presumed that it had been repeated only because great interest had been taken in it. She then said she had at the time felt shame for those women; she had herself been ashamed to be seen naked as long as she could remember. I had to regard this

[1] Cf. *Studien über Hysterie.*

shame as something obsessive and concluded that according to the defence-mechanism an experience had been repressed for which she did *not* feel shame; so I required her to let any memories come up relating to the topic of shame. She promptly reproduced a series of scenes from her seventeenth back to her eighth year in which she had been ashamed of her nakedness in the presence of her mother while bathing, her sister, or the family physician; the series, however, ended in a scene in her sixth year in which she undressed in the nursery on going to bed without feeling shame about her brother's presence. On being questioned she informed me that such scenes had often occurred and that the brother and sister had for years had the habit of showing themselves to each other naked before going to bed. I now understood the significance of the sudden idea that someone was watching her when she was going to bed. It was an unaltered fragment of the old memory evoking self-reproach and she was now making up for the shame which she had not felt as a child.

The conjecture that we were concerned with an affair between children, as so frequently also in the ætiology of hysteria, was strengthened by further progress in the analysis, which at the same time yielded solutions for several of the details frequently recurring in the clinical picture of paranoia. The beginning of her depression occurred at the time of a quarrel between her husband and her brother in consequence of which the latter no longer came to the house. She had always been very fond of this brother and missed him greatly when this happened. Further, she also referred to a certain period in her illness at which for the first time 'everything became clear to her'—that is to say, the time when she became convinced of the truth of her conjecture that she was generally scorned and deliberately insulted. This certainty came upon her during a visit from a sister-in-law, who in the course of conversation remarked casually, 'If anything of that kind happened to me I should simply shrug my shoulders'. Frau P. at first received this remark with indifference, but later, after the visitor had left, it occurred to her that the words contained a reproach, as if *she* was wont to make light of serious things; and from that moment she felt sure that she was the victim of universal slander. When I questioned her why she felt justified in applying these words to herself, she replied that it was the tone in which her sister-in-law had spoken which (although only later) had convinced her of it—a characteristically paranoiac detail. I now urged her to recollect the remarks which her sister-in-law had made *before* the expression complained of, and I learnt that the sister-in-law had related that in her home there had been all sorts of difficulties with the *brothers*, and had added the wise comment: 'In every family things occur over which one would gladly draw a veil, but if anything of the kind happened to me I should think nothing of it'. Frau P. had now to admit that her depression was related to these sentences before the last remark. Since she had repressed both the two sentences which might have aroused the memory of her relations with her brother and had retained in memory only the insignificant last sentence, she had had to connect her idea that her sister-in-law was intending a reproach against her with this last sentence; and as its contents offered no support to this interpretation she turned from the contents to the *tone* in which these words were spoken. Probably a typical piece of evidence that the misinterpretations of paranoia are based upon repression.

Her singular conduct in fixing appointments with her brother in which she had nothing to say to him was explained in a surprising way. Her explanation was that she thought that if she could only look at him he would understand her suffering because he knew the cause of it. Now since this brother was actually the only person who could know of the ætiology of her illness, it became clear that she had been acting in accordance with a motive which she did not herself consciously understand, but which was seen to be completely justified as soon as a meaning from the unconscious was supplied.

I then succeeded in inducing her to reproduce the various scenes in which the sexual relations with her brother had culminated (they had lasted certainly not less than from her sixth to her tenth year). During this work of reproduction the organic feeling in the genitals 'joined in the discussion'—a regular occurrence during the analysis of the memory-fragments of hysterics. The vision of naked female genitals (now, however, of childish proportions and without hair) appeared or stayed away according to whether the scene in question had occurred in bright light or in the dark. Her disgust in regard to eating, too, was explained by a repulsive detail in these proceedings. After we had come to an end of these scenes the hallucinatory sensations and visions disappeared and, up to the present at least, have not returned.[1]

---

[1] A subsequent exacerbation removed the success of the treatment, which was in any case not very great, and at this later stage she no longer saw the offensive images of strange genitals, but had the idea that strangers saw *her* genitals as soon as they were *behind* her.

Subsequent note by the Author for this Translation. 1922.

The fragmentary account of this analysis in the text above was written while the patient was still undergoing treatment. Very shortly after, her condition became so much more serious that the treatment had to be broken off. She was transferred to an institution and

I had discovered, therefore, that these hallucinations were nothing else but parts of the content of repressed experiences of childhood—symptoms of the return of the repressed.

I now directed my attention to the analysis of the voices In the first place it had to be explained why such an indifferent content as 'Here comes Frau P.', 'She's looking for a house now', and the like, could be so distressing to her; then I turned to the question how these particular harmless sentences had come to be selected for hallucinatory reinforcement. From the first it was clear that these 'voices' could not be hallucinatory reproductions of memories like the images and sensations, but were rather thoughts that had been 'said aloud'.

The first time that she heard the voices occurred under the following circumstances: she had been reading O. Ludwig's novel, *Die Heiterethei*, finding it very thrilling. and had noticed that while reading thoughts kept creeping into her mind. Immediately afterwards she went a walk along a country road and suddenly the voices said to her as she walked past a peasant's cottage: 'That's what Heiterethei's house looked like! There's the spring and there's the shrubbery! How happy she was in spite of all her poverty!' Then the voices repeated to her whole paragraphs from the book she had just read; but it

there went through a period of severe hallucinations having all the signs of dementia præcox. [The original footnote applies to this period.] Contrary to expectation, however, she recovered and returned home, had another child which was quite healthy, and was able for a long period (12 to 15 years) to carry out all her duties in a satisfactory manner. The only sign of her previous psychosis was said to be that she avoided the company of all relatives, whether of her own family or of her husband's. At the end of this period, affected by very adverse changes in her circumstances, she again became ill. Her husband had become unable to work and the relatives she had avoided were obliged to support the family. She was again sent to an institution and died there soon after, of a pneumonia which rapidly supervened.

was still quite unintelligible why the house, shrubbery and spring of Heiterethei, and just the most trifling and irrelevant parts of the novel should be forced on her attention with such pathological intensity. However, the solution of the puzzle was not difficult. The analysis showed that during her reading her mind had wandered and she had become excited by totally different passages in the book. Against this material—analogies between the couple in the novel and herself and her husband, memories of intimacies in her married life and family secrets—there arose a repressing resistance, because it was connected by easily demonstrable trains of thought with her sexual dread and finally amounted to an awakening of the old childhood-experience. In consequence of the censorship exercised by the repression the harmless and idyllic passages, which were connected with the proscribed ones by contrast and also by proximity, became strengthened in consciousness and were able to 'say themselves aloud'. The first of the repressed ideas, for instance, related to the gossip among the neighbours to which the heroine, who lived all alone, was exposed. She easily discovered the analogy with herself in this; she also lived in a small place, saw no one, and thought herself despised by her neighbours. This distrust of her neighbours had a foundation in real experience; for when she was first married she had at first been obliged to be content with a small dwelling, and the wall of the bedroom against which the bed of the young couple stood adjoined a room of the neighbours. Great sexual shyness first awoke in her at the time of her marriage—obviously by its rousing memories of the affair in her childhood when the two children played at man and wife; she was continually apprehensive lest the neighbours should distinguish words and noises through the intervening wall, and this shame turned itself into suspicions of the neighbours in her mind.

The voices therefore owed their origin to the repression of thoughts which, if followed to their conclusion, really signified self-reproaches in regard to experiences which had a significance analogous to that of the trauma in childhood; they were accordingly symptoms of the return of the repressed, at the same time, however, a compromise between the resistance of the ego and the strength of the idea under repression, which in this case had brought about an absolutely unrecognizable distortion. In other instances where I had an opportunity to analyse the voices in Frau P.'s case the distortion was not so great; nevertheless, the words always had the character of diplomatic indefiniteness; the distressing allusion was usually closely hidden, the connection between the particular sentences being disguised by a strange tone of voice, unusual forms of speech, and the like—characteristics common to the auditory hallucinations of paranoiacs and in which I see traces of the compromise-distortion. The remark, 'There goes Frau P., she's looking for a house' signified, for example, a threat that she would never be well again, because I had promised her that after treatment she would be able to return to the small town where her husband's business was;—she had taken a lodging in Vienna for some months.

In isolated instances Frau P. was also aware of more definite threats, for example, as proceeding from her husband's relations, but they were always so mildly expressed as to be in marked contrast to the pain which they caused her. In view of what is known about paranoia I am inclined to believe that gradual weakening of the resistance which is designed to keep the self-reproaches under takes place; so that finally the defence fails completely and the original reproach, the actual insulting word against which protection is being sought, returns in its original form. I do not know however whether this is a regular process, whether the censorship exerted over the reproaching speeches may not sometimes be absent from the beginning, or may not sometimes persist to the end.

It only remains for me now to turn to account what has been learned from this case of paranoia in a comparison between paranoia and the obsessional neurosis. In each of them repression has proved to be the nucleus of the psychical mechanism, and in each of them the repressed content is a sexual experience in childhood. And in this case of paranoia, too, every compulsion comes from repression; the symptoms of paranoia may be classified in the same way that has proved justifiable in regard to the obsessional neurosis. Part of the symptoms again originate in a primary defence—namely, all the delusions of distrust, suspicion and persecution by others. In the obsessional neurosis the initial self-reproach has undergone repression by the formation of the primary symptom: *self-distrust*. The self-reproach is thereby recognized as justified and, in compensation, a recognition of the conscientiousness in the healthy interval serves as a protection against belief in the reproaches when they return in the form of obsessions. In paranoia the reproach is repressed in a manner which may be described as *projection*;[1] by the defence-symptom of *distrust directed against others* being erected; in this way recognition of the reproach is withheld, and, as if in return, protection is lost against the self-reproaches which reappear in the delusions.

[1] [The first use of this technical term.—Ed.]

Other symptoms of my case of paranoia are to be described as symptoms of the return of the repressed and bear traces, as do those of the obsessional neurosis also, of a compromise which alone makes its entry into consciousness possible. Such are, for instance, the delusion that she is being observed while undressing, the visions, the sensory hallucinations and the hearing of voices. In the delusion mentioned, almost unaltered memories are present, which are only indefinite because a part of their content is omitted. The return of the repressed in visual images approximates more to the character of hysteria than to that of obsessional neurosis; although hysteria is wont to repeat its memory-symbols without modification, whereas the paranoiac memory-hallucination undergoes a distortion similar to that of the obsessional neurosis—an analogous current image takes the place of the repressed one (the genitals of an adult woman instead of that of a child, the hair on the former being particularly prominent because it was lacking in the original impression). A circumstance quite peculiar to paranoia and one that cannot be cleared up in this comparison is that the repressed reproaches return as thoughts spoken aloud. They must thereby suffer a two-fold distortion, first, through a censorship, which leads to their substitution by other associated ideas or to a disguise by indefinite kinds of expressions, and secondly, through their relation to current experiences which are merely analogous to the original.

The third group of symptoms found in the obsessional neurosis, those of a secondary defence, cannot be present in paranoia as such; because the symptoms of the return of the repressed are not opposed by any defence—indeed, they find acceptance. Paranoia, on the other hand, turns to another source in forming symptoms; the delusions which by means of a compromise succeed in becoming conscious (symptoms of the return of the repressed) absorb the thought-processes of the ego until they finally become accepted without contradiction. Since the delusions themselves are not to be influenced, the ego must accommodate itself to them; and thus the combinatory delusion-formations, such as *interpretation-delusions* ending in a *change within the ego*, correspond to the secondary defence in the obsessional neurosis. My case was in this respect not fully developed; at that time there was no sign of the attempts at interpretation which appeared later. But I do not doubt that it will still be possible to arrive at further important results if psycho-analysis is applied also to this stage of paranoia. It might then be proved that the so-called *weakness of memory* in paranoiacs is a tendencious manifestation, that is, that it is based upon repression and serves the ends of repression. Finally, even memories which are not in the least pathogenic, but which stand in contradiction to that change within the ego that the symptoms of the return of the repressed so tyrannically demand, become repressed and replaced.

X

THE ÆTIOLOGY OF HYSTERIA[1]

(1896)

I

When we endeavour to form some opinion about the causation of a morbid condition such as that of hysteria we first of all adopt the method of anamnestic enquiry, examining the patient or his friends about the harmful influences to which they themselves trace the appearance of the particular neurotic symptoms. The value of what we discover in this way is, of course, impaired by all the various circumstances which commonly conceal from a patient the knowledge of his own condition—his lack of scientific understanding of ætiological influences, the fallacy *post hoc, ergo propter hoc*, the distress it causes him to think or speak of certain noxiæ and traumas. Hence, in making any such enquiry we adhere to the principle of not adopting the patients' belief without a thorough critical examination and not allowing them to lay down for us our scientific opinion upon the ætiology of the neurosis. Although on the one hand we acknowledge certain constantly recurring statements, as that the hysterical condition is a long-persisting effect of an emotional disturbance which once took place, we have on the other hand introduced into the ætiology of hysteria a factor which the patient himself never cites and only reluctantly admits—namely, the disposition in-

[1] First published in the *Wiener klinische Rundschau*, 1896, Nr. 22 to 26. Amplification of a lecture delivered at the Society of Psychiatry and Neurology in Vienna, May 2, 1896. [Translated by Cecil M. Baines.]

herited from his parents. You know that in the opinion of the influential school of Charcot heredity alone is to be recognized as the real cause of hysteria, whilst all other harmful influences of the most varying kind and intensity only play the part of exciting causes, of '*agents provocateurs*'.

You will readily admit that it would be desirable to find another way of arriving at the ætiology of hysteria, one in which we should feel less dependent on the statements of the patients themselves. The dermatologist, for instance, is able to recognize the luetic character of a sore from the nature of its edges, of the crust upon it and from its shape, without being misled by the protestation of the patient who denies any source of infection. In forensic medicine, the physician can explain how an injury has been caused, even without any information from the injured person. Now in hysteria there exists a similar possibility of penetrating from the symptoms to knowledge of their causes. As for what concerns the relation which the method to be employed bears to the older method of anamnestic enquiry, I will put before you a simile taken from an advance which has in fact been made in another field of work.

Imagine that an explorer comes in his travels to a region of which but little is known and that there his interest is aroused by ruins showing remains of walls, fragments of pillars and of tablets with obliterated and illegible inscriptions. He may content himself with inspecting what lies there on the surface and with questioning the people who live near by, perhaps semi-barbaric natives, about what tradition tells of the history and meaning of these monumental remains, and taking notes of their statements—and then go his way. But he may proceed differently; he may have come equipped with picks, shovels and spades, and may press the inhabitants into his service and arm them with these tools, make an onslaught on the ruins, clear away the rubbish and, starting from the visible remains, may bring to light what is buried. If his work is crowned with success, the discoveries explain themselves; the ruined walls are part of the ramparts of a palace or a treasure-house, from the ruined pillars a temple can be constructed, the many inscriptions, which by good luck may be bilingual, reveal an alphabet and a language, and when deciphered and translated may yield undreamed-of information about the events of the past, to commemorate which these monuments were built. *Saxa loquuntur!*

If one tries in something the same way to let the symptoms of a case of hysteria tell the tale of the development of the disease, we must start from the momentous discovery of J. Breuer: that the symptoms of hysteria (apart from stigmata) are determined by certain experiences of the patient's which operate traumatically and are reproduced in his psychic life as memory-symbols of these experiences. We must adopt Breuer's method — or one of a similar kind—in order to lead the patient's attention from the symptom back to the scene in and through which it originated; and having thus discovered it, we proceed when the traumatic scene is reproduced to correct the original psychical reaction to it and thus remove the symptom.

It is no part of my intention to-day to treat of the difficult technique of this therapeutic method or the psychological revelations it has achieved. I had to start from this point, simply because analyses conducted on Breuer's method seem at the same time to open up the way to the causes of hysteria. If we subject a large number of symptoms in many people to this analysis, we shall come to know of a correspondingly large number of traumatically operative scenes. We have learnt to recognize in these experiences the efficient causes of hysteria; hence we may hope to discover from the study of these traumatic scenes by what influences and in what ways hysterical symptoms are produced.

That this expectation is justified follows from the fact that Breuer's theses, when put to the test in more numerous cases, prove to be actually correct. But the way from the symptoms of hysteria to its ætiology is longer and introduces us to all sorts of unexpected connections.

For let us be quite clear that tracing an hysterical symptom back to a traumatic scene assists our understanding only if the scene in question fulfils two conditions—if it possesses the required *determining quality* and if we can credit it with the necessary *traumatic power*. Let me give an illustration instead of a mere explanation of terms. Suppose that the symptom in question is that of hysterical vomiting, we think we can apprehend its cause (or at any rate leave only a certain part unexplained) if analysis traces the symptom to an experience which justifiably gave rise to a high degree of disgust, for instance the sight of a decomposing corpse. Supposing, instead of this, analysis traces back the vomiting to some great shock, e. g. a railway accident, this explanation will be unsatisfactory and we shall have to ask ourselves how it is that the shock led to the particular symptom of vomiting. This derivation of the symptom lacks determining quality. We have another instance of an unsatisfactory explanation when the vomiting is said to have originated in eating a fruit which had a rotten spot in it. Then the vomiting is indeed determined by disgust, but we cannot understand how the disgust in this case could be so powerful as to perpetuate itself in an hysterical symptom; the experience lacks traumatic power.

Now let us consider to what extent the traumatic scenes of hysteria which are revealed in analysis fulfil the two above requirements in a large number of symptoms and cases. Here we encounter our first great disappointment. It does sometimes happen that the traumatic scene in which the symptom originated really possesses both properties which we require in order to understand the symptom: determining quality and traumatic force. But far oftener—incomparably so—we find realized one of three other possibilities which are very difficult to understand: either the scene indicated by analysis in which the symptom first made its appearance seems to us not qualified to determine the symptom, for its content bears no relation to the form of that symptom; or the ostensibly traumatic experience whose content is so related proves to be a normally harmless impression, one which ordinarily would have no effect; or finally the 'traumatic scene' disconcerts us in both directions, appearing both harmless and altogether unrelated to the peculiar form of the hysterical symptom.

(Here I may remark in passing that Breuer's conception of the origin of hysterical symptoms is not affected by the discovery of traumatic scenes which represent experiences in themselves insignificant. For Breuer assumed—in agreement with Charcot—that even a harmless experience may acquire the significance of a trauma and may develop determining power when the subject is in a particular psychic condition, the so-called *hypnoid state*. I find, however, that often there are no grounds for presupposing such hypnoid states. What is definite is that the theory of hypnoid states contributes nothing to the solution of the other difficulties, namely, that so often the traumatic scenes are lacking in determining quality.)

Moreover, this first disappointment in the practice of Breuer's method is followed immediately by another which must be specially grievous to a physician. Such derivations as these which do not contribute to our understanding of the case in respect of determining quality and traumatic force are also of no therapeutic advantage; the patient keeps his symptoms unaltered, in spite of the first result yielded by analysis. You will understand how great the temptation then is to go no further with work which, apart from this, is laborious.

But perhaps we only need a fresh inspiration to help us out of our dilemma and lead to valuable results. Here it is:—we know indeed through Breuer that hysterical symptoms may be resolved if, starting from them, we can find our way back to the memory of a traumatic experience. If the memory so revealed does not answer our expectations, possibly we must pursue the same path a little further; perhaps there is hidden behind the first traumatic scene the recollection of a second, which satisfies our requirements better and the reproduction of which has a better therapeutic result, so that the scene first discovered has only the significance of a link in the chain of association. And perhaps this situation repeats itself, inoperative scenes being in several places interpolated as necessary transitions in the reproduction, till finally, starting from the hysterical symptom, we arrive at the scene which really operates traumatically and is in every respect, from both the therapeutic and the analytic point of view, satisfactory. Well, this supposition is correct. When the scene first revealed does not satisfy our requirements, we say to the patient that this experience does not explain anything, but that there must be hidden behind it an earlier and more significant experience, and, following the same technique, we direct his attention to that strand in the associations which unites both memories—that which we have found and that which we have still to find.[1] Continuation of the analysis then leads in every instance to the reproduction of new scenes of the kind we should expect: for example, to instance again the case of hysterical vomiting which I selected before and which was first referred by analysis to the shock of a railway accident. Now although this experience lacks the determining quality, I find on further analysis that this accident woke the memory of another which had happened previously, in which the patient had not, it is true, been himself involved, but which was the occasion of his seeing a corpse, a sight which aroused in him horror and disgust. It is as though the combined influence of these two scenes led to the fulfilment of our two postulates, the one experience supplying, in the shock, the traumatic force and the other, in its content, the determining influence. The other instance, where the vomiting was traced to eating an apple in which there was a rotten spot, is amplified through analysis somewhat as follows: the rotting apple roused the memory of a former experience of picking up fallen apples in a garden when the patient happened to come on the loathsome carcase of an animal.

[1] We purposely refrain from discussing what type of association unites the two memories (whether their relation is temporal, causal or that of similarity of content, etc.) and from asking what psychological character (conscious or unconscious) is to be attributed to these 'memories'.

I will not again return to these examples, for I must admit that they are not taken from any case in my experience, but that I invented them, and most probably they are bad inventions; I myself regard such explanations of hysterical symptoms as impossible. But there were several reasons why I had to make up examples, and one reason I can state at once. The real examples are all of them far and away more complicated; to relate a single one of them in detail would occupy the whole of this lecture hour. The chain of associations has always more than two links; the traumatic scenes do not form simple rows like a pearl necklace, but they branch out and are interconnected like genealogical trees, a new experience being influenced by two or more earlier ones in the form of memories; in short, to give an account of the resolution of a single symptom is practically synonymous with the task of giving a complete history of a case.

But now I must not neglect to lay special emphasisis on the one conclusion derived, quite unexpectedly, from analytic work by means of these chains of recollections. We have found out that no hysterical symptom can originate in one real experience alone, but that in every instance the memory roused by association co-operates with earlier experiences in causing the symptom. If this conclusion is (as I believe) *without exception* correct, it indicates the foundation upon which a psychological theory of hysteria is to be built.

You might think that those rare instances in which analysis can trace the symptom immediately to a traumatic scene of satisfactory determining quality and traumatic force and, by so tracing it, at the same time remove it (as described in Breuer's history of the case of Anna O.) would surely constitute powerful objections to the general validity of the conclusion just propounded. Certainly it looks as if that were so; but I can assure you I have the best of reasons for assuming that even in these cases there exists a chain of operative memories which stretches far back behind the traumatic scene, even though the reproduction of the latter alone may result in the removal of the symptom.

In my opinion it is really astonishing that hysterical symptoms should arise only where memories are at work, especially when we reflect that these memories, according to all the statements of the patients themselves, did not come into consciousness at the moment when the symptom first made its appearance. Here is food for much reflection, but for the present we must not let these problems deflect the course of our discussion of the ætiology of hysteria. Rather we must ask ourselves: where shall we get to if we follow the chain of associated memories revealed to us by analysis? How far do they go? Is there any point at which they come naturally to an end? Do they perhaps lead to experiences which are in any way similar, whether by relation of time or of content, so that in these universally similar factors we may discern that ætiology of hysteria for which we are seeking?

My experience up till now enables me already to answer these questions. Taking a case which presents several symptoms, from whatever symptom we start we arrive by means of analysis at a series of experiences the memories of which are linked together by association. At first the memory-chains are distinct from one another as they lead backwards, but, as we said before, they branch out; from a single scene two or more memories may be reached at the same time, and from these again there issue side-chains the single links of which may in their turn be joined by association to links of the main chain. The metaphor of a family tree of which the members have also intermarried is really not a bad one. Other complications in the linking up of the chains arise from the circumstance that a single scene in the same chain may be several times recalled to memory, so that it is related in more than one way to a later scene, and may prove both to be directly connected with it and also to be joined by means of intermediate links. In short, the connection is by no means a simple one, and the fact that the scenes are discovered in reverse chronological order (the very feature which justifies our comparison with the excavation of ruins) certainly does not contribute to a more rapid understanding of the process.

New complications are met if the analysis is pursued further. The chains of associations for the separate symptoms then begin to enter into relation with one another; the family trees intertwine. When we come to a certain experience in the memory-chain which has reference, for instance, to the symptom of vomiting, besides the backward-leading links in this chain, there is revived a memory which belongs to another chain and which is the basis of another symptom, perhaps that of headaches. So that experience belongs to both series and thus constitutes a *nodal point*, several of which are to be found in every analysis. Its clinical correlation may perhaps be that from a certain time on the two symptoms occur together, symbiotically, really without any inner mutual dependence. Still further back we find nodal points of another sort. There the chains of associations converge; we find experiences in which two or more symptoms have originated.

One chain has attached itself to one detail of the scene and a second chain to another detail.

But the most important result arrived at by such a consistent pursuit of analysis is this: whatever case and whatever symptom we take as our starting-point, *in the end we infallibly come to the realm of sexual experience.* So here for the first time we would seem to have discovered an ætiological condition of hysterical symptoms.

From previous experience I can foresee that it is just against this conclusion or against its universal validity that your opposition will be directed. Perhaps it would be more correct to say: your inclination to opposition, for probably none of you can refer to investigations which, if the same method had been employed, would have yielded a different result. On the actual matter in dispute I will only remark that in my case at least there was no preconceived opinion which led me to single out the sexual factor in the ætiology of hysteria. The two investigators as whose pupil I began my work on the subject, Charcot and Breuer, emphatically had no such presupposition, in fact they had a personal disinclination to it which I originally shared. Only the most laborious and detailed investigations have converted me, and that slowly enough, to the opinion which I defend to-day. If you subject to the closest scrutiny my assertion that the ætiology of hysteria is to be sought in the sexual life, it amounts to the statement that I can assure you that, in some eighteen cases of hysteria, I was able to recognize this connection to hold for every single symptom and, when circumstances permitted, to confirm the fact by therapeutic success. You may of course object that the nineteenth and twentieth analyses would perhaps show that hysterical symptoms can be derived from other sources also, and that thus the validity of the sexual ætiology would not be universal but would be reduced to 80 per cent. By all means let us wait and see, but since those eighteen cases are at the same time *all* those which I was able to analyse, and since nobody picked them out to please me, you will understand that I do not share any such expectation, but am prepared to let my belief outrun the evidential force of my discoveries up to the present time. Besides, I am influenced by yet another motive, which for the moment is of merely subjective value. In the single attempt to explain the physiological and psychical mechanism of hysteria that I have made for the purpose of embracing the results of my observations, I have found the participation of sexual impulses an indispensable hypothesis.

So, the memory-chains having converged, we come at last to sexual things and to some few experiences which for the most part occur at the same period of life, namely, the age of puberty. In these experiences we are to find the ætiology of hysteria and through them learn to understand how hysterical symptoms originate. But here we meet with a fresh disappointment and a grave one. It is true that these experiences which have been discovered and extracted from the whole mass of memories with such difficulty and seemed to be the ultimate traumata, have two characteristics in common: they are sexual and they occur at the time of puberty, but otherwise they are very different in kind and unequal in importance. In some cases it was a matter of experiences which must be recognized as serious traumata—an attempt at rape, revealing at one blow to the immature girl the whole brutality of sexual desire; or the involuntary witnessing of sexual acts on the part of the parents, which at one and the same time reveals unsuspected ugliness and wounds both the childish and the moral sensibility; and so forth. In other cases these experiences are astonishingly trivial. The experience on which the neurosis of one of my patients was shown to be based was that a boy friend had stroked her hand caressingly and on another occasion had pressed his leg against her dress as they sat side by side at table, his expression at the same time leading her to guess that this was something forbidden. With another young lady, hearing a riddle which suggested an obscene answer actually sufficed to call forth the first anxiety-attack with which the illness began. Clearly, discoveries such as these are not favourable to an understanding of the cause of hysterical symptoms. If both serious and trifling occurrences, experiences undergone by the patient in person as well as visual impressions and verbal communications may be recognized as the ultimate traumata of hysteria, we may perhaps put forward the explanation that hysterics are peculiarly constituted human beings—probably on account of some hereditary disposition or process of degeneration—in whom the shrinking from sexuality which normally plays a certain part at the age of puberty is developed to a pathological extent and is permanently retained; so to speak, persons who are not adequate mentally to the demands of sexuality. It is true that in this statement we pass over hysteria in men; but, even without such an obvious objection, it would scarcely be a very great temptation to halt at this solution. We are only too conscious intellectually that we have here something only half understood, something obscure and unsatisfactory.

Luckily for our explanation, certain of these sexual experiences at puberty display a further inadequacy likely to stimulate us to continue our analytic work. For we find that these experiences may also too lack the determining quality, though this is much rarer than in the traumatic scenes of later life. So, for example, the two patients whom I spoke of above as cases in which the experiences of puberty were actually harmless began, in consequence of those experiences, to suffer from peculiar painful sensations in the genital organs. These sensations had persisted as main symptoms of the neurosis, but it could not be shown that they were determined either by the scenes at puberty or by later ones; certainly they were neither normal organic sensations nor manifestations of sexual excitation. Does it not then seem obvious to say that we must look for the determining quality of these symptoms in yet other experiences, dating from an even earlier period; that here, for the second time, we must follow that saving inspiration which led us before from the first traumatic scenes to the memory-chains? To be sure, by so doing, we get back to the time of earliest childhood, the time before the sexual life developed, and this would seem to involve abandoning our sexual ætiology. But have we no right to assume that even the age of childhood is not without delicate sexual excitations, more, that perhaps the later sexual development is decisively influenced by childish experiences? Injuries sustained by an organ as yet immature, or a function in process of development, do indeed so often cause graver and more lasting effects than can ensue in riper years. Perhaps the abnormal reaction to sexual impressions which surprises us in hysterics at puberty is always due to such sexual experiences in childhood, experiences which might then prove to be significant and similar in kind? We should then come to the view that certain things must be regarded as having been acquired in early life which hitherto have been laid to the charge of some by no means clearly understood hereditary predisposition. And, since infantile experiences of a sexual nature can surely manifest a psychic influence only through their memory-traces, would not this view bear out in a gratifying manner the result reached in analysis—namely, that the influence of memories is essential for the production of hysterical symptoms?

II

You will doubtless have suspected that I should not have developed this last train of thought at such length, if I had not wished to prepare you for the idea that this path alone, after our many delays, can lead us to the goal. For now we really stand at the end of our lengthy and laborious analytic work and find fulfilled here all that we have so far maintained and expected. When we are persevering enough to carry our analysis back into early childhood, to the very furthest point which human memory can reach, we thereby in every instance cause the patient to reproduce the experiences which, on account both of their special features and of their relation to subsequent morbid symptoms, must be regarded as the ætiology for which we are looking. These *infantile* experiences are once more *sexual* in content, but are far more uniform in kind than was the case in the scenes of puberty which we had lately discovered; it is now no longer a question of sexual thoughts being awakened by any chance sensory impression, but of sexual experiences undergone by the patient personally, of sexual intercourse (in a wide sense). You will admit that the importance of such scenes needs no further argument; to this you may now add that in the details of this scene you can invariably discover the determining factors which were perhaps still lacking in those other scenes that had taken place later and were reproduced earlier.

I put forward the proposition, therefore, that at the bottom of every case of hysteria will be found one or more experiences of premature sexual experience, belonging to the first years of childhood, experiences which may be reproduced by analytic work though whole decades have intervened. I believe this to be a momentous revelation, the discovery of a *caput Nili* of neuropathology, but I hardly know from what point to continue the discussion of the situation. Shall I set out before you the actual material I have obtained from the analyses I have conducted, or ought I not rather first of all to try to meet the mass of objections and doubts which I am probably right in supposing to be at this moment absorbing your attention? I choose the latter course; perhaps we shall then be able to dwell on the facts with a more objective mind.

(*a*) Anyone who is altogether opposed to the psychological conception of hysteria, who is unwilling to give up the hope of one day tracing its symptoms to 'finer anatomical changes' and has rejected the view that the material foundations of hysterical changes must necessarily be similar in kind to those of our normal mental processes—anyone who adopts this attitude will naturally put no faith in the results of our analyses; but the difference in principle between his premisses and ours absolves us from any obligation to convince him on single points.

But someone else, less determined to reject psychological theories of hysteria, will when considering our analytical results be tempted to ask what degree of certainty the application of psycho-analysis involves; whether it is not very possible either that the physician forces such scenes upon the docile patient, alleging them to be recollections, or that the patient tells him things which he has purposely invented or spontaneous phantasies which the physician accepts as genuine facts. Well, my answer is that the general misgiving about the reliability of the psycho-analytic method can be appraised and removed only when a complete presentation of its technique and results is available; doubts about the genuine nature of the infantile sexual scenes, however, can be deprived of their force here and now by more than one argument. In the first place, the behaviour of the patients who reproduce these infantile experiences is in every respect incompatible with the assumption that the scenes are anything but a most distressing reality which is recalled with the utmost reluctance. Before they are analysed, the patients know nothing of these scenes; they are generally indignant if we tell them that something of the sort is now coming to light; they can be induced only under the very strongest compulsion of the treatment to engage in reproducing the scenes; whilst calling these infantile experiences into consciousness they experience the most violent sensations, of which they are ashamed and which they endeavour to hide, and they still try, even after going through them again in so convincing a fashion, to withhold belief by emphasizing the fact that they have no feeling of recollecting these scenes as they had in the case of other forgotten material.

Now this last attitude on their part seems absolutely decisive. Why should patients assure me so emphatically of their unbelief, if from any motive they had invented the very things that they wish to discredit?

It is less easy to refute the charge that the physician forces reminiscences of this sort upon the patient and influences him by suggestion to imagine and recount them; nevertheless I think this position is just as untenable. I have never yet succeeded in forcing on a patient a scene that I expected to find in such a way that he appeared to live through it again with all the appropriate emotions; perhaps others are more successful.

There is however a whole series ot further evidence which vouches for the reality of the infantile sexual scenes. First, they display just the uniformity in certain details that would necessarily follow from the identically-recurring conditions of the existence of these experiences; otherwise we should have to believe in a secret conspiracy between the individual patients. And again, patients often describe them as if they were harmless events, the significance of which they obviously do not perceive, for if they did they would be shocked; or they mention details to which they attach no importance but which only someone with experience of life knows of and can appreciate as subtle indications of reality.

Such occurrences strengthen the impression that patients must actually have experienced what they reproduce under the compulsion of analysis as scenes from childhood, and we have yet another and even more convincing proof when we examine the relation of the infantile scenes to the content of the whole subsequent history of the illness. Just as when putting together children's picture-puzzles, we finally after many attempts become absolutely certain which piece belongs to the gap not yet filled—because only that particular piece at the same time completes the picture and can be fitted in with its irregular edges to the edges of the other pieces in such a way as neither to leave a space nor to overlap —so the content of the infantile scenes proves to be an inevitable completion of the associative and logical structure of the neurosis; and only after they have been inserted does its origin become evident—one might often say, self-evident.

Without wishing to lay special stress on the fact, I will add that in a number of cases the therapeutic test also speaks for the genuine nature of the infantile scenes. There are cases in which a complete or partial cure can be achieved without going down as far as the infantile experiences; others in which there is no success at all until the analysis comes to its natural end with the discovery of the earliest traumata. I think that in the former cases we are not secure against relapses; my belief is that a complete psycho-analysis implies the radical cure of a case of hysteria. However, do not let us here anticipate what experience will show.

There would be yet one more proof, one which is really unassailable, of the genuineness of the childish sexual experiences—namely, the confirmation of the statements of the person analysed by the account of someone else who is, or is not, under treatment. These two persons must have taken part in the same experience in their childhood, perhaps had stood in a sexual relation to one another. Such relations between children are, as you will hear in a moment, by no means rare; moreover, it quite often happens that both persons concerned suffer subsequently from neuroses; and yet I regard it as a fortunate accident that I have had objective confirmation of this kind in two out of my eighteen cases. In one instance, the brother, who had not fallen ill, of his own accord confirmed for me not, it is true, the earliest sexual experiences with his sister, the patient, but at least scenes of this kind from their later childhood and the fact of sexual relations dating further back. Another time it happened that two women whom I was treating had as children had sexual intercourse with the same man, when certain scenes had occurred in which all three took part. A particular symptom which could be traced to these childish experiences had been developed in both cases and bore witness to this common experience.

(*b*) Sexual experiences in childhood consisting of stimulation of the genitals, coitus-like activities, etc. are therefore in the final analysis to be recognized as the traumata from which proceed hysterical reactions against experiences at puberty and hysterical symptoms themselves. Two objections which contradict each other are sure to be raised from different quarters against this statement. Some will say that such sexual abuses, practised on children or by children on one another, happen too seldom to be regarded as conditioning so common a neurosis as hysteria; others will perhaps maintain that such experiences are, on the contrary, very frequent, far too frequent for us to ascribe ætiological significance to them where their existence is proved. Further, it will be urged that it is easy enough on enquiry to find people who remember scenes of sexual seduction and abuse in their childhood, but yet have never suffered from hysteria; finally, as a weighty argument, that in the lower strata of the population hysteria certainly does not appear more frequently than in the highest, while surely everything goes to show that the rule of keeping a child from everything sexual is transgressed far more commonly among the proletariat.

Let us begin our defence with the easier part of our task. It seems to me certain that our children are far oftener exposed to sexual aggressions than we should suppose, judging by the scanty precautions taken by parents in this matter. When I first made enquiries about what was known on the subject, I learnt from colleagues that there are several publications by children's physicians in which the frequency of sexual practices by nurses and attendants with their charges, even with infants, is complained of and in the last few weeks I have come across a study by Dr. Stekel of Vienna on 'Coitus in Childhood.'[1] I have not had time to collect other published evidence, but even if only isolated testimony were forthcoming, we might expect that increased attention to this subject would confirm the great frequency of sexual experiences and sexual activity in childhood.

Lastly, the results of my analysis may speak for themselves. In all the eighteen cases (of pure hysteria and hysteria combined with obsessions: six men and twelve women) I have, as I said, discovered such sexual experiences in childhood. I may divide my cases into three groups, according to the source of the sexual excitation. In the first group it was a question of assaults—single or at any rate isolated instances of abuse by grown-up strangers (who took care to avoid gross mechanical injury) where consent by the children did not enter into the matter and the first and preponderating result of the experience was terror. A second group consists of those far more numerous cases in which some adult attendant of the child—a maid, nurse, governess, teacher, unhappily only too often a near relation—initiated the child into sexual intercourse and maintained a regular

[1] *Wiener Medizinische Blätter*. 18. April 1896.

love-relation with him, often for years, which had its mental counterpart. To the third group belong finally the real child-relations, sexual relations between two children of different sex, mostly between brother and sister, which are often continued past the age of puberty and have far-reaching consequences for the two concerned. In most of my cases I could trace the combined influences of two or more such ætiologies; in certain instances the accumulation of sexual experiences from different quarters was really amazing. You will understand this peculiarity in my observations more easily when you consider that the cases were all of severe forms of neurosis involving almost complete incapacity for life.

Where there had been a relation between two children I was sometimes able to prove that the boy—who played the aggressive part—had previously been seduced by a woman, and that then, urged on by his prematurely aroused libido and in consequence of the obsessive memory, he tried to repeat with the little girl exactly the same practices as he had learnt from the adult, without attempting any independent modification in the form of the sexual activity.

So I am inclined to assume that without previous seduction children cannot find the way to acts of sexual aggression. The foundation of the neurosis would accordingly have been laid in childhood by adults, and the children themselves have transmitted to one another the disposition to suffer later from hysteria. I ask you to pause for a moment upon the special frequency of sexual relations in childhood between brothers and sisters, or cousins, due to the opportunity afforded by their being constantly together; now suppose that ten or fifteen years later several of the younger generation of the same family are found to be ill, and then ask yourselves whether this familial type of neurotic manifestation would not naturally lead us to assume an hereditary disposition, where there is actually only *pseudo-heredity*, a transmission or infection having taken place in childhood.

Now let us turn to the other objection which is based upon the very frequency—freely admitted—of infantile sexual experiences and the fact that many people who have not developed hysteria remember such scenes.

We shall reply in the first place that excessive frequency in an ætiological factor cannot possibly be used as an objection to its ætiological significance. Is not the tubercle bacillus ubiquitous, inhaled by many more human beings than suffer from tuberculosis? And is its ætiological significance impaired by the fact that it clearly needs the concurrence of other factors to produce the disease that is its specific effect? It is enough to establish it as the specific cause that tuberculosis is never found where the bacillus is not active. The same is probably true of our problem also. It makes no difference that many people go through infantile sexual experiences without developing hysteria, so long as all those who do become hysterics have had such experiences. The radius of an ætiological factor may be wider, but not less wide than its effect. Not everyone who touches or comes near a smallpox patient develops smallpox, and yet infection from an actual case of it is almost the only known ætiology of the disease.

Of course if infantile sexual activity were an almost universal occurrence, it would prove nothing to find it in every case. But first, such a statement would be a grave exaggeration, and secondly, the ætiological pretensions of infantile scenes rest not only on their constant appearance in the anamnesis of hysterics, but above all on the evidence of the associative and logical connections between these scenes and the hysterical symptoms, connections which would be as clear as daylight to you if you had the complete history of the illness.

What are the other factors that are necessary to the 'specific ætiology' of hysteria in order actually to produce the neurosis? Now this is really a theme in itself, one which I do not propose to discuss; to-day I need only indicate the point of contact at which the sides of the question—the specific and the subsidiary ætiology—fit into one another. Probably a considerable number of factors will have to be considered: inherited and personal constitution; the importance of the infantile sexual experiences in themselves and particularly their number—a short relation with a boy outside the patient's family to whom she later becomes indifferent will not have so powerful an effect as intimate sexual relations with a brother lasting for several years. In the ætiology of the neurosis quantitative conditions are just as important as qualitative; there are thresholds which have to be crossed if the illness is to manifest itself. Moreover, I myself do not regard the ætiological series mentioned above as complete, nor do I think it solves the problem why hysteria is not more common in the lower classes. (You will remember, by the way, how surprisingly frequent Charcot declared it to be in the *men* of the working classes.) But I may also remind you that I myself a few years ago indicated a factor hitherto but little remarked, to which I ascribe the leading part in the production of hysteria *after* puberty. At that time I put forward the view that the outbreak of hysteria may almost invariably be traced to a *psychic conflict*, arising through an unbearable idea having called up the *defences* of the ego and demanding repression. In what circumstances this attempt at defence has the pathological effect of actually thrusting into the unconscious a memory painful to the ego and creating an hysterical symptom in its place I could not at that time say. I can complete my statement today: The defence achieves its purpose of thrusting the unbearable idea out of consciousness, if in the (hitherto normal) person concerned infantile sexual scenes exist in the form of unconscious memories and if the idea to be repressed can be brought into logical or associative connection with any such infantile experience.

Since the ego's attempt at defence depends on the whole moral and intellectual development of the person concerned, the fact that hysteria is so much rarer in the lower classes than would follow from its specific ætiology is no longer entirely incomprehensible.

Let us go back once more to the last group of objections, the answer to which has led us so far afield. We have heard and acknowledged that there are many people who have a very clear recollection of infantile sexual experiences and yet do not suffer from hysteria. This objection has really no weight at all, but it provides an occasion for a valuable comment. People of this type *should* not (according to our understanding of neurosis) be hysterical at all, at least not in consequence of scenes which they consciously remember. In our patients these memories are never conscious; we cure their hysteria, however, by converting their unconscious memories of infantile scenes into conscious recollection. We could not in any way alter the fact that they had such memories nor need we. From this you perceive that it is not merely a question of the existence of the infantile sexual experiences, but that a certain psychological condition enters into the case. These scenes must exist as *unconscious memories;* only so long and in so far as they are unconscious can they produce and maintain hysterical symptoms. But upon what the consciousness or unconsciousness of these memories depends, whether it be conditioned by their content, or by the time at which they occur, or by some later influences, is a fresh problem which we will take care to avoid. Let me just remind you that the first result of analysis is embodied in the conclusion: hysterical symptoms are derivatives of memories operating unconsciously.

(*c*) If we hold fast to the assumption that infantile sexual experiences are the fundamental condition of hysteria—constitute, if I may say so, the *disposition* to that disease—they yet do not produce hysterical symptoms directly, for in the first instance they have no effect and exercise a pathogenic influence only later when they are roused after puberty in the form of unconscious memories—then we have to deal with the numerous observations which prove that hysterical illness may already make its appearance in childhood and before puberty. But this difficulty is solved when we examine more closely the particulars gathered in analysis about the period when these infantile sexual experiences took place. We then find that in our severe cases the formation of hysterical symptoms begins, not exceptionally but regularly, with the eighth year, and that those sexual experiences which show no direct result invariably date further back, to the third and fourth or even the second year. Since in no single instance does the chain of effective experiences break off with the eighth year, I must assume that this time of life, the period of growth in which the second dentition occurs, forms a boundary line for hysteria, which cannot be caused when once this line is passed. Anyone who has not had sexual experiences before this cannot be disposed to hysteria after this; anyone who has had them is ready to develop hysterical symptoms. The isolated instances of the occurrence of hysteria on the other side of the dividing line of age (before eight years) may be interpreted as evidence of premature development. The existence of this dividing line has probably some connection with processes of development in the sexual system. Premature sexual development on the physical side may often be observed and we may even suppose that it may in general be promoted by premature sexual excitation.

So we have an indication that a certain infantile condition of the psychic functions, as of the sexual system, is necessary in order that a sexual experience occurring within this period should subsequently, in the form of a memory, exercise a pathogenic influence. Still I do not as yet venture to make any more precise statement about the nature of this psychic infantilism and its temporal limits.

(*d*) Another of our critics might possibly take exception to the idea that the memory of infantile sexual experiences should have so tremendous a pathogenic effect, while the experience itself had none. True, we are not accustomed to find that a memory-picture has a power that the real impression lacked. Here, however, we note, by the way, with what consistency the proposition that symptoms can only proceed from memories is borne out in hysteria. All the later scenes at which the symptoms begin are not the causative ones: those which really are causative do not at first have any effect. But here we are confronted by a problem which we may justifiably keep separate from our main theme. We feel indeed that synthesis is required of us when we reflect upon the number of remarkable conditions we have come to recognize: that in order to form an hysterical symptom there must be an effort of defence against a painful idea; that this idea must be shown to have an associative and logical connection with an unconscious memory, many or few links being present, all of which remain unconscious too for the time being; that the content of the unconscious memory must be sexual; that that content is an experience which occurred at a certain infantile period of life; and we cannot help asking how it comes about that this memory of an experience which was harmless at the time can subsequently have the abnormal effect of conducting to a pathological issue a psychic process like that of defence, while itself remaining all the time unconscious.

But one must say to oneself that this is a purely psychological problem, the solution of which may perhaps require certain assumptions about normal psychic processes and the part played in them by consciousness; for the time, however, it may remain unsolved without robbing of its value the insight so far acquired into the ætiology of hysterical phenomena.

III

The problem I have just formulated concerns the *mechanism* of hysterical symptom-formation. But I have to present the causation of these symptoms without taking this mechanism into consideration, and the conclusions are consequently bound to forfeit something in clearness and completeness. Let us go back to the part played by the infantile sexual scenes. I am afraid that I may have misled you in the direction of over-estimating their power to form symptoms. So I will again emphasize the fact that every case of hysteria displays symptoms which are determined not by infantile, but by later, often by recent experiences. Other symptoms, of course, date from the very earliest experiences, have, so to speak, the longest pedigree. Such are especially the numerous and manifold sensations and paræsthesias of the genital organs and other parts of the body, sensations which simply correspond to those belonging to the infantile scenes, reproduced in hallucinatory fashion and often intensified to a painful degree.

Another series of exceedingly common hysterical phenomena—painful bladder pressure, painful sensations in defecation, intestinal disturbances, choking and vomiting, indigestion and nausea—could similarly be recognized in my analyses (and that with surprising regularity) as derivatives of the same childhood-experiences and were explained without difficulty by certain invariable features of these episodes. Now the feeling of a sexually normal human being recoils from the idea of these infantile sexual scenes, containing, as they do, all the abuses known to libertines and impotent persons, whose sexual practices include the improper use of the mouth and the rectum. The physician's astonishment at this soon gives place to complete understanding. We cannot expect that people who do not scruple to gratify their sexual desires upon children will be repelled by any lack of refinement in the manner of that gratification, and the natural sexual impotence of childhood inevitably impels towards those surrogate activities to which the adult degrades himself in the case of acquired sexual impotence. All the peculiar circumstances in which the ill-matched pair carry on their love-relation: the adult—who cannot escape his share in the mutual dependence inherent in a sexual relation and yet is endued with complete authority and the right of punishment, and can exchange the one rôle for the other in unbridled gratification of his moods; the child—helpless victim of this capriciousness, prematurely awakened to every kind of sensation and exposed to every kind of disappointment, often interrupted in the practice of the sexual activities assigned to him by his imperfect control of his natural needs—all these grotesque, yet tragic, incongruities become stamped upon the further development of the person concerned and his neurosis, manifesting themselves in innumerable lasting consequences which deserve to be carefully traced out. Where the relation is one between two children, the character of the sexual scenes is still repulsive, since every relation of the sort between children postulates a previous seduction of one of them by an adult. The psychic consequences of such a childhood-relation are quite extraordinarily far-reaching; the two persons remain all their lives united by an invisible bond.

Sometimes it is the accidental circumstances of these infantile sexual scenes which in later years exercise a determining influence upon the symptoms of the neurosis. Thus in one of my cases the circumstance that the child was required to stimulate the genitals of an adult woman with his foot sufficed for years to fix neurotic attention on the legs and their functions and finally to produce an hysterical paraplegia. In another case a patient suffering from anxiety-attacks which tended to come on at certain hours of the day could not be calmed unless one particular sister remained at her side. It would have remained a problem why she would not allow this one of her many sisters to leave her, had not analysis revealed that formerly the man who seduced the patient used to ask every time he came whether this sister, from whom he anticipated an interruption, was at home.

It may happen that the determining power of the infantile scenes disguises itself so effectually that it would certainly be overlooked in a superficial analysis. We imagine that we have found the explanation of a certain symptom in the content of one of the later scenes, but in the course of the analysis we come upon the same content in one of the infantile scenes, so that finally we have to admit that after all the later scene owes its power of determining the symptoms only to its agreement with the earlier one. I do not wish for this reason to represent the later scene as of no importance; if my task were to discuss the laws of hysterical symptom-formation, I should have to recognize as one of these laws that the idea chosen as the basis of a symptom will be one which various factors combine to arouse and which is stirred up from several directions simultaneously; —a state of affairs I have elsewhere tried to formulate by saying that *hysterical symptoms are over-determined*.

One thing more. It is true that so far I have set aside the relation between recent and infantile ætiology as a theme apart; nevertheless I cannot leave the subject without making at least one remark on this point. You will admit that there is one fact in particular which is apt to mislead us in the understanding of the psychology of hysterical phenomena, which so often seem to warn us not to judge by the same standard psychic acts in hysterics and in normal people. I refer to the discrepancy between psychic excitation and psychic reaction which we observe in hysterics and for which we try to account by assuming in them a general abnormal sensibility to stimulation; we often attempt to explain it in terms of physiology, as though in such patients certain organs of the brain which serve to transmit stimuli were in a peculiar morbid state (something like the spinal centres of a frog which has been injected with strychnine) or else had withdrawn from the influence of the higher, inhibiting centres, as in animals experimented upon in vivisection. Here and there either of these conceptions may be a perfectly valid explanation of hysterical phenomena: I do not deny it. But the most important part of the phenomenon, that is, of the abnormal, exaggerated, hysterical reaction to psychic stimuli admits of another explanation, supported by countless instances taken from the analyses of patients. This explanation is as follows: the reaction of hysterics only appears exaggerated; it is bound to appear so to us, because we know only a small part of the motive forces behind it.

In reality, this reaction is proportionate to the exciting stimulus, and therefore normal and psychologically intelligible. We immediately perceive this when analysis has added to the manifest causes of which the patient is conscious those other causes which have contributed to the result, though the patient knows nothing about them and is therefore unable to tell us anything.

I could spend hours demonstrating the validity of this important assertion for the whole range of psychic activity in hysterics, but here I must confine myself to a few examples. You will remember the mental 'hypersensitiveness' so common in hysterics, which leads them to react to the least suggestion of depreciation as to a deadly insult. Now what would you think if you observed such a readiness to take offence in two normal people, for instance husband and wife? You would certainly infer that the conjugal scene you witnessed was not simply the result of the present trifling occasion, but that, for a long time, inflammable material had been accumulating and that the whole mass had now been brought to an explosion by this last shock.

Now apply this train of thought to hysterics. It is not the last, in itself infinitesimal, mortification which produces the fit of crying, the outbreak of despair, the attempted suicide—regardless of the axiom that effect must be proportioned to cause, but this trivial actual mortification has roused and set working the memories of so many, far more intense, previous mortifications, behind all of which lies the memory of a serious one in childhood, one which the patient never got over. Or, when a young girl reproaches herself most bitterly for allowing a boy secretly to caress her hand, and from that moment is the victim of neurosis, you can of course explain it by pronouncing her to be an abnormal, eccentric, hypersensitive person; but you will take a different view when analysis shows that the touch reminded her of a similar one felt in very early youth, which was part of a less harmless story, so that really the reproaches belong to that former occasion. Finally, the problem of hysterogenic areas is another of the same kind; if you touch one particular spot, you do something you did not intend: i. e. you wake a memory which may bring on an hysterical attack, and since you know nothing of the psychic connecting link you refer the attack directly to your touch. The patients are equally ignorant and therefore fall into similar errors; they constantly establish 'false connections' between the last recent cause of which they are conscious and the effect which depends on so many intermediate links. But if the physician succeeds in linking up the unconscious and the conscious determinants of an hysterical reaction, he nearly always has to recognize that this seemingly exaggerated reaction is appropriate and is abnormal only in form.

You may now rightly object to this justification of the hysterical reaction to psychic stimuli that it is none the less abnormal, for why do healthy people behave differently? Why do not all the long-past excitations in them also combine afresh to operate when there is a real new excitation? We do indeed get the impression that in hysterics all the former experiences, to which there has so often already been such a violent reaction, retain their power of producing an effect, as though these people were incapable of discharging psychic stimuli. That is so; we must indeed assume something of the sort. Do not, however, forget that the former experiences of hysterics become operative on some actual occasion, in the form of *unconscious memories*. It seems as though the difficulty of discharge, the impossibility of transforming an actual impression into a powerless memory, was related to the nature of the unconscious part of the mind. You see that the rest of the problem is again psychology, a psychology too for which philosophers have done little to prepare the way.

To this psychology, which has yet to be constructed to meet our requirements—the future *patho-psychology*—I must also refer you when in conclusion I tell you something which at first will make you apprehensive lest it should confuse our dawning understanding of the ætiology of hysteria. For I must state that the ætiological rôle of infantile sexual experiences is not confined to hysteria, but holds good equally for the remarkable obsessional neurosis and perhaps even for the different forms of chronic paranoia and other functional psychoses. I express myself on this point less definitely, because I have analysed far fewer cases of obsessional neurosis than of hysteria; I have actually only a single full analysis and several fragmentary ones of cases of paranoia to which to refer. But what I discovered in these cases seemed to me reliable evidence and gave me confident expectations for future cases. You will perhaps remember that I had already placed both hysteria and obsessions under the single heading of 'defence neuroses', even before I knew of common features in the infantile ætiology of both. Now I must add—though this is a thing which of course need not be of general occurrence—that every one of my cases of obsessional neurosis revealed a substratum of hysterical symptoms, mainly sensations and pains, which were traced to those earliest experiences of childhood. What then determines whether the subsequent developments of the infantile sexual scenes shall take the form of hysteria or obsessional neurosis, or even paranoia, when the other pathogenic factors supervene? These additions to our knowledge would seem to diminish the ætiological significance of these scenes, for the ætiological relation would lose its specific character.

I am not yet able to give a positive answer to this question. The number of cases I have analysed is not large enough, nor have the conditioning factors been sufficiently various. So far I have noted that obsessional ideas can regularly be shown by analysis to be disguised and transformed self-reproaches for sexual aggressions in childhood, that they are therefore more frequently met with in men than in women, and that men develop them more often. From this I might conclude that the character of the infantile scenes—whether the experience was pleasurable or was merely passively submitted to—has a determining influence upon the choice of the subsequent neurosis, but again I do not wish to underestimate the significance of the age at which these childish activities take place, and of certain other factors. On these points we need discussion of further analyses to guide us to a conclusion; but when it becomes clear which are the decisive factors in the choice between the possible forms of defence neurosis, the mechanism by which that particular form develops will once more be a purely psychological problem.

I have now come to the end of my subject for today's discussion. I am prepared for contradiction and unbelief, and will therefore say one thing more in support of my position. Whatever you may think of my conclusions, I have the right to ask you not to look upon them as the fruit of idle speculation. They are based on laborious individual examination of patients, which in most cases has taken a hundred hours and more of work. Even more important to me than your estimation of my results is the direction of your attention to the method I have used, which is novel, difficult to handle and yet irreplaceable for scientific and therapeutic purposes. I am sure you will realize that one cannot gainsay the conclusions reached by the use of this modification of Breuer's original method if one neglects that method and uses only the ordinary one of questioning the patient. To do so would be like trying to refute the discoveries of histological technique by the aid of macroscopic investigations. Since the new method of research gives access to a new element in psychic processes, namely, to that which remains unconscious or, to use Breuer's expression, is *incapable of entering consciousness*, it beckons to us with the hope of a new and better understanding of all functional mental disturbances. I cannot believe that psychiatry will long hold back from this new path to knowledge.

XI

SEXUALITY IN THE ÆTIOLOGY OF THE NEUROSES[1]

(1898)

Detailed investigations during the last few years have led me to the conviction that factors arising in sexual life represent the nearest and practically the most momentous causes of every single case of nervous illness. This theory is not entirely novel; a certain amount of ætiological importance has always been allowed to sexual factors by all writers on the subject. Many of the side-currents of medicine assure us of a cure for 'sexual complaints' and for 'nervous debility' in one and the same breath. Once its validity is no longer denied, it will not be hard, therefore, to dispute the originality of the theory.

In several short papers which have appeared in the last few years in the *Neurologisches Zentralblatt*, the *Revue Neurologique* and the *Wiener klinische Rundschau*, I have endeavoured to give some account of the material and the points of view which offer scientific support to the doctrine of the 'sexual ætiology of the neuroses'. Detailed presentation of them, however, has not yet been undertaken, mainly because, while attempting to explain the observed actual interrelations between the phenomena, new problems arise, for the solution of which the necessary preliminary researches are lacking. It does not seem to me, however, at all premature to attempt

---

[1]) First published in the *Wiener klinische Rundschau*, 1898, Nos. 2, 4, 5, and 7. [Translated by J. Bernays.]

to direct the attention of practitioners to the circumstances that, as I maintain, exist, so that they may convince themselves of the accuracy of my conclusions and at the same time of the benefits to be derived in medical practice by a knowledge of them.

I know that efforts will be made, based upon arguments of an ethical nature, to prevent physicians from pursuing this topic further. Anyone who wishes to assure himself whether or not his patients' neuroses are really connected with their sexual life cannot avoid the necessity of questioning them about it and demanding a truthful account from them. But in this, it is asserted, lies the danger, both for the individual and for society. I hear it said that a physician has no right to intrude upon his patients' privacy in sexual matters, or to wound their modesty (especially that of his women patients) so grossly as such an interrogation would do. His clumsy hand would only ruin family happiness, and with youthful patients destroy innocence and undermine the authority of parents; with adults he would become the uncomfortable possessor of disquieting knowledge and his relations with his patients would suffer in consequence. It is therefore his ethical duty to hold himself aloof from the whole question of their sexual life.

One may well reply to this that it is nothing but prudery, concealing scanty justification behind very weak arguments, and is unworthy of a medical man. If factors arising in sexual life are definitely recognizable as causes of disease, then investigation and discussion of them come on this ground alone without further ado into the range of a physician's professional duty. The offence against modesty which he thereby commits is no different and no worse, I imagine, than when he insists on examining a woman's genital organs in order to treat a local affection—a demand which his training itself binds him to make. Even to-day one hears that older women whose youth was spent in country places often become reduced by excessive genital hæmorrhages to a state of severe prostration, because they cannot make up their minds to permit a physician to see them uncovered. As a result of the educative influence exercised in the course of a single generation by the medical world upon the general public, an objection of this kind is only in the rarest cases exhibited by young women at the present time. Whenever it does occur it is condemned as unreasonable prudishness—modesty out of place—and the husband might well ask: 'Are we living in Turkey, where a sick wife may only show her arm to a doctor through a hole in the wall?'

It is not true that interrogation and communications referring to sexual matters give the physician a dangerous power over his patient. The same objection might with more justification have been alleged in earlier days against the use of anæsthetics, which deprive the patient of consciousness and will-power and leave it to the physician to decide when and whether they are to return. And yet we cannot do without anæsthetics to-day, because they enable the physician to render help better than anything else; he has taken over the responsibility for them along with his other weighty professional duties.

A physician can always do harm if he is clumsy or unscrupulous, no more and no less in probing into the sexual life of his patients than in other directions. Naturally, if anyone discovers by a meritorious endeavour to arrive at self-knowledge that he is deficient in the tact, seriousness and discretion necessary for interrogating neurotic patients, if anyone knows that revelations of a sexual character will evoke in himself only lewd thoughts instead of scientific interest, he will do right to keep away from the subject of the ætiology of the neuroses. We only ask in addition that he should avoid treatment of nervous patients altogether.

Neither is it true that patients themselves raise insuperable objections to an investigation of their sexual life. After some slight hesitation, grown-up persons usually adjust themselves to the situation by saying: 'I am at the doctor's; I can say anything to him.' Numerous women who find it difficult enough to go through life with the task of concealing their sexual feelings are relieved to find that to the physician their recovery is the paramount issue, and are grateful to him for allowing them for once to behave quite naturally in regard to sexual matters. A dim comprehension of the overwhelming importance of sexual factors in producing neurosis (a recognition which I am trying to formulate anew for medical science) seems actually never to have quite passed out of the consciousness of the laity. How often do scenes like this take place: A married couple comes for consultation, one of the two suffering from neurosis. After some introductory remarks and explanations to the effect that no conventional barriers should be allowed to interfere when a physician wishes to help in such a case, and so forth, one tells them one's surmise that the origin of the malady will be found to lie in an unnatural and harmful form of sexual intercourse, which they have probably been practising since the wife's last confinement. Physicians are not in the habit of concerning themselves with these matters, but this attitude on their part is ill-advised, notwithstanding the fact that patients don't wish to discuss these things; and so forth. Then one partner nudges the other and says, 'You see, I told you all along it would make me ill', and the other partner answers, 'Well, I know, I thought so too, but what is one to do?'

In certain other circumstances, such as, for instance, with young girls who are systematically trained to conceal their sexual life, the physician will have to content himself with a very modest measure of sincerity in the patient's admissions. But an important consideration that has to be taken into account on the other side is that an experienced physician does not meet his patients unprepared and as a rule asks of them not elucidation but merely confirmation of his surmises. Anyone who will follow these indications of mine, in the matter of how the morphology of the neuroses is to be regarded and translated into ætiological terms, will require but little more in the way of confessions from his patients; in the very description of their symptoms, which they volunteer only too readily, they will usually have acquainted him with the sexual factors hidden behind.

It would be a great advantage if patients could know the extent to which physicians will henceforth be able to interpret their neurotic complaints with certainty, and to infer from them the sexual ætiology at work; it would undoubtedly stimulate them, from the moment they have made up their minds to seek relief for their troubles, to throw off their secretiveness. Moreover, it is to the interest of us all that a higher measure of sincerity in sexual matters should obtain among us than is demanded at the present time. Sexual morality can only gain by this; in matters of sexuality at present we are all, every one of us, hypocrites, whether we be ill or well.

It will only be advantageous if a certain amount of tolerance in sexual matters results from more widespread honesty in this regard.

Medical practitioners have usually very little interest in many of the questions discussed among neuropathologists with regard to the neuroses: for instance, whether it is justifiable to differentiate strictly between hysteria and neurasthenia, whether a hystero-neurasthenia may also be distinguished beside these forms, whether obsessional ideas should be classified with neurasthenia or recognized as a special form of neurosis, and so on. In actual life such distinctions may well be a matter of indifference if nothing further results from the decision—no deeper insight, no landmark pointing out a direction for therapeutic efforts—so long, too, as the patient is invariably sent off to a hydrotherapeutic establishment—or told that there is nothing the matter with him! It would be otherwise, however, if the point of view advanced here about the causative relations between sexuality and the neuroses were adopted; fresh interest is then aroused by the symptomatology of the various neurotic ailments, and an ability to analyse the complicated picture correctly into its component parts and to classify these correctly becomes of practical importance. For the morphology of neurosis may be translated into its ætiology with very little difficulty, and with a knowledge of the latter new therapeutic indications spring to life as a matter of course.

Now it is always possible, in every instance, by careful consideration of the symptoms to reach a decision which is important, namely, whether the case bears the characteristic marks of neurasthenia or of some form of psychoneurosis (hysteria, obsessions). (Very frequently composite-formations occur, in which signs of neurasthenia are intermingled with those of a psychoneurosis; we will, however, leave consideration of them till later.) Only in the various forms of neurasthenia does interrogation result in disclosing the ætiological factors belonging to sexual life; these factors are naturally known to the patient and belong to the present, or more properly, to the period since maturity (although this limitation in time does not cover all cases). With cases of psychoneurosis an interrogation of this kind has little result, though it may perhaps gain for us a knowledge of factors which must be recognized as exciting or contributory and may or may not be related to sexual life. When they are so related they manifest themselves as of the same type as the ætiological factors of neurasthenia, that is, they entirely lack any specific relation to the cause of the psychoneurosis. And yet the ætiology of the psychoneuroses, too, in every instance lies in the patient's sexual life. By a curious by-path, which will be considered later, it is possible to arrive at a knowledge of this ætiology and to understand why the patient could not tell us anything about it; for the events and influences which lie at the root of every psychoneurosis belong not to the present time, but to a long-past period, to a prehistoric period of life, so to say—to early childhood, and that is why the patient knows nothing of them. He has—but only in a certain sense—forgotten them.

Thus we have a sexual ætiology in all cases of neurosis; in neurasthenia, however, this is of present-day origin, whereas in the psychoneuroses the factors belong to infancy; this is the first important contrast in the ætiology of the neuroses. A second contrast appears when we take account of a distinction in the symptomatology of neurasthenia itself.

On the one hand, we find cases in which definite symptoms characteristic of neurasthenia are conspicuous: cranial pressure, tendency to fatigue, dyspepsia, constipation, irritation of the spine, and so forth. On the other hand, in certain cases these indications are of minor importance and the syndrome is composed of other symptoms which all show a relation to one main symptom, to 'anxiety' (free-floating anxiety, restlessness, expectant anxiety, complete, rudimentary or supplementary anxiety-attacks, locomotor vertigo, agoraphobia, sleeplessness, exacerbation of pains, etc.). I have left to the former type of neurasthenia its designation, but have distinguished the second as 'anxiety-neurosis' and have justified this separation elsewhere, there also taking into account the fact that both neuroses commonly appear together. For the present purpose it is sufficient to emphasize that a distinction in the ætiology runs parallel with a symptomatic differentiation in the two forms. Neurasthenia may always be traced back to a condition of the nervous system such as is induced by excessive masturbation, or may arise spontaneously on account of frequent emissions. In the anxiety-neurosis there may regularly be found conditions relating to the sexual life which all have in common the element of abstinence or of incomplete satisfaction: such as coitus interruptus, abstinence with strong libido, so-called frustrated excitation, and so forth. In the short paper intended to introduce the anxiety-neurosis I put forward the view that anxiety actually was libido diverted from its usual course.

Wherever symptoms of neurasthenia are mingled in any one case with those of anxiety-neurosis, that is, where a composite-formation appears, the thesis (which has been empirically arrived at) may be adopted that a combination of neuroses represents the co-operation of several ætiological factors; in every instance this expectation is confirmed. It would be well worth while to discuss in detail how often these ætiological factors are closely interwoven organically by the interrelation of sexual processes, as, for instance, coitus interruptus or insufficient potency of the husband with masturbation.

Having accurately diagnosed a case of neurasthenic neurosis under observation, and correctly classified its symptoms, one may proceed to transpose into ætiology the symptomatological knowledge so gained and may fearlessly require the patient's confirmation of one's surmises. Denial at the beginning should not mislead the physician; every resistance is finally overcome by firmly insisting on what has been inferred, and by emphasizing the unshakable nature of one's convictions. In this manner one learns all kinds of things about the sexual life of men and women which might well fill a useful and instructive volume; we learn, too, to regret from every point of view that scientific knowledge of sexual matters is still regarded as opprobrious. Since minor digressions from the normal *vita sexualis* are much too frequent for the discovery of them to constitute a factor of much importance, only serious and long-continued abnormality in the sexual life of neurotic patients will be allowed to weigh as an explanatory agent; and, also, it may safely be regarded as an imaginary danger that a patient who is psychically normal could be induced by a physician's persistence to accuse himself falsely of sexual misdemeanours.

If we proceed in this manner with our patients we also gain the conviction that no cases of neurasthenia are negative in respect to a sexual ætiology. In my mind, at least, the conviction has become so fixed that I have turned to account the negative result of an interrogation in making a diagnosis; that is, I have conluded that such negative cases could not be neurasthenia. In this way I arrived in several instances at a diagnosis of general paralysis instead of neurasthenia, because it was not possible to demonstrate the frequent masturbation required according to my theory; and the further course of these cases confirmed my judgement as correct. In another instance when the patient, in the absence of any apparent organic lesions, complained of cranial pressure, headache and dyspepsia and met my suspicions regarding his sexual life with honesty and serene certainty, it occurred to me to suspect a latent suppuration in one of the nasal sinuses, and a specialist colleague of mine confirmed this conclusion—which I had arrived at through the negative results of the interrogation on the sexual life—by relieving the patient of his ailment through the removal of putrid matter from the antrum.

The illusion that negative cases do exist, in spite of all this, can arise in other ways as well. Sometimes interrogation reveals a normal sexual life in persons whose neurosis, superficially viewed, really resembles neurasthenia or anxiety-neurosis very closely. More penetrating investigation, however, regularly reveals the true state of affairs. Behind such cases, which have been taken for neurasthenia, there lies a psychoneurosis: an hysteria or obsessional neurosis. Hysteria in particular, which apes so many organic affections, can with ease assume the appearance of one of the forms of actual neurosis by giving hy terical value to the symptoms of the latter. Such forms of hysteria coming under the guise of neurasthenia are not even very infrequent. To fall back on a psychoneurosis wherever neurasthenia shows a negative result sexually is, however, not a cheap way out of the difficulty, and the proof that it is so lies in the only process which unmasks hysteria completely—namely, in the method of psycho-analysis, which will be discussed later.

There may, however, be many who are quite willing to take the sexual ætiology into account with their neurasthenic patients, but who will yet regard it as going too far if they are not required to consider as well the other factors which are always mentioned by medical writers as the causes of neurasthenia. Now it would never occur to me to suggest that we should substitute a sexual ætiology in the neuroses for all the others and thereby declare the latter entirely inoperative. That would be a misunderstanding of my attitude. What I mean is simply that the sexual factors, which have hitherto not been properly estimated, are to be taken into account in addition to all the well-known ætiological factors mentioned by the medical authors, which have probably been quite correctly recognized as such. These sexual factors, however, according to my view of them, deserve a special position in the series of ætiological factors. For they alone are never absent in any case of neurasthenia; they alone are capable of producing neurosis without other contributory factors, so that these other factors seem to be reduced to the position of a supplementary or auxiliary ætiology; they alone permit the physician to recognize the constant interrelation between the manifold forms in which they appear and the many varieties of clinical pictures. When, on the other hand, I review the cases in which neurasthenia has apparently developed because of over-work or emotional excitement, or as the after-effect of typhoid fever and similar diseases, the various symptoms they show appear to have nothing in common; I am not able to form any expectation about the symptoms from the special character of the ætiology, nor can I derive anything about the ætiology at work from the clinical picture presented.

The sexual factors are also those which most readily lend themselves as starting-points for therapeutic efforts. Heredity is doubtless a momentous factor when it is present; it can enable a serious morbid effect to develop where otherwise only an insignificant one would have appeared. But heredity is not amenable to the influence of the physician; every human being has his own hereditary morbid tendencies from birth; we cannot alter anything in them. Nor should we forget that, precisely in the ætiology of neurasthenia, we are bound of necessity to forego the first place to the influences of heredity; neurasthenia, both forms of it, is among those diseases which anyone may readily acquire without being hampered by heredity. If it were otherwise, the prodigious increase in neurasthenia of which all writers on medical subjects complain would be inconceivable. As far as civilization is concerned, too, it is possible that these authorities may be judging correctly in so often reckoning the causation of neurasthenia in the list of its crimes (although this probably comes about in a very different way from that which they suppose); yet the state of our civilization again is unalterable for the individual. Incidentally, this factor, being as it is of the same importance for all the members of one community, can in no way explain the fact of selection in the incidence of the disease. The physician himself actually lives, unaffected by neurasthenia, under the same conditions in this apparently morbific civilization as the neurasthenic patient whom he is to treat.—The significance of exhausting influences remains intact, after allowing for the limitation mentioned above. But the factor of 'over-work', which physicians are so fond of allowing their patients to regard as the cause of their neuroses, is unduly misused. It is quite true that anyone who has become disposed to neurasthenia through an injurious mode of sexual life tolerates intellectual work and the emotional stress of existence very badly, but it never happens that work or excitement alone makes anyone neurotic. Intellectual effort is rather a protection against neurasthenic illness; the most unremitting of intellectual workers are precisely the people who remain untouched by neurasthenia, and what neurasthenics call 'dangerous over-work' does not as a rule deserve the name of 'brain work' at all, regarded either qualitatively or quantitatively. Physicians will have to accustom themselves to explain to an official who has been 'over-done' at the office, or to a housewife whose duties in her home have become too much for her, that they have fallen ill not because they have tried to fulfil tasks which for the brain of a civilized person are really quite easy, but because all the time they have sorely neglected and played havoc with their sexual life.

Further, the sexual ætiology alone makes it possible to comprehend all the details of the clinical history of neurasthenics, the mysterious improvement in the course of the illness and the equally incomprehensible relapses, both of which are usually referred by physicians and patients to the therapy that has been undertaken. In my records, embracing the histories of more than two hundred cases, there is, for example, the story of a man who, when the treatment prescribed by the family physician had failed, had recourse to Father Kneipp and, beginning with this therapy, showed an extraordinary improvement in the very middle of his illness. A year later, however, the troublesome symptoms grew worse and he again sought relief at Wörishofen, but the second treatment failed to bring any improvement. A glance into the history of this patient's family affairs solved the double riddle. Six and a half months after his first return from Wörishofen the patient's wife gave birth to a child (in fact, without knowing it, he had left her at the beginning of a pregnancy) and after his return he was able to have normal intercourse with her. At the close of this period, which was beneficial to his neurosis, his ailment was rekindled by recourse to coitus interruptus again, so that the second treatment was bound to show negative results, for the pregnancy mentioned above was the last that occurred.

Another case in which a similar unexpected influence of treatment called for explanation took an even more instructive form; for a strange alternation in the symptoms of the neurosis showed itself. A young neurotic patient had been sent by his physician for a typical neurasthenia to a well-conducted hydrotherapeutic establishment. In this establishment his condition at first improved so much that he was justifiably expected soon to depart as a grateful convert to hydrotherapeutic methods. In the sixth week a sudden change occurred; the patient 'couldn't stand the water any longer', became more and more nervous, and finally left the establishment after two more weeks, dissatisfied and unrelieved of his trouble. When he complained to me about the deceptive action of the therapy, I asked him a few questions about the symptoms which had set in during it. Strange to say, there had been a complete change in them. He had come to the sanatorium complaining of cranial pressure, lassitude and dyspepsia; the disturbances in the course of the treatment had been excitement, attacks of dypsnœa, locomotor vertigo and troubled sleep. Now I was able to tell the patient: 'You are not fair to hydrotherapy. You fell ill, as you know yourself, on account of long-continued masturbation. In the sanatorium you gave up this form of gratification and therefore improved rapidly. But when you felt well you unwisely sought the company of a lady, let us say one of your fellow-patients, and started a relationship with her which without normal satisfaction could only lead to excitement. The beautiful walks in the neighbourhood of the institution gave you many opportunities. Your relapse is due to this relationship, and not to a sudden inability to tolerate hydrotherapy. From your present condition I should conclude, by the way, that you are continuing this relationship here in town as well.' I can assure the reader that the patient confirmed my supposition point for point.

The present treatment of neurasthenia, carried out perhaps most successfully in hydrotherapeutic establishments, aims at amelioration of the nervous condition by means of two factors, rest and recuperation. I know of nothing against this therapy, except that it does not take into account the circumstances of the patient's sexual life. According to my experience, it would be highly desirable for the medical directors of such establishments to become fully aware that they are dealing not with victims of civilization or of heredity, but—*sit venia verbo*—with persons disabled by their sexuality. They would then, on the one hand, more readily find explanations both for their successes as well as their failures, and on the other hand, achieve new results, which are now dependent upon chance or upon the patient's undirected course of action. If a neurasthenic woman suffering from anxiety is taken away from home and sent to a hydrotherapeutic establishment, freed from all duties, able to bathe, to take gymnastic exercise and plenty of food, one is naturally inclined to give the credit for the splendid improvement which often sets in within a few weeks or months to the quiet life which the patient has been enjoying and to the invigoration which hydrotherapy has brought about. That may be so: but it is apt to be overlooked, that with the separation from home there is also an interruption in marital relations and that it is precisely this temporary removal of the originating cause of the ailment which makes it possible for her to recuperate under the influence of favourable treatment. Neglect of this point of view in regard to the ætiology avenges itself, too, when the apparently satisfactory cure proves to be a very transitory one. Soon after the patient has returned to her ordinary way of life, the symptoms of the trouble reappear and force her from time to time to spend a part of her existence unproductively in establishments of this kind, or else to turn in another direction for hope of recovery. It is therefore clear that in neurasthenia the therapy must take its starting-point within the radius of the patient's ordinary existence, and not in sanatoria.

This ætiological theory will also explain the source of failures which medical superintendents of sanatoria would greatly like to prevent—failures of the treatment within the establishment itself. Masturbation among grown-up girls and adult men is far more frequent than is commonly supposed and has a harmful effect not only by producing neurasthenic symptoms, but also because the patient is kept under the oppression of a secret which he feels to be shameful. Physicians who are not accustomed to translate neurasthenia into masturbation account for the diseased condition by referring it back to some catchword like anæmia, over-work, and so on, and then expect the patient to recover after undergoing a therapy devised to remedy such things. To their astonishment, however, periods of improvement alternate with periods in which all the symptoms grow worse and are accompanied by severe depression. The outcome of such a therapy is generally doubtful. If the physician knew that all the time the patient was struggling with this bad habit and is in despair because he has once again been overcome by it, if he understood how to relieve the patient of his secret, to diminish its importance in the patient's eyes and to support him in his fight against the habit, the success of the therapeutic efforts might well be assured.

To induce the patient to abandon the habit of masturbation is only one of the new therapeutic tasks which confronts the physician upon consideration of a sexual ætiology, and this one seems, in common with every other attempt to wean people from some form of indulgence, practicable only in an institution under medical supervision. Left to himself, whenever things are at all depressing the masturbator usually turns to the gratification that he finds so easy and comforting. Medical treatment can then only set itself the goal of leading the neurasthenic who has recovered his health back to normal forms of sexual satisfaction; for, once it has been aroused and satisfied for any length of time, sexual need is not to be silenced again but can only be transferred to another object. Incidentally, the same thing applies to all abstinence-treatments, which will succeed only superficially as long as physicians content themselves with removing the narcotic from the patient without troubling about the source of this imperative need for the drug. 'Habit' is merely an empty phrase without any explanatory significance; not everybody who has occasion to take morphine, cocaine, chloral-hydrate and the like for a space of time thereby acquires a craving for them. More searching examination generally shows that these narcotics are intended as substitutes (directly or indirectly) for the missing sexual gratification, and wherever normal sexual life cannot be re-established a patient who has been weaned from his habit may be expected quite certainly to slide back into it.

The other task set the physician by this ætiology refers to the anxiety-neurosis; it consists in bringing the patient to abandon all injurious varieties of sexual intercourse and to enter into normal sexual relations. As will be readily understood, this duty falls to the lot of the patient's confidential adviser, that is, the family physician, who is seriously at fault in his duty to the patient if he considers it beneath his dignity to meddle in such matters.

Since he has most often to deal with married couples in these instances, he at once finds his efforts confronted by the current malthusian tendencies to limit the offspring of marriage. I have not the least doubt that these principles are gaining ground more and more among our middle classes; I have come across couples who began to practise the prevention of conception as soon as the first child was born, and others who intended that sexual intercourse should accord with these principles from the wedding-night itself. The problem of malthusianism is a far-reaching and complicated one; I have no intention of treating it here in the exhaustive manner which would really be necessary for the therapy of the neuroses. I shall only discuss how a physician who recognizes the importance of sexual ætiology in the neuroses can best face this problem.

Obviously, the worst thing he can do is to ignore it, no matter under what pretence. A thing that is necessary cannot be beneath my professional dignity, and it is necessary to give the assistance of medical advice to a married couple who are planning to limit their offspring, if you wish to prevent one or both of the partners being exposed to a neurosis. It cannot be denied that contraceptive measures become a necessity in married life at some time or other, and theoretically it would be one of the greatest triumphs of mankind, one of the most tangible liberations from the bondage of nature to which we are subject, were it possible to raise the responsible act of procreation to the level of a voluntary and intentional act, and to free it from its entanglement with an indispensable satisfaction of a natural desire.

A clear-sighted physician will therefore take it upon himself to decide under what conditions the use of contraceptive measures is justified, and will require to distinguish between the harmful and the harmless forms among these measures. Everything is harmful that hinders the fulfilment of gratification; it is well-known, however, that at present we possess no method of preventing conception which satisfies all the requirements which may properly be asked of it, that is, which is certain, convenient, does not diminish pleasurable sensation during coitus, nor wound feminine sensibilities. This is a practical problem which physicians might well apply their energy to solve; they would thereby reap great gratitude. Anyone who could fill this gap in our medical technique would be the means of preserving the joy of living and good health for countless men and women, though it is true he would at the same time have initiated a profound change in our social conditions.

This does not exhaust the list of the sources of inspiration which lie in a recognition of the sexual ætiology of the neuroses. The main benefit which we obtain from it for neurasthenia falls in the sphere of prophylaxis. If masturbation is the cause of neurasthenia in youth, and later on also has its ætiological significance in the anxiety-neurosis by its action in reducing potency, then the prevention of masturbation in both sexes is a task that deserves more attention than it has received up to the present time. On considering both the slight and the serious disabilities that have their root in neurasthenia, which is apparently growing more and more prevalent, it becomes evident that it is positively to the public interest *that men should enter upon sexual relations with full potency*. In matters of prophylaxis, however, the individual is almost helpless. The whole community must take an interest in the matter and give its assent to the construction of measures valid for all. At present we are still far removed from a state of things holding out such hope of relief, so that the increase in neurasthenia may quite rightly be accounted to our civilization. There is a great deal which must be changed. The opposition of a generation of physicians who can no longer remember their own youth must be broken down, the pride of fathers who are unwilling to descend to the level of common humanity in the eyes of their children will have to be overcome, the unreasonable prudery of mothers, who at present quite generally regard it as an incomprehensible and also undeserved stroke of fate that 'just their children should be nervous', would have to be met. Above all, popular opinion would have to make room for the discussion of problems of sexual life; it must become possible to speak of such things without being stamped as a disturber of the peace or as a person whose aim is to arouse the lower instincts. And so there still remains plenty of work in this direction for the next century—in which our civilization will have to learn to become compatible with the claims of our sexuality!

The value of a correct diagnostic differentiation between the psychoneuroses and neurasthenia is also shown by the fact that the former need to be regarded differently in practice and require special therapeutic measures. Psychoneuroses appear under two kinds of conditions, either independently or in the wake of actual neuroses (neurasthenia and anxiety-neurosis). In these latter cases we are dealing with a new type, incidentally very frequent, of mixed neurosis. The ætiology of the actual neuroses has become a supplementary ætiology of the psychoneuroses, and a clinical picture results in which, for example, anxiety-neurosis predominates, but which in other respects shows features of real neurasthenia, of hysteria and of the obsessional neurosis. Even when faced with such a combination, it is not profitable to abandon the distinctions between the various single clinical pictures of neuroses, since it is really not so very difficult to analyse the result into the following constituents: The predominance of the anxiety-neurosis shows that the morbid condition has arisen under the influence of an actual sexual noxia. The person concerned was, however, besides this, predisposed by a particular ætiology to one or more forms of psychoneurosis, and would have developed a psychoneurosis at some time or other, either spontaneously or under the influence of some other weakening cause. Thus the still lacking supplementary ætiology of the psychoneurosis has been supplied by the current ætiology of the anxiety-neurosis.

For such cases it has quite correctly come to be a therapeutic practice to disregard the psychoneurotic components in the clinical picture and to treat exclusively the 'actual' neurosis. In very many cases it is possible to overcome the accompanying neurosis if the neurasthenic condition is handled in the right manner. A different estimate is required in those cases of psychoneurosis which appear either spontaneously or at the close of a long illness composed of neurasthenia and psychoneurosis, and remain as an independent condition. When I speak of the 'spontaneous' appearance of a psychoneurosis, I do not mean, for example, that every ætiological element is lacking after anamnestic research. Though that may well be so, it may also be that attention is drawn to some more commonplace factor, for instance, an emotional crisis, an enfeebled condition after organic illness and the like. It must, however, be remembered with all these cases that the real ætiology of the psychoneuroses does not rest upon these factors, but remains outside the reach of ordinary anamnestic examination.

As is well known, this is the gap that some have attempted to bridge by the assumption of a special neuropathic temperament which, if it existed, would indeed not leave much hope for the success of any therapy with these morbid conditions. The neuropathic disposition itself is conceived of as a sign of general degeneration and then this convenient term is levelled broadcast against the poor sufferers whom medical men are quite powerless to aid. Fortunately, this is not at all the true state of affairs. Although the neuropathic temperament doubtless exists, I deny that it is adequate alone to produce a psychoneurosis. Moreover, I must further deny that a neuropathic temperament in conjunction with the contributory causes exciting an outbreak of illness in adult life together represent a sufficiently adequate ætiology of psychoneurosis. In referring the fate of an individual who shows a morbid condition back to the experiences of his ancestors we have gone too far; we have forgotten that between conception and maturity there lies a long and important period in the life of a man—childhood—in which the seeds of later disease may be acquired. That is what in fact happens with the psychoneuroses. Their real ætiology is to be found in experiences during childhood, and again—exclusively, too—in those impressions which have to do with sexual matters. We do wrong entirely to ignore the sexual life of children; in my experience children are capable of all the mental and many of the physical activities. Just as the whole sexual apparatus of man is not comprised in the external genital organs and the two reproductive glands, so his sexual life does not begin only with the onset of puberty, as to casual observation it may appear to do. It is true, however, that the organization and evolution of the species man strives to prevent extensive sexual activity during childhood; apparently the sexual instincts of the human animal are to be stored up in order that at the time of their release at puberty they may serve important cultural ends (W. Fliess). It is perhaps possible to understand, through considerations of this kind, why sexual experiences in childhood are bound to have a pathogenic effect. This effect, however, displays itself only in the slightest degree at the actual time of their occurrence; far more important is their subsequent effect, which can show itself only in later periods of maturity. This subsequent effect can only originate in the mental traces which have been left behind by the infantile sexual experiences. In the interval between the occurrence of these experiences and their reproduction (we ought rather to say the later intensification of the libidinous impulses aroused by them) not only the physical sexual but also the mental apparatus has undergone an important development, and therefore an abnormal mental reaction now follows upon the effect produced by these earlier sexual experiences; that is, psychopathological formations appear.

In these introductory remarks I can only mention the main elements on which the theory of the psychoneuroses is based: the subsequence of the effect, the infantile condition of the sexual apparatus and of the mental organism. In order to attain full comprehension of the mechanism by which the psychoneuroses come into being, more detailed exposition would be necessary; above all, it would be indispensable to regard as credible certain assumptions concerning the composition of the mental instrument and the way in which it works, which seem to me to be novel. In a book on the interpretation of dreams at which I am now working, I shall find occasion to touch upon these principles of a psychology of the neuroses. For dreams belong to the same category of psychopathological formations as the *idée fixe* of hysteria, obsessions and delusions.

Since the manifestations of the psychoneuroses arise through the subsequent action of unconscious mental traces, they are amenable to psychotherapy, which, however, must seek other methods than the only one followed so far, that of suggestion with or without hypnosis. In recent years I have worked out almost completely a therapeutic procedure, based on the 'cathartic' method initiated by J. Breuer, which I intend to call the 'psycho-analytic' method; I owe countless successes to it and may reasonably hope to increase its effectiveness considerably yet. The first account of this method—its technique and applicability—was given in the *Studien über Hysterie* written in conjunction with J. Breuer and published in 1895. Much of it, I may say, has since then been altered for the better. Whereas at that time we modestly declared that we could undertake to remove only the symptoms of hysteria and not the disease itself, I have since perceived that this distinction is without significance, so that the prospect of an effectual cure of hysteria and obsessions lies ahead. I have therefore been most interested to read statements like the following in the writings of my colleagues: 'In this case the ingenious method devised by Breuer and Freud has failed', or 'The method has not fulfilled the promise it seemed originally to hold out'. On these occasions I have had something of the sensations of a man who comes across an obituary notice of himself in the newspapers, but ventures to feel reassured by his better knowledge of the situation. For the method is so difficult that serious study of it is indispensable, and I cannot remember that any one of my critics expressed any wish to learn it from me; nor do I believe that they have applied themselves to the matter, as I have done, with sufficient intensity to come upon it of their own accord. The remarks in the *Studien über Hysterie* are totally inadequate to give the reader a mastery of this technique, nor are they in any way intended to furnish complete instruction in it.

The psycho-analytic method is not at present applicable to all cases; I recognize the following limitations in regard to it: it demands a certain measure of clearsightedness and maturity in the patient and is therefore not suited for youthful persons or for adults who are feeble-minded or uneducated. With persons who are too far advanced in years it fails because, owing to the accumulation of material, so much time would be required that the end of the cure would be reached at a period of life in which much importance is no longer attached to nervous health. And finally it is possible only if the patient is capable of a normal mental condition from the vantage-point of which he may overlook the pathological material. During an hysterical confusion or interpolated mania or melancholia nothing can be effected by psycho-analytic means. Such cases can, nevertheless, be subjected to the treatment after the violent manifestations have yielded to the customary methods. In practice, the chronic cases of psychoneuroses are altogether more tractable by this method than cases with acute crises, in which the greatest weight is naturally laid on the speed with which the latter can be subdued. Hysterical phobias and the different forms of obsessional neurosis are consequently the most favourable field of work for this new therapy.

That the method is restricted by these limitations is to a great extent explicable by the conditions under which I had to work it out. My material does in fact consist of chronic nervous cases recruited from the more cultivated classes. I consider it very probable that supplementary methods may be arrived at for treating young persons and for those who seek relief in hospitals. I should also mention that up to the present I have tried my treatment exclusively on severe cases of hysteria and obsessional neurosis; I cannot tell how it would react on those slight cases which appear to be cured in a few months by some neutral kind of treatment. It will readily be understood that a new therapy which requires many sacrifices can reckon on only such patients as have already tried the generally accepted methods without success, or by those whose condition justified the inference that they could expect nothing from these apparently more convenient and shorter therapeutic methods. I was obliged to attack at once the hardest tasks with imperfect instruments; the test has therefore proved all the more convincing.

The essential difficulties which still stand in the way of the psycho-analytic method of cure are due, not to its own character, but rather to the lack of comprehension among laymen and physicians in regard to the real character of the psychoneuroses. It is only an inevitable corollary of this complete ignorance that physicians should consider themselves justified in consoling the patient or in persuading him to try various therapeutic measures with the most flimsy assurances, 'Come to my sanatorium for six weeks and you will get rid of your symptoms (phobias, obsessions and the like).' Sanatoria are, as a matter of fact, indispensable for subduing acute conditions arising in the course of a psychoneurosis and effect this by means of diversion, care and rest; towards removing chronic conditions they achieve nothing, and this is as true of the distinguished sanatoria which are supposed to be scientifically conducted as of ordinary hydrotherapeutic establishments.

It would be more dignified as well as more helpful to the patient (who after all has somehow to reconcile himself to his ailments) if physicians would tell the truth as they see it day by day: the psychoneuroses as a genus are by no means slight illnesses. When hysteria has once begun no one can foretell when it will end. One mostly seeks in vain to comfort oneself with the prophecy, 'Some day it will suddenly come to an end.' Often enough recovery proves to be a mere compromise, a condition of mutual toleration between the sound and the unsound elements in the patient, or comes about by way of the transformation of the symptom into a phobia. An hysteria in a young girl, which has with difficulty been relieved, will be resuscitated, after a short interruption due to a new-found happiness, in the hysteria of the wife; with one difference, that this time another person, the husband, will be impelled by his own interests to keep silent about the illness. Even if no manifest incapacity for life results, there almost always follows a loss of power to make free use of the energies of the mind. Obsessions recur again and again during the patient's whole life; phobias and other restrictions of will-power have hitherto proved inaccessible to every kind of treatment. All these facts are kept from the knowledge of the public, so that the father of an hysterical girl is horrified when he is told that he ought to consent to a year's treatment for his daughter, though the illness may perhaps be of only a few months' duration. The layman is deeply convinced inwardly of the unnecessariness, so to speak, of all these psychoneuroses, and therefore regards the course of the disease with little patience and is unwilling to make sacrifices for the treatment. He behaves more reasonably with a case of typhoid lasting three weeks, or a fracture which requires six months to heal, or he regards it as proper that orthopædic treatment should be undergone for several years when his child shows the first signs of curvature of the spine; and the difference in his behaviour is due to the better understanding shown by physicians in these matters, about which they honestly impart their knowledge to the lay public. Sincerity on the part of physicians and tractability in the public will be achieved in regard to the psychoneuroses also, when once insight into the essential character of these complaints becomes the common property of medicine. A thorough psychotherapeutic treatment of these ailments will no doubt always require a special training and will be incompatible with other kinds of medical practice. As a compensation, this group of physicians, which in the future will doubtless be a large one, has before it the prospect of noteworthy achievements and of a gratifying insight into the mental life of mankind.

XII
ON PSYCHOTHERAPY
(1904)

About eight years have passed since I had the opportunity, on the invitation of your lamented chairman, Professor von Reder, of speaking here on the subject of hysteria. Shortly before that occasion I had published, in 1895, in collaboration with Dr. Joseph Breuer, the *Studien über Hysterie* in which, on the basis of the new knowledge which we owe to this investigator, an attempt was made to introduce a novel therapy for the neuroses. Fortunately, I may say, the efforts of our 'Studies' have been successful; the ideas expressed in them concerning the action of psychical traumas through retention of affect, as well as the conception of hysterical symptoms which explains them as the result of an emotion transposed from the realm of the mental to the physical—ideas for which we created the terms 'abreaction' and 'conversion'—are to-day generally known and understood. There is, at least in German-speaking countries, no presentation of hysteria to-day that does not to some extent take them into account, and we have no colleagues who do not follow at least for a short distance the road pointed out by us. And yet, while they were still new, these propositions and the terms for them must have sounded not a little strange!

---

[1] First published in the *Wiener Medizinische Presse*, 1905, No. 1. Lecture delivered before the College of Physicians, in Vienna, December 12, 1904. [Translated by J. Bernays.]

I cannot say the same of the therapeutic method which was introduced to our colleagues at the same time as our theory; it is still struggling for recognition. There may be special reasons for this. At that time the technique of the process was as yet undeveloped; it was impossible for me to give medical readers of the book the directions necessary to enable them to carry through this method of treatment completely. But causes of a general nature have certainly also played a part. To many physicians, even to-day, psychotherapy seems to be the offspring of modern mysticism and, compared with our physico-chemical specifics which are applied on the basis of physiological knowledge, appears quite unscientific and unworthy of the attention of a serious investigator. Allow me, therefore, to defend the cause of psychotherapy before you, and to point out to you what may be described as unjust or mistaken in this condemnation of it.

In the first place, let me remind you that psychotherapy is in no way a modern method of healing. On the contrary, it is the most ancient form of therapy in medicine. In Löwenfeld's instructive work (*Lehrbuch der gesamten Psychotherapie*) many of the methods of primitive and ancient medical science are described. The majority of them must be classed under the head of psychotherapy; in order to effect a cure a condition of 'expectant faith' was induced in sick persons, the same condition which answers a similar purpose for us to-day. Even since physicians have come upon other therapeutic agents, psychotherapeutic endeavours of one kind or another have never completely disappeared from medicine.

Secondly, let me draw your attention to the fact that we physicians cannot discard psychotherapy altogether, simply because the other person so intimately concerned in the process of recovery—the patient—has no intention of giving it up. You will know of the increase in knowledge on this subject that we owe to the Nancy school, to Liébeault and Bernheim. An element dependent on the psychical disposition of the patient enters as an accompanying factor, without any such intention on our part, into the effect of every therapeutic process initiated by a physician; most frequently it is favourable to recovery, but often it acts as an inhibition. We have learned to use the word 'suggestion' for this phenomenon, and Möbius has taught us that the unreliability which we deplore in so many of our therapeutic measures may be traced back actually to the disturbing influence of this very powerful factor. All physicians, therefore, yourselves included, are continually practising psychotherapy, even when you have no intention of doing so and are not aware of it; it is disadvantageous, however, to leave entirely in the hands of the patient what the mental factor in your treatment of him shall be. In this way it is uncontrollable; it can neither be measured nor intensified. Is it not then a justifiable endeavour on the part of a physician to seek to control this factor, to use it with a purpose, and to direct and strengthen it? This and nothing else is what scientific psychotherapy proposes.

And, in the third place, I would remind you of the well-known experience that certain diseases, in particular the psychoneuroses, are far more readily accessible to mental influences than to any other form of medication. It is not a modern dictum but an old saying of physicians that these diseases are not cured by the drug but by the physician, that is by the personality of the physician, inasmuch as through it he exerts a mental influence. I am well aware that you favour the view which Vischer, the professor of æsthetics, expressed so well in his parody of Faust:

"Ich weiß, das Physikalische
Wirkt öfters aufs Moralische"[1].

But is it not more reasonable and more likely to happen that moral, that is, mental means can influence the moral side of a human being?

There are many ways and means of practising psychotherapy. All that lead to recovery are good. Our usual word of comfort, which we dispense very liberally to our patients—'Never fear, you will soon be all right again'—corresponds to one of these psychotherapeutic methods; only, now that deeper insight has been won into the neuroses, we are no longer forced to confine ourselves to the word of comfort. We have developed the technique of hypnotic suggestion, and psychotherapy by diversion of attention, by exercise, and by eliciting suitable affects. I despise none of these methods and would use them all under proper conditions. If I have actually come to confine myself to one form of treatment, to the method that Breuer called *cathartic*, which I myself prefer to call 'analytic', it is because I have allowed myself to be influenced by purely subjective motives. Because of the part I have played in founding this therapy, I feel a personal obligation to devote myself to closer investigation of it and to the development of its technique. And I may say that the analytic method of psychotherapy is the one that penetrates most deeply, and carries farthest, the one by means of which the most extensive transformations can be wrought in patients. Putting aside for a moment the therapeutic point

---

[1] [I know that the physical
Often influences the moral.]

of view, I may also say of it that it is the most interesting method, the only one which informs us at all about the origin and interrelation of morbid manifestations. Owing to the insight which we gain into mental illness by this method, it alone should be capable of leading us beyond its own limits and of pointing out the way to other forms of therapeutic influence.

Permit me now to correct several mistakes that have been made in regard to this cathartic or analytic method of psychotherapy, and give a few explanations on the subject.

(*a*) I have observed that this method is very often confounded with hypnotic treatment by suggestion; I have noticed this because it happens comparatively often that colleagues who do not ordinarily confide their cases to me send me patients—refractory patients, of course—with a request that I should hypnotise them. Now I have not used hypnosis for therapeutic purposes for the last eight years (except for a few special experiments) so that I habitually send back these cases with the recommendation that anyone who relies upon hypnosis may perform it himself. There is, actually, the greatest possible antithesis between suggestive and analytic technique—the same antithesis that in regard to the fine arts the great Leonardo da Vinci summed up in the formulas: *Per via di porre* and *per via di levare*. Painting, says Leonardo, works *per via di porre*, for it applies a substance—particles of colour—where there was nothing before, on the colourless canvas; sculpture, however, proceeds *per via di levare*, since it takes away from the rough stone all that hides the surface of the statue contained in it. The technique of suggestion aims in a similar way at proceeding *per via di porre;* it is not concerned with the origin, strength and meaning of the morbid symptoms, but instead, it superimposes something—a suggestion—and expects this to be strong enough to restrain the pathogenic idea from coming to expression. Analytic therapy, on the other hand, does not seek to add or to introduce anything new, but to take away something, to bring out something; and to this end concerns itself with the genesis of the morbid symptoms and the psychical context of the pathogenic idea which it seeks to remove. It is by the use of this mode of investigation that analytic therapy has increased our knowledge so notably. I gave up the suggestive technique, and with it hypnosis, so early in my practice because I despaired of making suggestion powerful and enduring enough to effect permanent cures. In all severe cases I saw the suggestions which had been applied crumble away again; and then the disease or some substitute for it returned. Besides all this I have another reproach against this method, namely, that it conceals from us all insight into the play of mental forces; it does not permit us, for example, to recognize the *resistance* with which the patient clings to his disease and thus even fights against his own recovery; yet it is this phenomenon of resistance which alone makes it possible to comprehend his behaviour in daily life.

(*b*) It seems to me that among my colleagues there is a widespread and erroneous impression that this technique of searching for the origins of the symptoms and removing the manifestations by means of this investigation is a easy one which can be practised off-hand, as it were. I conclude this from the fact that not one of all those who show an interest in my therapy and pass definite judgements upon it has ever asked me how I actually go about it. There can be but one reason for this, namely, that they think there is nothing to enquire about, that the thing is perfectly obvious. Again, I am now and then astonished to hear that in this or that ward of a hospital a young assistant has received an order from his chief to undertake a 'psycho-analysis' of an hysterical patient. I am sure he would not be allowed to examine an extirpated tumour until he had convinced his chiefs that he was conversant with histological technique. Similarly, a report reaches my ears that this or that colleague has arranged appointments with a patient in order to undertake a mental treatment of the case, though I am certain that he knows nothing of the technique of any such therapy. His expectation must be therefore that the patient will offer him his secrets as a present, as it were, or perhaps he looks for salvation in some sort of confession or confidence. I should not be surprised if an invalid were injured rather than benefited by being treated in such a fashion. For it is not so easy to play upon the instrument of the soul. I am reminded at this point of a world-famed neurotic, although certainly he was never treated by a physician but existed only in a poet's imagination: I mean Hamlet, Prince of Denmark. The King appointed the two courtiers, Rosenkranz and Guildenstern, to follow him, to question him and drag from him the secret of his depression. He wards them off; then flutes are brought on the stage and Hamlet, taking one of them, begs one of his torturers to play upon it, telling him that it is as easy as lying. The courtier excuses himself for he knows no touch of the instrument, and when he cannot be persuaded to try it, Hamlet finally breaks out with these words: 'Why, look you now, how unworthy a thing you make of me, you would play upon me.—You would pluck out the heart of my mystery; you would sound me from my lowest note to the top of my compass; and there is much music, excellent voice, in this little organ; yet you cannot make it speak. '*Sblood, do you think I am easier to be played on than a pipe? Call me what instrument you will, though you can fret me you cannot play upon me.*' (Act III, scene 2.)

(*c*) From certain of my remarks you will have gathered that there are many characteristics in the analytic method which prevent it from being an ideal form of therapy. *Tuto, cito, jucunde*: investigation and probing do not indicate speedy results, and the resistance already mentioned would prepare you to expect unpleasantness in various ways. Psycho-analytic treatment certainly makes great demands upon the patient as well as upon the physician. From the patient it requires perfect sincerity—a sacrifice in itself; it absorbs time and is therefore also costly; for the physician it is no less time-absorbing, and the technique which he must study and practise is fairly laborious. I consider it quite justifiable to resort to more convenient methods of healing as long as there is any prospect of attaining anything by their means. That, after all, is the only point at issue. If the more difficult and lengthy method accomplishes considerably more than the short and easy one, then, in spite of everything, the use of the former has its justification. Just consider how much more inconvenient and costly is the Finsen therapy of lupus than the method of cauterizing and scraping previously employed; and yet the use of the former signifies a considerable advance, for it performs a radical cure. Although I do not wish to carry this comparison to all lengths, the psycho-analytic method may claim a similar privilege. Actually, I have been able to elaborate and to test my therapeutic method only on severe, nay, the severest cases; at first my material consisted entirely of patients who had tried everything else without success, and had spent long years in sanatoria. I have scarcely been able to bring together sufficient material to enable me to say how my method would work with those cases of lighter, episodically appearing invalidism which we see recover under all kinds of influences and even spontaneously. Psycho-analytic therapy was created through and for the treatment of patients permanently unfitted for life, and its great triumph has been that by its measures a satisfactorily large number of these have been rendered permanently fit for existence. In the face of such an achievement all the effort expended seems trivial. We cannot conceal from ourselves what, as physicians, we are in the habit of denying to our patients, namely, that a severe neurosis is no less serious for the sufferer than any cachexia, any of the dreaded major diseases.

(*d*) The conditions under which this method is indicated, or contra-indicated, can scarcely be definitely laid down as yet, because of the many limitations to which the scope of my activities have been subjected in practice. Nevertheless, I will attempt to discuss a few of them here:

1. It is important that the morbid condition of the patient should not be allowed to blind one in making an estimate of his whole personality; those patients who do not possess a reasonable degree of education and a fairly reliable character should be refused. It must not be forgotten that there are healthy persons as well as unhealthy ones who are good for nothing in life, and that there is much too prompt an inclination to ascribe to their malady

everything which makes such people unfit, if they show the slightest symptoms of a neurosis. In my opinion a neurosis is by no means a stamp of degeneracy, though it may often enough be found in one person in conjunction with the manifestations of degeneration. Now analytic psychotherapy is not a process suited to the treatment of neuropathic degeneration; on the contrary, degeneracy acts as a hindrance to its effectiveness. Nor is the method applicable to any who are not urged to seek a cure by their own sufferings, but who undergo treatment only because they are forced into it by the authority of relatives. The qualification which is the determining factor of fitness for psycho-analytic treatment—that is, whether the patient is educable—must be discussed from yet another standpoint.

2. To be quite safe, one should limit one's choice of patients to those who possess a normal mental condition, since in the psycho-analytic method this is used as a foothold from which to obtain control of the morbid manifestations. Psychoses, states of confusion and deeply-rooted (I might say toxic) depression are therefore not suitable for psycho-analysis; at least not for the method as it has been practised up to the present. I do not regard it as by any means impossible that by suitable changes in the method we may succeed in advancing beyond these hindrances—and so be able to initiate a psychotherapy of the psychoses.

3. The age of patients has this importance in determining their fitness for psycho-analytic treatment, that, on the one hand, near or above the fifties the elasticity of the mental processes, on which the treatment depends, is as a rule lacking—old people are no longer educable—and, on the other hand, the mass of material to be dealt with would

prolong the duration of the treatment indefinitely. In the other direction the age limit can be determined only individually; youthful persons, even under the age of adolescence, are often exceedingly amenable to influence.

4. Psycho-analysis should not be attempted when the speedy removal of dangerous symptoms is required, as for example, in a case of hysterical anorexia.

By this time you will have received the impression that the field of analytic psychotherapy is a very narrow one, since you have really heard nothing from me except the indications which point against it. There remain, however, cases and types of disease enough on which this therapy may be tested, as for instance, all chronic forms of hysteria with residual manifestations, the broad field of obsessive conditions, aboulias, and the like.

It is gratifying that precisely the most valuable and most highly developed persons are best suited for these curative measures; and one may also safely claim that in cases where analytic psychotherapy can achieve but little, any other therapy would certainly not have been able to effect anything.

(*e*) You will no doubt wish to enquire about the possibility of doing harm by undertaking a psycho-analysis. In reply to this I may say that if you are willing to judge impartially, if you will consider this procedure in the same spirit of critical fairness that you show to our other therapeutic methods, you will have to agree with me that no injury to the patient is to be feared when the treatment is conducted with real comprehension. Anyone who is accustomed, like the lay public, to blame the treatment for whatever happens during an illness will doubtless judge differently. It is not so very long ago since the same prejudice was directed against our hydropathic establishments. Many a patient who was advised to go into an establishment of the kind hesitated because he had known someone who had entered the place as a nervous invalid and had become insane there. As you will imagine, these were cases of early general paralysis that could still in the first stage be sent to a hydropathic establishment; once there, they had run their inevitable course until manifest mental derangement supervened: but the public blamed the water as the originator of this disastrous change. When it is a matter of new kinds of therapeutic influence even physicians are not always free from such errors of judgement. I recall once making an attempt at psychotherapy with a woman who had passed the greater part of her life in a state alternating between mania and melancholia. I took on the case at the close of a period of melancholia and for two weeks things seemed to go smoothly; in the third week we were already at the beginning of the next attack of mania. This was undoubtedly a spontaneous transformation of the symptoms, since in two weeks analytic psychotherapy cannot accomplish anything. And yet the eminent physician (now deceased) who saw the case with me could not refrain from the remark that psychotherapy was probably to blame for this 'relapse'. I am quite conviced that he would have shown himself possessed of more critical judgement in other circumstances.

(*f*) Finally, I must confess that it is hardly fair to take up your attention for so long on the subject of psycho-analytic therapy without telling you in what this treatment consists and on what it is based. Still, as I am forced to be brief, I can only hint at this. This therapy, then, is based on the recognition that unconscious ideas—or better, the unconsciousness of certain mental processes—constitutes the direct cause of the morbid symptoms. We hold this opinion in common with the French school (Janet) which, by the way, owing to too crude a schematization, refers the cause of hysterical symptoms to an unconscious *idée fixe.* Now please do not be afraid that this is going to land us in the depths of philosophical obscurities. Our unconscious is not quite the same thing as that of philosophers and, moreover, the majority of philosophers decline all knowledge of 'unconscious mentality'. If, however, you will look at the matter from our point of view, you will understand that the transformation of this unconscious material in the mind of the patient into conscious material must have the result of correcting his deviation from normality and of lifting the compulsion to which his mind has been subjected. For conscious will-power governs only the conscious mental processes, and every mental compulsion is rooted in the unconscious. Nor need you ever fear that the patient will be harmed by the shock accompanying the introduction of the unconscious into consciousness, for you can convince yourselves theoretically that the somatic and emotional effect of an impulse that has become conscious can never be so powerful as that of an unconscious one. It is only by the application of our highest mental energies, which are bound up with consciousness, that we can command all our impulses.

There is, however, another point of view which you may take up in order to understand the psychoanalytic method. The discovery of the unconscious and the introduction of it into consciousness is performed in the face of a continuous *resistance* on the part of the patient. The process of bringing this unconscious material to light is associated with 'pain' *(Unlust)*, and because of this pain the patient again and again rejects it. It is for you then to interpose in this conflict in the patient's mental life. If you succeed in persuading him to accept, by virtue of a better understanding, something that up to now, in consequence of this automatic regulation by pain, he has rejected (repressed), you will then have accomplished something towards his education. For it is an education even to induce a person who dislikes leaving his bed early in the morning to do so all the same. Psycho-analytic treatment may in general be conceived of as such a *re-education in overcoming internal resistances.* Re-education of this kind is, however, in no respect more necessary to nervous patients than in regard to the mental element in their sexual life. For nowhere else have civilization and education done so much harm as in this field, and this is the point, as experience will show you, at which to look for those ætiologies of the neuroses that are amenable to influence; since the other ætiological factor, the constitutional component, consists of something fixed and unalterable. And from this it comes that one important qualification is required of the physician in this work: not only must his own character be irreproachable—'As to morals, that goes without saying', as the hero of Vischer's novel *Auch Einer* was wont to say—but he must also have overcome in his own mind that mixture of lewdness and prudery with which, unfortunately, so many people habitually consider sexual problems.

At this juncture another remark is perhaps not out of place. I know that the emphasis which I lay upon the part played by sexuality in creating the psychoneuroses has become generally known. But

I know, likewise, that qualifications and exact particularization are of little use to the general public; there is very little room in the memory of the multitude; it really only retains an undigested kernel of any proposition and fabricates an extreme version which is easy to remember. It may be that this has happened with many physicians, too, so that they vaguely apprehend the content of my doctrine to be that I regard sexual privation as the ultimate cause of the neuroses. In the conditions of life in modern society there is certainly no lack of sexual privation. This being so, would it not be simpler to aim directly at recovery by recommending the satisfaction of sexual needs as a therapeutic measure, instead of undertaking the circuitous path of mental treatment? I know of nothing which could impel me to suppress such an inference if it were justified. The real state of things, however, is otherwise. Sexual need and privation are merely one factor at work in the mechanism of neurosis; if there were no others the result would be dissipation, not disease. The other, no less essential, factor, which is all too readily forgotten, is the neurotic's aversion from sexuality, his incapacity for loving, that feature of the mind which I have called 're-pression'. Not until there is a conflict between the two tendencies does nervous illness break out, and therefore to counsel the active gratification of sexual needs in the psychoneuroses can only very rarely be described as good advice.

Let me conclude with the following defensive remark. We will hope that, when freed from every prejudice, your interest in psychotherapy may lend us support in this way—that you also will then achieve success even with severe cases of psycho-neurosis.

XIII

FREUD'S PSYCHO-ANALYTIC METHOD[1]

(1904)

The particular method of psychotherapy which Freud practises and terms psycho-analysis is an outgrowth of the so-called cathartic treatment discussed by him in collaboration with J. Breuer in the *Studien über Hysterie*, published in 1895. This cathartic therapy was Breuer's invention and was first employed by him when treating an hysterical patient about ten years before; in so doing he had obtained an insight into the pathogenesis of her symptoms. At the personal suggestion of Breuer, Freud revived this method and tried it with a large number of patients.

The cathartic mode of treatment presupposed that the patient could be hypnotised and was based on the widening of consciousness which occurs in hypnosis. Its goal was to remove the morbid symptoms, and it attained this end by making the patient revert to the psychic state in which the symptom had appeared for the first time. In this state there came up in the hypnotised patient's mind memories, thoughts and impulses which had previously dropped out of his consciousness, and, as soon as he had related these to the physician, accompanying this expression with intense emotion, the symptom was overcome and its return done away with. This experience, which could regularly be made, was taken

---

[1] From Löwenfeld: *Psychische Zwangserscheinungen.* 1904. [This chapter was written at Dr. Löwenfeld's request as a part of the section on psychotherapy in the latter's book.—Translated by J. Bernays.]

by the authors in their joint paper to signify that the symptom represents suppressed processes which had not reached consciousness, that is, that it represents a transformation ('conversion') of these processes. They explained the therapeutic effectiveness of their treatment by the discharge of the previously 'strangulated' affect attaching to the suppressed mental acts ('abreaction'). But in practice the simple outline of the therapeutic operation was almost always complicated by the circumstance that it was not a single ('traumatic') impression, but in most cases a series of impressions—to be viewed in its entirety only with difficulty—which had participated in the creation of the symptom.

The main characteristic of the cathartic method, in contrast to all other methods used in psychotherapy, consists in the fact that its therapeutic efficacy does not lie in the suggestive prohibitive command of the physician. The expectation is rather that the symptoms will disappear automatically as soon as the operation, based on certain hypotheses concerning the psychic mechanism, succeeds in diverting the course of mental processes from the direction which previously had found an outlet in the formation of the symptom.

The changes which Freud introduced in Breuer's cathartic method of treatment were at first changes in technique; these, however, brought about new results and have finally necessitated a different though not contradictory conception of the therapeutic task.

The cathartic method had already renounced suggestion; Freud went one step further and gave up hypnosis as well. At the present time he treats his patients as follows: without exerting any other kind of influence he invites them to recline in a comfortable position on a couch, while he himself is seated on a chair behind them outside their field of vision. He does not ask them to close their eyes, and avoids touching them as well as any other form of procedure which might remind them of hypnosis. The consultation thus proceeds like a conversation between two equally wakeful persons, one of whom is spared every muscular exertion and every distracting sensory impression which might draw his attention from his own mental activity.

Since it depends upon the will of the patient whether he is to be hypnotised or not, no matter what the skill of the physician may be, and since a large number of neurotic patients cannot be hypnotised by any means whatever, it followed that with the abandonment of hypnosis the applicability of the treatment was assured to an unlimited number of patients. On the other hand, the widening of consciousness, which had supplied the physician with just that psychic material of memories and images by the help of which the transformation of the symptoms and the liberation of the affects was accomplished, was now missing. Unless a substitute could be found for this missing element all therapeutic effect was out of the question.

Freud now found an entirely adequate substitute in the 'associations' of the patients; that is, in the involuntary thoughts most frequently regarded as disturbing elements and therefore ordinarily pushed aside whenever they cross an intention of following a definite train of thought.

In order to secure these ideas and associations he asks the patient to 'let himself go' in what he says, 'as you would do in a conversation which leads you "from cabbages to kings".' Before he asks them for a detailed account of their case-history he admonishes them to relate everything that passes through their minds, even if they think it unimportant or irrelevant or nonsensical; he lays special stress on their not omitting any thought or idea from their story because to relate it might be embarrassing or painful to them. In the task of collecting this material of otherwise neglected ideas Freud made the observations which became the determining factors of his entire theory. There were gaps in the patient's memory even in narrating his case: actual occurrences were forgotten, the chronological order was confused, or causal connections of events were broken, yielding unintelligible effects. No neurotic case-history is without amnesia of some kind or other. If the patient is urged to fill these gaps in his memory by serious application of his attention it is noticed that all the ideas which occur to him are pushed back by him with all critical means available, until at last he feels actual discomfort when the memory has really returned. From this experience Freud concludes that the amnesias are the result of a process which he calls *repression* and the motivation of which he finds in feelings of 'pain' *(Unlust)*. The psychical forces which have brought about this repression are traceable, according to him, to the *resistance* which operates against the re-integration of these memories.

The factor of resistance has become one of the cornerstones of his theory. The ideas otherwise pushed aside with all kinds of excuses—as those mentioned above—he regards as derivatives of the repressed psychical manifestations (thoughts and impulses), as distortions of these because of the resistance which is exerted against their reproduction.

The greater the resistance, the greater is the distortion. The value for the therapeutic technique of these unintentional thoughts lies in their relation to the repressed psychical material. If one possesses a procedure which makes it possible to arrive at the repressed from the associations, at the distorted material from the distortions, then what was formerly unconscious in mental life may be made accessible to consciousness even without hypnosis.

Freud has developed on this basis an art of interpretation which takes on the task of freeing, as it were, the pure metal of the repressed thoughts from the ore of the unintentional ideas. The objects of this work of interpretation are not only the patient's ideas but also his dreams, which open up the straightest road to the knowledge of the unconscious, his unintentional as well as his purposeless actions (symptomatic acts) and the blunders he makes in every-day life (slips of the tongue, erroneous acts, and the like). The details of this technique of interpretation or translation have not yet been published by Freud. According to the hints he has given they comprise a number of rules, reached empirically, of how the unconscious material may be reconstructed from the associations, directions how to interpret the fact when the patient's ideas cease to flow, and experience concerning the most important typical resistances that arise in the course of such a treatment. A bulky volume called *Die Traumdeutung*, published by Freud in 1900, may be regarded as the forerunner of an initiation into his technique.

From these remarks concerning the technique of the psycho-analytic method the conclusion could be drawn that its inventor has given himself needless trouble and has made a mistake in abandoning the less complicated hypnotic mode of procedure. However, in the first place, the technique of psycho-analysis is much easier in practice once one has learnt it than any description of it would indicate, and secondly, there is no other way which leads to the desired goal, so the hard road is still the shortest one to travel. The objection to hypnosis is that it conceals the resistance and for this reason has obstructed the physician's insight into the play of psychic forces. Hypnosis does not do away with the resistance but only avoids it and therefore yields only incomplete information and transitory therapeutic success.

The task which the psycho-analytic method tries to perform may be formulated in different ways, which are, however, in their essence equivalent. It may, for instance, be stated thus: the task of the cure is to remove the amnesias. When all gaps in memory have been filled in, all the enigmatic products of mental life elucidated, the continuance and even the renewal of the morbid condition is impossible. Or the formula may be expressed in this fashion: all repressions are to be undone; the mental condition is then the same as if all amnesias are removed. Another formulation reaches further; the problem consists in making the unconscious accessible to consciousness, which is done by overcoming the resistances. But it must be remembered that such an ideal condition is not present even in the normal and further that it is only rarely possible to carry the treatment to a point approaching this condition. Just as health and sickness are not qualitatively different from each other but are only gradually separated in an empirically determined way, so the aim of the treatment will never be anything else but the practical recovery of the patient, the restoration of his ability and capacity for enjoyment and an active life. In a cure which is incomplete or in which success is not perfect, one at any rate achieves a considerable improvement in the general mental condition, while the symptoms (though now of smaller importance to the patient) may continue to exist without stamping him as an invalid.

The therapeutic process remains the same, apart from insignificant modifications, for all the symptom-formations of the varied manifestations of hysteria, and all forms of the obsessional neurosis. This does not imply, however, that there can be an unlimited application of this method. The nature of the psycho-analytic method involves indications and contra-indications with respect to the person to be treated as well as with respect to the clinical picture. Chronic cases of psychoneuroses with few violent or dangerous symptoms are the most favourable ones for psycho-analysis: so in the first place all forms of the obsessional neurosis, obsessive thinking and acting, and cases of hysteria in which phobias and aboulias play the most important part; further, all somatic expressions of hysteria whenever they do not, as in anorexia, require the physician to attend promptly to the speedy removal of symptoms. In acute cases of hysteria it will be necessary to await a calmer stage; in all cases where nervous exhaustion dominates the clinical picture a treatment which in itself demands effort, brings only slow improvement and for a time cannot consider the persistence of the symptoms, is to be avoided.

Various qualifications are demanded in the person if he is to be beneficially affected by psycho-analysis. To begin with, he must be capable of a psychically normal condition; during periods of confusion or melancholic depression nothing can be accomplished even in cases of hysteria. Furthermore, a certain measure of natural intelligence and ethical development may be required of him; with worthless persons the physician soon loses the interest which makes it possible for him to enter profoundly into the mental life of the patient. Deep-rooted malformations of character, traits of an actually degenerative constitution show themselves during treatment as sources of a resistance that can scarcely be overcome. In this respect the constitution of the patient does in fact set a limit to the curative effect of psychotherapy. If the patient's age is near or above the fifties the conditions for psycho-analysis become unfavourable. The mass of psychical material can then no longer be thoroughly inspected; the time required for recovery is too long; and the ability to undo psychic processes begins to grow weaker.

In spite of all limitations the number of persons suitable for psycho-analytic treatment is extraordinarily large and the extension which has come to our therapeutic knowledge from this method is, according to Freud, very considerable. Freud requires long periods, six months to three years, for an effective treatment; yet he informs us that up to the present, from various circumstances which may easily be divined, he has for the most part been in a position to try his treatment only on very severe cases; patients have come to him after many years of illness, completely incapacitated for life, and after being disappointed by all kinds of treatments have had recourse to his new and much-suspected method as to a last resort. In cases of less severe illness the duration of the treatment might well be much shorter, and momentous advantage in the way of prevention for the future might be gained.

XIV

MY VIEWS ON THE PART PLAYED BY SEXUALITY IN THE ÆTIOLOGY OF THE NEUROSES[1]

(1905)

I am of opinion that the best idea of my theory concerning the ætiological significance of the sexual factor in neurosis is obtained by examining its evolution. For I have no sort of wish to deny that this theory has passed through a process of development and has undergone a transformation during this process. My colleagues could regard this admission as evidence that the doctrine is nothing but the result of continued and constantly extended experience; for anything that arises from speculation may very easily appear once for all complete in form and then remain unalterable.

The theory originally applied merely to the morbid states embraced under the term neurasthenia; among these, I noticed two which occasionally appeared in a pure form and which I have named 'neurasthenia proper' and 'anxiety-neurosis'. It was indeed always a matter of general knowledge that sexual factors may play a part in the causation of these forms of disease, but neither were these factors found to be regularly active nor was there any thought of allotting them a preferential position among other ætiological influences. I was surprised to begin with at the frequency of grave disturbances in the *vita sexualis* of nervous invalids; the more I enquired into

[1] First published in Löwenfeld's *Sexualleben und Nervenleiden*, IV te Auflage, 1906. [Translated by J. Bernays.]

such disturbances (bearing in mind that all men conceal the truth in these matters) and the more adept I became at persisting in my interrogations in spite of denials at the beginning, the more regularly did pathogenic factors from sexual life disclose themselves, until there seemed to me little to prevent an assumption of their general occurrence. Nevertheless, it was necessary to be prepared at the outset for a frequent incidence of sexual irregularities such as this, in view of the pressure of present-day social conditions, and one might still be doubtful what degree of deviation from normal sexual functioning was to be regarded as pathogenic. I therefore could attribute less importance to the regular, demonstrable appearance of sexual noxiæ than to another observed phenomenon which seemed to me less ambiguous in character. It appeared that each type of ailment, whether neurasthenia or anxiety-neurosis, showed a constant relation to the type of sexual noxia. In typical cases of neurasthenia evidence of masturbation or frequent pollutions would come to light; in anxiety-neurosis, factors such as coitus interruptus and 'frustrated excitation' could be shown which appeared to contain one common element, namely, an unsatisfying discharge of the libido aroused. Only after this recognition, which was easily observed and could at will be frequently confirmed, had I the courage to accord a preferential position to sexual influences in the ætiology of the neuroses. In addition, a combination of the ætiologies ascribed to these manifestations was discoverable in the cases of combined neurasthenia and anxiety-neurosis which often occur; and it appeared that such a dualism in the manifestations of neurosis accorded well with the polar character of sexuality, male and female.

At the time that I attributed to sexuality this part in the creation of simple neuroses[1] I still adhered as regards the psychoneuroses (hysteria and obsessions) to a purely psychological doctrine in which sexual factors had no more significance than other sources of emotion. In conjunction with J. Breuer, and based upon observations made by him at least a decade before on an hysterical patient, I had studied, by means of awakening memories in hypnotic states, the mechanism of the origin of hysterical symptoms. We had reached inferences which helped to bridge the gap between Charcot's traumatic hysteria and the common, non-traumatic hysteria.[2] We had arrived at the conception that the symptoms of hysteria were lasting effects of psychic traumas, whose sum of affect had by peculiar circumstances been prevented from being worked off in consciousness and had therefore forced an abnormal outlet into bodily innervation. The terms 'strangulated affect', 'conversion' and 'abreaction' embrace the distinctive points of this conception.

In view of the close relation of the psychoneuroses to the simple neuroses, which can go so far that an unpractised physician often finds it difficult to make a diagnostic distinction, it became inevitable that the knowledge acquired in one field would throw light as well on the other. Moreover, quite apart from such a correlation, closer examination of the psychical mechanism of hysterical symptoms led to the same result. For, as the psychical traumas which were the starting-point of the hysterical symptoms were followed—by means of the cathartic method initiated by Breuer and myself—further and further back into the patient's past, experiences were finally

[1] See No. V of this volume, p. 76.
[2] See *Studien über Hysterie,* 1895.

reached which belonged to his infancy and concerned his sexual life; and this was so even where an ordinary emotion, not of a sexual kind, had led to the outbreak of the disease. Without taking into account these sexual traumas of childhood it was impossible to explain the symptoms, comprehend their determination, or prevent their return. After this, the unique significance of sexual experiences in the ætiology of the psychoneuroses seemed incontestably established; and this fact remains to-day one of the cornerstones of the theory.

When this theory is described in the statement that the cause of a life-long hysterical neurosis lies in sexual experiences of infancy, usually commonplace in themselves, it may indeed sound strange enough. Yet if allowance is made for the historical development of the theory, if its main content be summarised in the thesis that hysteria is the expression of a peculiar behaviour of the sexual function in the person concerned and that this behaviour is already decisively determined by the first impressive influences and experiences during infancy, we shall indeed be the poorer by a paradox, yet the richer by a motive for directing our attention to these most significant after-effects of infantile impressions which have hitherto been so grossly neglected.

Reserving for a later, more detailed discussion the question whether the ætiology of hysteria and the obsessional neurosis is to be regarded as contained in the sexual experiences of childhood, I will return to the form the theory assumed in some short preliminary papers published in the years 1895 and 1896[1]. By emphasizing the ætiological factors already inferred, it was possible at that time to contrast the common neuroses, which had a current

[1] See Nos. VIII and IX of this volume, pp. 138 and 155.

ætiology, with the psychoneuroses, the ætiology of which lay particularly in sexual experiences of the remote past. The doctrine culminated in the sentence: No neurosis is possible with a normal *vita sexualis*.

Although even to-day I do not regard these statements as incorrect, it is surely not surprising that during ten years of constant work towards elucidation of these problems I should have travelled some distance beyond my previous point of view and now believe that further more extensive experience has placed me in a position to correct the incompleteness, the displacements and the misconceptions under which the theory then laboured. It happened by chance that my earlier, not verv plentiful material contained a disproportionately large number of cases in whose infantile history seduction by adults or other older children had played the chief part. I overestimated the frequency of these occurrences, which are otherwise quite authentic, and all the more so since I was not at this period able to discriminate between the deceptive memories of hysterics concerning their childhood and the memory-traces of actual happenings. I have since learned to unravel many a phantasy of seduction and found it to be an attempt at defence against the memory of sexual activities practised by the child himself (masturbation of children). This explanation deprived the 'traumatic' element in the sexual experiences of childhood of their importance, and there remained a recognition that the form of the infantile sexual activity (whether spontaneous or provoked) determines the direction taken by later sexual life after maturity. This same explanation, by which I was able to correct the most momentous of my early errors, necessitated a change in the conception of the mechanism of hysterical symptoms. These now no longer appeared as direct derivations of repressed memories of sexual experiences in childhood; but, on the contrary, it appeared that between the symptoms and the infantile impressions were interpolated the patient's phantasies (memory-romances), created mostly during the years of adolescence and relating on one side to the infantile memories on which they were founded, and on the other side to the symptoms into which they were directly transformed. Only after the factor of the hysterical phantasies had been introduced did the structure of the neurosis and its relation to the patient's life become perspicuous; at the same time a really surprising analogy came to light between these unconscious phantasies of hysterics and the romances which become conscious as delusions in paranoia.

After this correction, the 'infantile sexual traumas' were in a sense supplanted by the 'infantilism' of the sexuality in these cases. It was not a far step to a second modification of the original theory. When the frequency of seduction in childhood was no longer assumed, there vanished also the over-emphasis on the 'accidental', external influencing of the sexuality to which I had attributed the chief part in the causation of the disease, without, however, denying the existence of constitutional and hereditary elements. In connection with the details of the various sexual experiences of childhood, I had even hoped to solve the problem of the 'choice of neurosis', that is, to ascertain what form of psychoneurosis would develop from each type of experience; I believed at that time, though with some reservations, that passivity in such experiences produced a specific predisposition to hysteria, and activity to obsessional neurosis. These views I was later compelled to abandon entirely, although many actual facts seem to suggest that the supposed correlation between passivity and hysteria and activity and the obsessional neurosis should be retained in some form or other. With the decline in importance of the influences experienced accidentally the constitutional and hereditary elements again won the upper hand; with this difference, however, from prevailing opinion, that in my conception the 'sexual constitution' took the place of a general neuropathic disposition. In my recently published *Drei Abhandlungen zur Sexualtheorie* (1905) I have attempted to describe the many aspects and varieties of this sexual constitution, as well as the composite nature of the sexual instinct as a whole and its origin from various contributory sources in the organism.

While still maintaining the modifications imposed by the altered conception of the 'infantile sexual traumas', the theory now advanced in a direction which had already been indicated in the publications of the years 1894—96. Already at that time, and even before sexuality had been accorded its proper position in the ætiology, I had put it forward as a condition of the pathogenic effectiveness of a given experience that it must seem to the ego intolerable and must evoke an effort towards defence[1]. To this defence I had referred the mental dissociation—or as it was then called, the dissociation of consciousness—of hysteria. If the defence succeeded, then the unbearable experience and its affective consequences were banished from consciousness and from the memory of the ego; but under certain conditions the banished material—now become unconscious—became operative and returned into consciousness by way of the symptoms and the affects attached to them, so that the outbreak of the disease re-

[1] See No. IV of this volume, p. 59.

presented a failure of the defence. This conception had the merit of taking into account the interplay of the mental forces, thereby bringing the mental processes of hysteria nearer to the normal, instead of reducing the characteristic of the neurosis to a mysterious disturbance incapable of further analysis.

Investigation into the mental life of normal persons then yielded the unexpected discovery that their infantile history in regard to sexual matters was not necessarily different in essentials from that of the neurotic, and that seduction particularly had played the same part in it; the result was that the accidental influences receded still further into the background in favour of the influence of 'repression', as I had begun to call what I had formerly termed 'defence'. The important thing, therefore, was evidently not the sexual stimulation that the person had experienced during childhood; what mattered was, above all, how he had reacted to these experiences, whether he had responded to them with 'repression' or not. With regard to spontaneous sexual activity it became evident that in the course of development it was often broken off by an act of repression. Thus the sexually mature neurotic regularly carried within him a fragment of 'sexual repression' from his childhood days, which came to expression under the stress imposed upon him by real life. And psychoanalysis of hysterics showed that their illness was the result of a conflict between the libido and the sexual repression, their symptoms being equivalent to compromises in the conflict between these two mental currents.

I could not expound this part of my theory further without a detailed discussion of my views on the subject of repression. It must suffice to bring the reader's notice at this point to my *Drei Abhand-*

lungen zur Sexualtheorie, in which I have attempted to throw some light, even if only a meagre ray, on the somatic processes in which the essence of sexuality lies. I have there described how the constitutional disposition of the child is by far more variegated than we might have expected, how it deserves to be called 'polymorphously perverse' and how what is called the normal sexual function develops from this disposition through certain components of it becoming repressed. The infantile characteristics of sexuality provided a clue which enabled me to establish a simple correlation between health, perversion, and neurosis. It appeared that normality developed as the result of repression of certain component-instincts and components of the infantile disposition, and of a subordination of the remainder under the primacy of the genital zone in the service of the reproductive function; perversions represented disturbances in this process of coalescence caused by an excessive (obsessive, as it were) development of certain of the component-instincts; and neurosis could be traced back to unduly severe repression of libidinal tendencies. Since almost all the perverse impulses comprising the infantile disposition demonstrably constitute the symptom-forming forces of neurosis, though in the latter they are in a state of repression, I was able to designate neurosis as the 'negative' of perversion.

I consider it worth emphasis that, in spite of all changes in them, my views concerning the ætiology of the psychoneuroses have never yet caused me to disavow or abandon two points of view: namely, the importance of sexuality and of infantilism. In other respects, constitutional factors have supplanted accidental influences; sexual repression' has taken the place of the concept of 'defence' which was intended purely psychologically. Now if anyone should enquire where he is to look for an incontestable proof of the ætiological importance of sexual factors in the psychoneuroses—since these maladies are observed to ensue after the most commonplace emotional, or even somatic disturbances, and since a specific ætiology in the form of particular infantile experiences is not forthcoming—then I would indicate psycho-analytic investigation of neurotics as the source from which the disputed conviction springs. When this irreplaceable method of investigation is used one learns that the *symptoms represent the patient's sexual activity*, either the whole of it or a part of it, and are rooted in the normal or the perverse component-instincts of sexuality. Not only does a considerable portion of hysterical symptomatology spring directly from the manifestations of sexual excitement; not only does a series of erotogenic zones assume the importance of genital organs in the neurosis by intensification of their infantile qualities; but even the most complicated symptoms reveal themselves as 'converted' representations of phantasies which have a sexual situation as their content. Whoever knows how to interpret the language of hysteria can perceive that the neurosis deals only with the patient's repressed sexuality. Only one must conceive of the sexual function in its true range, as circumscribed by the infantile disposition. Wherever a commonplace emotion must be included among the causative factors of the illness, analysis will regularly show that the pathogenic effect has been exercised by the ever-present sexual element in the traumatic occurrence.

This has led us imperceptibly away from the question of the causation of the psychoneuroses to the problem of their nature. On the basis of the knowledge acquired by means of psycho-analysis one can only say that the nature of these maladies lies in disturbances of the sexual processes, of those organic processes which determine the development and form of expression of the sexual craving. One can scarcely avoid, in the last analysis, picturing those processes as chemical, so that we might recognize the so-called actual neuroses as the somatic effects of disturbances in sexual metabolism, and the psychoneuroses as, in addition, the psychical effects of these disturbances. The similarity of the neuroses to the phenomena of intoxication and abstinence following upon certain alkaloids, as well as to Graves' and to Addison's diseases, is readily apparent on the clinical side; and, just as we can no longer describe as 'nervous diseases' the two maladies mentioned, so the 'actual neuroses' also, despite their name, will probably soon have to be removed from this category.

Thus, whatever has a harmful effect on the processes serving the sexual function belongs to the ætiology of the neuroses. In the first place, accordingly, there are the noxiæ affecting the sexual function itself, in so far as they are felt to be harmful by the sexual constitution, which varies with social culture and education. In the next place, there are all the other noxiæ and traumas which are capable of injuring the sexual processes secondarily through general injury to the whole organism. It should not, however, be forgotten that the ætiological problem presented by the neuroses is at least as complicated as the causative factors of any other disease. A single pathogenic influence is scarcely ever adequate to cause disease; most often a number of ætiological factors supporting one another are necessary and these are consequently not to be opposed to one another. This is the reason why a condition of neurotic invalidism is not sharply distinguished from that of normal health. The malady results from a summation of causes, and the measure of the ætiological conditions may be filled from various accessory sources. To seek the ætiology of the neuroses exclusively in heredity or in the constitution would be no less one-sided than to attempt to find this ætiology only in the accidental modifications undergone by sexuality during life, although investigations show that the nature of these disorders consists only of a disturbance of the sexual processes within the organism.

ON THE HISTORY OF THE PSYCHO-ANALYTIC MOVEMENT

(1914)

ON THE HISTORY OF THE PSYCHO-ANALYTIC MOVEMENT[1]

(1914)

I

Fluctuat nec mergitur.

No one need be surprised to find a subjective element in the contribution I propose to make here to the history of the psycho-analytic movement, nor need anyone wonder at the part I play in it. For psycho-analysis is my creation; I was for ten years the only person who concerned himself with it, and all the dissatisfaction which the new doctrine aroused in my contemporaries has been poured forth in the form of criticisms on my head. Although it is long now since I was the only psycho-analyst, I regard myself as justified in maintaining that even to-day no one can know better than I what psycho-analysis is, how it differs from other ways of investigating the life of the mind, and precisely what should be called psycho-analysis and what would better be described by some other name. In thus rejecting what seems to me a cool act of usurpation, I am indirectly informing the readers of this *Jahrbuch* of the events leading to the changes in editorship and in character that it has undergone.

In 1909, in the lecture-hall of an American university, I had my first opportunity of speaking in public about psycho-analysis[2]; the occasion was a

[1] First published in the *Jahrbuch der Psychoanalyse*, Bd. VI. 1914. [Translated by Joan Riviere.]

[2] *Über Psychoanalyse.* Fünf Vorlesungen. Dritte Auflage, 1916. Appeared simultaneously in English in the *American Journal of Psychology*, March, 1910; translated into Dutch, Hungarian, Polish, Russian and Italian.

momentous one for my work, and moved by this thought I then declared that it was not I who had brought psycho-analysis into existence. The credit for this was due to another, to Josef Breuer, whose work had been done at a time when I was still a student occupied with my examinations (1880—82). Since I gave those lectures, however, well-meaning friends have suggested to me a doubt whether my gratitude should not have been expressed less extravagantly on that occasion. According to them, I should have done as I had previously been accustomed to do, and regarded Breuer's 'cathartic procedure' as a forerunner of psycho-analysis, the latter beginning with my discarding the hypnotic method and introducing that of free association. It is of no great importance in any case whether the history of psycho-analysis is reckoned as beginning with the cathartic method or with my modification of it; I refer to this uninteresting point merely because certain opponents of psycho-analysis have the habit of recollecting occasionally that the art of psycho-analysis was after all not invented by me, but by Breuer. This of course happens only when for once in a way they are able to find something worthy of attention in it; when they impose no such limits to their general rejection of it, however, psycho-analysis is always without question my work alone. I have never heard that Breuer's great share in psycho-analysis has earned him a corresponding measure of criticism and abuse; and as it is long ago now since I recognized that to stir up contradiction and arouse bitterness is the inevitable fate of psycho-analysis, I conclude that I must be the real originator of all that is particularly characteristic in it. I am happy to be able to add that none of the efforts to minimize my part in creating this much-reviled analysis have ever come from Breuer himself or have met with any support from him.

Breuer's discovery has so often been described that I can dispense with discussing it in detail here. The fundamental fact was that the symptoms of hysterical patients are founded upon highly significant, but forgotten, scenes in their past lives (traumas); the therapy founded upon this consisted in causing them to remember and reproduce these scenes in a state of hypnosis (catharsis); and the fragment of theory inferred from this was that these symptoms represented an abnormal form of discharge for quantities of excitation which had not been disposed of otherwise (conversion). Whenever Breuer, in his theoretical contribution to the *Studien über Hysterie*, referred to this process of conversion, he always added my name in brackets after it, as though the priority for this first attempt at theoretic evaluation belonged to me. I believe that actually this distinction relates only to the name, and that the conception was evolved by us simultaneously together.

It is known that after Breuer made his first discovery of the cathartic method he let it rest for a number of years, and took it up again only after I returned from studying with Charcot and induced him to do so. He had a large consulting practice in medicine which made great claims on him; I had only unwillingly taken up the profession of medicine, but I had at that time a strong motive for helping nervous persons or at least for wishing to understand something about nervous states. I had already devoted myself to physical therapy, and had felt absolutely helpless after the disappointing results I had experienced with Erb's 'electrotherapy', which was so full of detailed indications. If I did not at the time arrive on my own account at the conclusion which Möbius later established, that the successes of electrical treatment in nervous patients are the effects of suggestion, certainly only the total absence of these promised successes was to blame. Treatment by suggestion during deep hypnosis, which I learned from Liébeault's and Bernheim's highly impressive demonstrations, then seemed to offer a satisfactory substitute for the failure of electrical treatment. But the method of investigating patients in a state of hypnosis, which I learned of from Breuer—with its automatic effectiveness and the satisfaction it afforded to scientific interest—was bound to be incomparably more attractive than the monotonous, arbitrary prohibitions used in treatment by suggestion, which stood in the way of all research.

We have lately received an admonition purporting to represent one of the latest developments of psycho-analysis, to the effect that the current conflict and the exciting cause of illness are to be brought into the foreground in the analysis. Now this is exactly what Breuer and I used to do at the beginning of our work with the cathartic method. We led the patient's attention directly to the traumatic scene in which the symptom had arisen, endeavoured to find the mental conflict inherent in it and to release the suppressed affect. In the course of this we discovered the mental process, so characteristic of the neuroses, which I later named regression. The patient's associations led back from the scene which one was trying to elucidate to earlier experiences, and compelled the analysis, which had to correct the present, to occupy itself with the past. This regression led constantly further backwards; at first it seemed regularly to bring us to puberty; later on, failures and points which still awaited explanation beckoned the analytic work still further back into years of childhood which had hitherto been inaccessible to any kind of exploration. This regressing trend became an important character of analysis. It appeared that psycho-analysis could explain nothing current without referring back to something past; more, that every pathogenic experience implied a previous one which, though not in itself pathogenic, had yet endowed the later one with its pathogenic quality. The temptation to confine attention to the known actual exciting cause was so strong, however, that even in later analyses I gave way to it. In the analysis of the patient I named 'Dora', carried out in 1899, I had knowledge of the event which occasioned the outbreak of the actual illness. I tried innumerable times to analyse this experience, but even direct demands always failed to produce from her anything more than the same meagre and incomplete description of it. Not until a long détour, leading back over her earliest childhood, had been traversed, did a dream present itself which on analysis brought to mind the hitherto forgotten details of this scene, so that comprehension and a solution of the current conflict became finally possible.

This one example shows how very misleading is the advice just now referred to, and what a degree of scientific regression is represented by the neglect of regression in analytic technique thus enjoined upon us.

The first difference between Breuer and myself came to light in regard to a question concerning the finer psychical mechanism of hysteria. He gave preference to a theory which was still to some extent physiological, as one might call it; he wished to explain the mental dissociation of hysteria by the absence of communication between various psychical states (states of consciousness, as we called them at that time), and he therefore constructed the theory of 'hypnoid' states, the effects of which were supposed to penetrate into waking consciousness like unassimilated foreign bodies. I had taken the matter less academically; everywhere I seemed to discern motives and tendencies analogous to those of everyday life, and I looked upon mental dissociation itself as an effect of a process of rejection which at that time I called *defence*, and later called *repression*. I made a shortlived attempt to allow the two mechanisms a separate existence side by side, but as observation showed me always and only one thing, it was not long before my 'defence' doctrine took up its stand opposite his 'hypnoid' theory.

I am quite sure, however, that this opposition between our views had nothing to do with the severance of our relations which followed shortly after. This severance had deeper causes, but it came about in such a way that at first I did not understand it; it was only later that I learnt from many sure indications how to account for it. It will be remembered that Breuer said of his famous first patient that the sexual element was amazingly undeveloped in her and had contributed nothing to the very rich clinical picture of the case. I have always wondered why the critics did not more often cite this assurance of Breuer's as an argument against my contention of a sexual ætiology in the neuroses, and even to-day I do not know whether I should regard the omission as evidence of tact or of carelessness on their part. Anyone who reads the history of Breuer's case now in the light of the knowledge gained in the last twenty years will at once perceive the symbolism in it—the snake, the stiffening, the disabling of the arm—and, on taking into account the situation at the bedside of the sick father, will easily guess the real interpretation of her symptom-formation; his opinion of the part played by sexuality in the young woman's mental life will then be very different from that of her physician. In his treatment of her case, Breuer could make use of a very intense suggestible *rapport* on the part of the patient, which may serve us as a prototype of what we call 'transference' today. Now I have strong reasons for surmising that after all her symptoms had been relieved Breuer must have discovered from further indications the sexual motivation of this transference, but that the universal nature of this unexpected phenomenon escaped him, with the result that, as though confronted by an 'untoward event', he broke off all further investigation. He never told me this in so many words, but he gave me at various times indications enough to justify this reconstruction of what happened. When I later began more and more resolutely to put forward the significance of sexuality in the ætiology of neurosis, he was the first to show that reaction of distaste and repudiation which was later to become so familiar to me, but which at that time I had not yet learnt to recognize as my inevitable fate.

The fact of the transference appearing, although neither desired nor induced by either physician or patient, in every neurotic who comes under treatment, in its crude sexual, or affectionate, or hostile form, has always seemed to me the most irrefragable proof that the source of the propelling forces of neurosis lies in the sexual life. This argument has never received anything approaching the degree of attention that it merits, for if it had, there would really be no choice but acceptance. In my own conviction of the truth it remains, beside and above the more specific results of analytic work, the decisive factor.

There was some consolation for the bad reception accorded even among my intimate friends to my contention of a sexual ætiology in the neuroses—a vacuum rapidly formed itself about my person—in the thought that I was taking up the fight for a new and original idea. But, one day, certain memories collected in my mind which disturbed this pleasing notion, and gave me instead a valuable insight into the processes of human activity and the nature of human knowledge. The idea for which I was being made responsible had by no means originated with me. It had been imparted to me by no less than three people whose opinion had commanded my deepest respect—by Breuer himself, by Charcot, and by the gynæcologist of Vienna University, Chrobak, perhaps the most eminent of all our Viennese physicians. These three men had all communicated to me a piece of knowledge which, strictly speaking, they themselves did not possess. Two of them later denied having done so when I reminded them of the fact; the third (Charcot) would probably have done the same if it had been granted to me to see him again. But these three identical opinions, which I had heard without understanding, had lain dormant in my mind for years until one day they awoke in the form of an apparently original idea.

One day when I was a young house-physician I was walking with Breuer through the town, when a man came up who evidently wished urgently to speak to him. I fell back; as soon as Breuer was free, he told me in his friendly instructive way that this man was the husband of a patient and had brought him some news of her. The wife, he added, was behaving in such an extraordinary way in society that she had been brought to him for treatment as nervous. Then he concluded: 'These things are always *secrets d'alcove!*' Astonished, I asked him what he meant, and he answered by telling me the meaning of the word *alcove* (marriage-bed), for he did not realize how extraordinary his remark had seemed to me.

Some years later, at one of Charcot's evening receptions, I happened to be standing near the great teacher at a moment when he appeared to be telling Brouardel some very interesting story from his day's work. I hardly heard the beginning, but gradually my attention was seized by what he was saying. A young married couple from the far East: the woman a confirmed invalid: the man either impotent or exceedingly awkward. '*Tâchez donc*, I heard Charcot repeating, *je vous assure, vous y arriverez.*' Brouardel, who spoke less loudly, must have expressed his astonishment that symptoms such as the wife's could have been produced in such circumstances. For Charcot suddenly broke in with great animation, '*Mais, dans des cas pareils c'est toujours la chose génitale, toujours . . . toujours . . . toujours*'; and he crossed his arms over his stomach, hugging himself and jumping up and down on his toes several times in his own characteristic lively way. I know that for one second I was almost paralyzed with amazement and said to myself, 'Well, but if he knows that, why does he never say so?' But the impression was soon forgotten; brain anatomy and the experimental induction of hysterical paralyses absorbed all available interest.

A year later, I had begun medical practice in Vienna as a *Privatdozent* for nervous diseases, and in everything relating to the ætiology of the neuroses I was still as ignorant and innocent as one could only expect of a promising student trained at a university. One day I had a friendly message from

Chrobak, asking me to take a patient of his to whom he could not give enough time, owing to his new appointment as University lecturer. I arrived at the patient's house before he did and found that she was suffering from attacks of insensate anxiety, and could only be soothed by the most detailed information about where her physician was at every moment of the day. When Chrobak arrived he took me aside and told me that the patient's anxiety was due to the fact that although she had been married for eighteen years she was still *virgo intacta*. The husband was absolutely impotent. In such cases, he said, there was nothing for a medical man to do but to shield this domestic misfortune with his own reputation, and put up with it if people shrugged their shoulders and said of him, 'He is no good if he can't cure her after so many years'. The sole prescription for such a malady, he added, is familiar enough to us, but we cannot order it. It runs:

R. Penis normalis
dosim
repetatur!

I had never heard of such a prescription and would have liked to shake my head over my kind friend's cynicism.

I have certainly not disclosed the illustrious parentage of this scandalous idea in order to saddle others with the responsibility for it. I am well aware that it is one thing once or twice, or even oftener, to give words to an idea that comes in the form of a fleeting inspiration, and quite another to intend it seriously, to take it literally, to pursue it in spite of all difficulties into every detail and to win it a place among accepted truths. It is the difference between a casual flirtation and solemn matrimony with all its duties and difficulties. 'To be wedded to an idea' is not an uncommon figure of speech.

Among the other new factors which were added to the cathartic procedure as a result of my work, transforming it into psycho-analysis, I should mention particularly: The doctrine of repression and resistance, the recognition of infantile sexuality, and the interpreting and making use of dreams as a source of knowledge of the unconscious.

The doctrine of repression quite certainly came to me independently of any other source; I know of no outside impression which might have suggested it to me, and for a long time I imagined it to be entirely my own, until Otto Rank showed us the passage in Schopenhauer's *World as Will and Idea* in which the philosopher is trying to give an explanation of insanity[1]. What he says there about the struggle against acceptance of a painful part of reality fits my conception of repression so completely that I am again indebted for having made a discovery to not being a wide reader. And yet others have read the passage and passed it by without making this discovery, and perhaps the same would have happened to me if in my young days I had had more taste for reading philosophical works. In later years I have denied myself the very great pleasure of reading the works of Nietzsche from a deliberate resolve not to be hampered in working out the impressions received in psycho-analysis by any sort of expectation derived from without. I have to be prepared, therefore—and am so, gladly—to forego all claim to priority in the many instances in which laborious psycho-analytic investigation can merely confirm the truths which this philosopher recognized intuitively.

The doctrine of repression is the foundation-stone on which the whole structure of psycho-analysis rests,

[1] *Zentralblatt für Psychoanalyse,* Bd. I, S. 69.

the most essential part of it, and yet it is nothing but a theoretical formulation of a phenomenon which may be observed to recur as often as one undertakes an analysis of a neurotic without resorting to hypnosis. One notices a resistance then making itself evident in opposition to the work of analysis and inducing a failure to recall memories in order to frustrate it. The use of hypnosis is bound to hide this resistance; the history of psycho-analysis proper, therefore, begins with the new technique that dispenses with hypnosis. Considered theoretically, the fact that this resistance coincides with an amnesia leads inevitably to that view of unconscious mental activity which is peculiar to psycho-analysis and after all distinguishes it quite clearly from philosophical speculations about the unconscious. It may thus be said that the theory of psycho-analysis is an attempt to account for two observed facts that strike one conspicuously and unexpectedly whenever an attempt is made to trace the symptoms of a neurotic back to their sources in his past life: the facts of transference and of resistance. Any line of investigation, no matter what its direction, which recognizes these two facts and takes them as the starting-point of its work may call itself psycho-analysis, though it arrives at results other than my own. But anyone who takes up other sides of the problem while avoiding these two premisses will hardly escape the charge of misappropriating by attempted impersonation, if he persists in calling himself a psycho-analyst.

If anyone should seek to regard the theory of repression and of resistance as assumptions instead of as results following from psycho-analysis, I should oppose him most emphatically. Such assumptions of a general psychological and biological nature do exist, and it would be useful to consider them on some other occasion; but the doctrine of repression is the outcome of psycho-analytic work, a theoretic inference legitimately drawn from innumerable observations. The formulation of infantile sexuality is another of these products, acquired, however, at a much later date; in the early days of tentative investigation by analysis no such thing was thought of. At first one merely remarked that the effect of current experiences had to be traced back to something in the past. Only, 'enquirers often find more than they bargain for'. One was drawn further and further back into the past; one hoped at last to be able to halt at puberty, the period in which sexuality is traditionally supposed to awake. But in vain; the tracks led on still further backwards, into childhood and into its earliest years. On the way an obstacle had to be overcome that was almost fatal to the young science. Influenced by Charcot's view of the traumatic origin of hysteria, one was readily inclined to accept as true and ætiologically significant the statements made by patients in which they ascribed their symptoms to passive sexual experiences in early childhood — broadly speaking, to seduction. When this ætiology broke down under its own improbability and under contradiction in definitely ascertainable circumstances, the result at first was helpless bewilderment. Analysis had led by the right paths back to these sexual traumas, and yet they were not true. Reality was lost from under one's feet. At that time I would gladly have given up the whole thing, just as my esteemed predecessor, Breuer, had done when he made his unwelcome discovery. Perhaps I persevered only because I had no choice and could not then begin again at anything else. At last came the reflection that, after all, one has no right to despair because one has been deceived in one's expectations; one must revise them. If hysterics trace back their symptoms to fictitious traumas, this new fact signifies that they create such scenes in phantasy, and psychical reality requires to be taken into account alongside actual reality. This was soon followed by the recognition that these phantasies were intended to cover up the auto-erotic activity of early childhood, to gloss it over and raise it to a higher level; and then, from behind the phantasies, the whole range of the child's sexual life came to light.

With this sexual activity during early childhood the inherited constitution at last came into its own. Predisposition and experience were here linked up in an indissoluble ætiological unity; impressions which were entirely commonplace, and would otherwise have had no effect, became exaggerated by the predisposition into traumas giving rise to excitation and fixations; while experiences stimulated factors in the disposition which, without them, might have remained long dormant and perhaps never have awakened. The last word on the subject of traumatic ætiology was spoken later by Abraham, when he pointed out that the peculiarity of the sexual constitution in children is precisely calculated to provoke sexual experiences of a certain kind, namely, traumas.

In the beginning my formulations regarding infantile sexuality were founded almost exclusively upon the results of analysis in adults, leading as they did back into the past. I had no opportunity of direct observations on children. It was therefore a very great triumph when it became possible years later to confirm almost all my inferences by direct observation and analysis of children, a triumph that lost some of its magnitude as one gradually realized that the nature of the discovery was such that one should really be ashamed of having to make it. The further one carried these observations on children, the more self-evident the facts became, and the more astonishing was it too that so much trouble was taken to overlook them.

Such a certain conviction of the existence and significance of infantile sexuality can, it is true, only be obtained by the path of analysis, pursuing the symptoms and peculiarities of neurotics back to their ultimate sources, the discovery of which then explains whatever is explicable in them and enables whatever is modifiable in them to be changed. I can understand that one would arrive at different results if, as C. G. Jung has recently done, one first forms a theoretical conception of the nature of the sexual instinct and then seeks to explain the life of children on this basis. A conception of this kind is bound to be selected arbitrarily or in accordance with secondary considerations, and runs the risk of not corresponding adequately to the field in which it is applied. It is true that the road of analysis leads also to certain final difficulties and obscurities in regard to sexuality and its relation to the whole life of the individual: but these problems cannot be dealt with by speculation; they must await solution by other observations or by observations in other fields.

I need say little about the interpretation of dreams. It came as the first-fruits of the new technique, when, following a dim presentiment, I had decided to exchange hypnosis for free association. My desire for knowledge had not been directed to start with towards understanding dreams. I do not know of any outside influence which drew my interest to them or inspired me with any helpful expectations. Before Breuer and I ceased to meet there had only just been time for me to tell him in one sentence that I now understood how to translate dreams. Since this was how the discovery came about, it followed that the symbolism in the language of dreams was almost the last thing to become clear to me, for the dreamer's associations help very little towards understanding symbols. I have held fast to the habit of always studying things themselves before looking for information about them in books, and therefore I was able to establish the symbolism of dreams for myself before I was led to it by Scherner's work on the subject. It was only later that I came to appreciate to its full extent this mode of expression in dreams—partly through the influence of Stekel, who at first did such very creditable work but afterwards went totally astray. The close connection between psycho-analytic dream-interpretation and the art of interpreting dreams as practised and held in such high esteem by the ancients only became clear to me much later. I found the essential charateristic and most significant part of my dream theory—the reduction of dream-distortion to an inner conflict, a kind of inward dishonesty—later in a writer who was familiar with philosophy though not with medicine, the engineer J. Popper, who published his *Phantasien eines Realisten* under the name of Lynkeus.

The interpretation of dreams became a solace and a support to me in those arduous first years of analysis, when I had to master the technology, clinical phenomena and therapy of the neuroses all at the same time; I was then completely isolated, and in the network of problems and accumulation of difficulties often dreaded losing my way and also my confidence. It was often a long time before the test of my hypothesis, that a neurosis must become intelligible by analysis, was realized in the patient; in their dreams, which might be regarded as analogues of their symptoms, this hypothesis was confirmed almost without exception.

It was only my success in this direction that enabled me to persevere. The result is that I have acquired the habit of gauging the measure of a psychologist's understanding by his attitude to dream-interpretation; and have observed with satisfaction that most of the opponents of psycho-analysis avoid this question altogether or else display remarkable clumsiness if they attempt to deal with it. I soon saw the necessity of an analysis of myself and this I carried out with the help of a series of my own dreams which led me back through all the events of my childhood; I am still to-day of the opinion that this kind of analysis may suffice for anyone who is a prolific dreamer and not too abnormal.

I think that by narrating this history of its development I have shown what psycho-analysis is better than by a systematic description of it. I did not at first perceive the peculiar nature of what I had discovered. Without thinking, I sacrificed at its inception my popularity as a physician, and the growth of a large consulting practice among nervous patients, by enquiries relating to the sexual factors involved in the causation of their neuroses; this brought me a great many new facts which definitively confirmed my conviction of the practical importance of the sexual factor. Unsuspectingly, I spoke before the Vienna Neurological Society, then under the presidency of Krafft-Ebing, expecting to be compensated by the interest and recognition of my colleagues for the material losses I had willingly undergone. I treated my discoveries as ordinary contributions to science and hoped to be met in the same spirit. But the silence with which my addresses were received, the void which formed itself about me, the insinuations that found their way to me, caused me gradually to realize that one cannot count upon views about the part played by sexuality in the ætiology of the neuroses meeting with the same reception as other communications. I understood that from now onwards I belonged to those who have 'disturbed the sleep of the world', as Hebbel says, and that I could not reckon upon objectivity and tolerance. Since, however, my conviction of the general accuracy of my observations and conclusions grew and grew, and as my confidence in my own judgement was by no means slight, any more than my moral courage, there could be no doubt about the outcome of the situation. I made up my mind that it had been my fortune to discover particularly important connections, and was prepared to accept the fate that sometimes accompanies such discoveries.

I imagined the future somewhat as follows: I should probably succeed in sustaining myself by means of the therapeutic success of the new method, but science would ignore me entirely during my lifetime. Some decades later, someone else would infallibly come upon the same things—for which the time was not yet ripe—, would achieve recognition for them and bring me to honour as a forerunner whose failure had been inevitable. Meanwhile I settled down, like Robinson, as comfortably as possible on my lonely island. When I look back to those lonely years, away from the pressure and preoccupations of to-day, it seems to me like a glorious 'heroic era'; my 'splendid isolation' was not lacking in advantages and in charms. I had not to read any publications, nor to listen to any ill-informed opponents; I was not subject to influence from any quarter; no one attempted to hurry me. I learnt to restrain speculative tendencies and to follow the unforgotten advice of my master, Charcot—to look at the same things again and again until they themselves begin to speak. There was no need for my writings, for which with some difficulty I found a publisher, to keep pace with my knowledge; they could be postponed as long as I pleased; there was no doubtful 'priority' to be secured. *Die Traumdeutung,* for instance, was complete in all essentials at the beginning of 1896; it was not written out until the summer of 1899. The analysis of 'Dora' was over at the end of 1899; the case was noted down in the next two weeks, but not published until 1905. All this time my writings were not reviewed in the medical journals, or, if by an exception this happened, they were scouted with contemptuous or pitying arrogance. Occasionally a colleague would make some reference to me in one of his publications; it would be very short and not at all flattering—such as 'eccentric', 'extreme', 'very peculiar ideas'. It happened once that an assistant at the clinic in Vienna where I gave lectures asked me for permission to attend one of the courses. He listened very attentively and said nothing; after the last lecture was over he offered to accompany me. As we walked, he told me that with the knowledge of his chief he had written a book against my views, but regretted very much that he had not first learnt more about them from my lectures, as in that case he would have written very differently. He had indeed enquired at the clinic whether he had not better first read the *Die Traumdeutung*; but had been advised against it, as it was not worth the trouble. He then himself compared the solidity of the structure of my doctrine with that of the Catholic church. In the interests of his salvation I take this as an expression of acknowledgement. But, he concluded by saying, it was too late to alter anything; his book was already printed. Nor did this man think it necessary later on to make known anything of the change in his opinion of psycho-analysis, but in his capacity of reviewer for a medical journal chose rather to follow its development with flippant comments.

Whatever personal sensitiveness I possessed was blunted in those years, to my advantage. From embitterment I was saved, however, by one circumstance that is not always present to help lonely discoverers. Many a one is tormented by the need to account for the lack of sympathy or the repudiation expressed by his contemporaries, and feels their attitude painfully as a contradiction of his own secure conviction. There was no need for me to feel so; for psycho-analytical principles enabled me to understand this attitude in my contemporaries and to see it as a necessary consequence of fundamental analytic premisses. If it was true that the associated connections I had discovered were kept from the knowledge of patients by inward resistances of an affective kind, then these resistances would be bound to appear in the healthy also, as soon as, from some external source, they became confronted with what is repressed. It was not surprising that they should be able to justify on intellectual grounds this rejection of my ideas though it was actually affective in nature. The same thing happened just as often in patients, and the arguments they advanced were just the same and not precisely brilliant—reasons are as plenty as blackberries, as Falstaff says. The only difference was that with patients one was in a position to bring pressure to bear on them, so as to induce them to realize their resistances and overcome them, but had to do without this advantage in dealing with those who were apparently healthy. How to compel these normal persons to examine the matter in a cool, objective scientific spirit was an insoluble problem which was best left to time to accomplish. In the history of science one can clearly see that often the very proposition that at first called out nothing but contradiction came later on to be accepted, although no new proofs in support of it were forthcoming.

One would hardly, however, expect me, during those years when I alone represented psycho-analysis, to have developed any particular respect for the opinion of the world or any propensity to intellectual compromise.

II

From the year 1902 onwards, a number of young medical men gathered round me with the express intention of learning, practising, and spreading knowledge of psycho-analysis. The stimulus came from a colleague who had himself experienced the beneficial effect of analytic therapy. Regular meetings were held on certain evenings at my house; discussions were arranged according to certain rules; the guests endeavoured to orient themselves in this new and strange field of research and to interest others in it. One day a young man who had passed through the technical training school introduced himself with a manuscript which showed very unusual comprehension. We induced him to go through the *Gymnasium* and the University and to devote himself to the non-medical side of psycho-analytic investigation. The little society acquired in him a zealous and dependable secretary and I gained in Otto Rank a faithful helper and co-worker.

The little circle soon expanded, and in the course of the next few years often changed its composition.

On the whole I could regard it as hardly inferior, in wealth and variety of talent, to the staff of any clinical lecturer one could think of. It included from the beginning those men who were later to play such a considerable, if not always an agreeable, part in the history of the psycho-analytic movement. At that time, however, one could not imagine these developments. I had every reason to be satisfied, and I think I did everything possible to impart to the others my own knowledge and experiences. There were only two inauspicious circumstances which at last estranged me inwardly from the group. I could not succeed in establishing among the members those friendly relations that ought to obtain between men who are all engaged upon the same difficult work, nor could I crush out the disputes about priority for which there were manv opportunities under these conditions of work in common. The difficulties in the way of instructing beginners in the practice of psycho-analysis, which are quite particularly great and are responsible for much in the present dissensions among us, were evident already in this private Vienna Psycho-Analytical Society. I myself did not venture to put forward a technique which was still incomplete, or a theory which was still in the making, with that authority which, if I had, would perhaps have spared the others many a pitfall and many a fatal error. The self-reliance of intellectual workers, their early independence of their teacher, is always gratifying psychologically; it is an advantage scientifically only when the workers personally fulfil certain conditions which are none too common. For psycho-analysis in particular a long and severe discipline and training in self-discipline was actually required. In view of the courage displayed by devotion to a subject so despised and so poor in prospects, I was disposed to tolerate much among the members to which I should otherwise have made objection. The circle also included others besides medical men—cultured persons who had recognized something important in psycho-analysis—writers, painters and so on. *Die Traumdeutung* and the book on wit (*Der Witz*), among others, had shown from the beginning that the principles of psycho-analysis cannot be limited to the medical field, but are capable of application to various other mental sciences.

In 1907 the situation changed at one stroke, contrary to all expectations. It appeared that psycho-analysis had unobtrusively awakened interest and gained friends, and that even some scientific workers existed who were ready to acknowledge an allegiance to it. A communication from Bleuler had informed me before this that my works had been studied and made use of in Burghölzli. In January 1907, a physician of the Zurich clinic, Dr. Eitingon, came to Vienna for the first time and other visits followed which led to an animated exchange of ideas. Finally, on the invitation of C. G. Jung, at that time still assistant physician at Burghölzli, a first meeting took place at Salzburg in the spring of 1908 which included friends of psycho-analysis from Vienna, Zurich and other places. One of the results of this first psycho-analytical Congress was the founding of a periodical called the *Jahrbuch für psycho-analytische und psychopathologische Forschungen*, published by Bleuler and Freud, and edited by Jung, which first appeared in the year 1909. A close community in the work of Vienna and Zurich found expression in this publication.

I have repeatedly acknowledged with gratitude the great efforts made towards the spread of psycho-analysis by the Zurich School of Psychiatry, in particular by Bleuler and Jung, and I have no hesitation in doing so again, even in such altered circumstances. It was not indeed the partisanship of the Zurich School which led the attention of the scientific world to psycho-analysis at that time. The latency period had expired and everywhere psycho-analysis was becoming the object of ever-increasing interest. But in all other places this accession of interest at first produced nothing but very emphatic repudiation, mostly quite violent; whereas in Zurich, on the contrary, agreement was on the whole the dominant note. Moreover, nowhere else could such a compact little group of adherents be found, or a public clinic be placed at the service of psycho-analytic researches, or was there a clinical lecturer who embodied psycho-analytical principles as an integral part in his psychiatric course. The Zurich group became as it were the nucleus of the little band who were fighting for the recognition of analysis. The only opportunity of learning the new art and working at it in practice lay there. Most of my followers and co-workers at the present time came to me by way of Zurich, even those who were geographically much nearer to Vienna than to Switzerland. For western Europe, which contains the great centres of culture, the position of Vienna is an outlying one; and its prestige has for many years been affected by strong prejudices. Representatives of all the most important nations congregate in Switzerland where mental activity is so great; an infective spot there was bound to be of great importance for the spread of the 'psychical epidemic', as Hoche of Freiburg has called it.

According to the evidence of a colleague who witnessed developments at Burghölzli, it appears that psycho-analysis awakened interest there very early. In Jung's work on occult phenomena, published in

1902, there was already an allusion to my book on dream-interpretation. From 1903 or 1904, says my informant, psycho-analysis was in the forefront of interest. After personal relations between Vienna and Zurich had been established in the middle of 1907, an informal society was also started in Burghölzli where the problems of psycho-analysis were discussed at regular meetings. In the alliance between the Vienna and the Zurich schools the Swiss were by no means mere recipients. They had already produced very creditable scientific work, the results of which were of service to psycho-analysis. The association experiments started by the Wundt School had been interpreted by them in a psycho-analytic sense, and had proved applicable in unexpected ways. By this means it had been possible to arrive at rapid experimental confirmation of psycho-analytic observations and to demonstrate to students certain connections which the analyst would only have been able to describe to them. The first bridge linking up experimental psychology with psycho-analysis had been constructed.

In psycho-analytic treatment association-experiments enable a provisional, qualitative analysis of the case to be made, but they furnish no essential contribution to the technique and can be dispensed with in carrying out analyses. More important, however, was another achievement by the Zurich school, or its leaders, Bleuler and Jung. The former showed that light could be thrown on a large number of purely psychiatric cases by reference to the same processes as have been recognized through psycho-analysis to obtain in dreams and neuroses (Freudian mechanisms); and Jung successfully applied the analytic method of interpretation to the most alien and obscure phenomena of dementia præcox, so that their sources in the life and interests of the patient came clearly to light. After this it was impossible for psychiatrists to ignore psycho-analysis any longer. Bleuler's great work on schizophrenia (1911), in which the psycho-analytical point of view was placed on an equal footing with the systematic clinical one, completed this success.

I will not omit to point out a divergence which was already at that time noticeable in the direction taken by the work of the two schools. I had published as early as 1897 the analysis of a case of schizophrenia, which however took a paranoid form, so that the solution of it could not have anticipated the results of Jung's analyses. But to me the important point had been, not so much the possibility of interpreting the symptoms, as the psychical mechanism of the disease, and above all the similarity of this mechanism with that of hysteria which was already known. At that time no light had yet been thrown on the differences between the two disorders. I was in fact already aiming at a libido theory of the neuroses, which should explain all neurotic and psychotic manifestations as abnormal directions taken by libido, that is, as deviations of it from its normal course. This point of view was overlooked by the Swiss investigators. As far as I know, Bleuler maintains the view even to-day that the various forms of dementia præcox have an organic causation; and Jung, whose book on this disease appeared in 1907, at the Congress at Salzburg in 1908 supported the toxic theory of its causation which takes no account of the libido theory, although it is true that it does not exclude it. Later on (1912) he came to grief on this point, by making too much of what he had previously ignored.

There is a third contribution made by the Swiss School, and probably to be ascribed entirely to Jung, which I do not value so highly as others do whose concern with these matters is more remote. I mean the theory of 'complexes' which grew out of the *Diagnostische Assoziationsstudien* (1906 to 1910). It has neither produced a psychological theory in itself, nor has it proved capable of easy incorporation into the context of psycho-analytical theory. The word 'complex', on the other hand, has become naturalized, so to speak, in psycho-analytic language; it is a convenient and often indispensable term for summing up descriptively a psychological state. None of the other terms coined by psycho-analysis for its own needs has achieved such widespread popularity, or been so misapplied to the detriment of formulating clear concepts. Analysts began to speak among themselves of a 'return of a complex' where they meant a 'return of the repressed'; or got into the habit of saying 'I have a complex against him', where correctly they could only have said 'a resistance against him'.

In the years following 1907 when the schools of Vienna and Zurich were united, psycho-analysis made that extraordinary plunge forward, the momentum of which is felt even to-day; this is shown both by the spread of psycho-analytic literature and by the constant increase in the number of medical men who are practising or studying it, and also by the frequency of the attacks upon it made at Congresses and in learned societies. It has penetrated into the most distant lands and everywhere has not merely startled psychiatrists but has commanded the attention of the cultured public and of scientific workers in other fields. Havelock Ellis, who has followed its development with sympathy without ever calling himself an adherent, wrote in 1911 in a report for the Australasian Medical Congress: 'Freud's psycho-analysis is now championed and carried out not only in Austria and in Switzerland, but in the United States, in England, in India, in Canada, and, I doubt not, in Australasia[1].' A physician from Chile (probably a German) spoke at the International Congress at Buenos Ayres in 1910 in support of the existence of infantile sexuality and commended highly the effects of psycho-analytic therapy for obsessional symptoms[2]. An English neurologist in Central India informed me, through a distinguished colleague who was coming to Europe, that the analyses of Mohammedan Indians which he had carried out showed the same ætiology of neuroses in them as we find in our European patients.

The introduction of psycho-analysis into North America took place with very special marks of honour. In the autumn of 1909, Stanley Hall, the President of Clark University, Worcester, Massachusetts, invited Jung and myself to take part in the celebration of the twentieth anniversary of the foundation of the University by giving addresses in the German language. To our great surprise, we found the members of that small but highly respected University for the study of pedagogy and philosophy so unprejudiced that they were acquainted with all the literature of psycho-analysis and had given it a place in their lectures to students. In prudish America it was possible, at least in academic circles, to discuss freely and scientifically everything that in ordinary life is regarded as objectionable. The five lectures which I improvised in Worcester appeared in English in the American Journal of Psychology, and were shortly after published in German under the

---

[1] Havelock Ellis: The Doctrines of the Freud School.

[2] G. Greve: Sobre Psicologia y Psicoterapia de ciertos Estados angustiosos. *Zentralblatt für Psychoanalyse,* Bd. I, S. 594.

title *Über Psychoanalyse*. Jung read a paper on 'Diagnostic Association-experiments' and one on 'Conflicts in the Mind of the Child'. We were rewarded with the honorary degree of Doctor of Laws. In that week at Worcester, psycho-analysis was represented by five persons; besides Jung and myself, there was Ferenczi, who had joined me as travelling companion, Ernest Jones, then at the University of Toronto (Canada), now returned to London, and A. A. Brill, who was already practising psycho-analysis in New York.

The most important personal relationship which arose from the meeting at Worcester was that with James J. Putnam, Professor of Neuropathology at Harvard University. Some years before, he had expressed an unfavourable opinion of psycho-analysis, but now he rapidly reconciled himself to it and recommended it to his countrymen and his colleagues in a series of lectures which were as rich in content as they were brilliant in form. The esteem he enjoyed throughout America on account of his high moral character and unflinching love of truth was of great service to psycho-analysis and protected it against the denunciations which might otherwise have early overwhelmed it. Later on, yielding too much to the strong ethical and philosophical bent of his nature, Putnam made what seems to me an impossible demand—he expected psycho-analysis to place itself in the service of a particular moral-philosophical conception of the Universe—but he remains the chief pillar of the psycho-analytic movement in his native land.

For the further spread of this movement Brill and Jones deserve the greatest credit; they achieved this by repeatedly with self-denying assiduity bringing to the notice of their countrymen in their writings the easily observable fundamental facts of everyday life, of dreams and neurosis. Brill has contributed still further to this effect by medical practice and by his translations of my works, and Jones by erudite lectures and by his skill in debate at congresses in America.[1] The absence of any deep-rooted scientific tradition in America and the much less stringent rule of official authority there have been decidedly advantageous to the movement which Stanley Hall started. It was characteristic of that country that from the beginning both professors and superintendents of mental hospitals as well as independent practitioners were all equally interested in analysis. But it is clear that precisely for this reason the centres of ancient culture, where the greatest resistance has been displayed, must be the scene of the final decisive battle for psycho-analysis.

Among European countries France has hitherto shown itself the least disposed to welcome psycho-analysis, although useful work in French by A. Maeder of Zurich has provided easy access to its doctrines. The first indications of allegiance came from the provinces; Morichau-Beauchant (Poitiers) was the first Frenchman to subscribe publicly to psycho-analysis. Régis and Hesnard (Bordeaux) have recently (1913) attempted to disperse the prejudices of their countrymen against the new ideas by an exhaustive and intelligent presentation which takes exception only to symbolism. In Paris itself, a conviction still seems to reign (to which Janet himself gave eloquent expression at the Congress in London in 1913) that everything good in psycho-analysis is

[1] The publications of both authors have appeared in a collected form. A. A. Brill: *Psychoanalysis, its Theories and practical Applications*, 1912. (Third edition, 1922; Saunders, Philadelphia.) Ernest Jones: *Papers on Psycho-Analysis*, 1912. (Third edition, 1923; Baillière, Tindall & Cox, London.)

a repetition of Janet's views with insignificant modifications, and that everything else in it is bad. At this congress, indeed, Janet had to submit to a number of corrections by Ernest Jones, who was able to point out to him his insufficient knowledge of the subject. Even though we deny his claims, however, we cannot forget the value of his work on the psychology of the neuroses.

In Italy, after several promising starts, no real interest was forthcoming. In Holland, analysis found an early hearing by way of personal relationships; Van Emden, Van Ophuijsen, Van Renterghem (*Freud en zijn School*) and the two Stärckes are actively occupied with it both practically and theoretically.[1] In scientific circles in England interest in analysis has developed very slowly, but there is reason to expect that the sense for the practical and the passionate love of justice in the English will ensure it a brilliant future there.

In Sweden, P. Bjerre, who succeeded to Wetterstrand's practice, gave up hypnotic suggestion, at least for the time, in favour of analytic treatment. R. Vogt (Christiania) had already in 1907 appreciated psycho-analysis in his book *Psykiatrien's grundtraek*, so that the first text-book of psychiatry to refer to psycho-analysis was a Norwegian one. In Russia, psycho-analysis has become generally known and has spread widely; almost all my writings, as well as those of other adherents of analysis, have been translated into Russian. But a really penetrating comprehension of analytical principles has not yet been evinced in Russia; so that the contributions of Russian physicians are at present not very notable.

[1] The first *official* recognition of dream-interpretation and psycho-analysis in Europe was extended to them by the psychiatrist Jelgersma, Rector of the University of Leiden, in his official address on February 9, 1914.

The only skilled analyst there is M. Wulff who practises in Odessa. It is principally due to L. Jekels that psycho-analysis has been introduced to Polish scientific and literary circles. Hungary, so near geographically to Austria, and so far from it scientifically, has produced only one collaborator, S. Ferenczi, but one that indeed outweighs a whole society.

The position of psycho-analysis in Germany can only be described by saying that it forms the centre-point of scientific discussions and evokes the most emphatic repudiation from both medical men and laity; these controversies, however, have come to no conclusion, but are continually being revived and intensified. No official seat of learning there has up to the present recognized psycho-analysis; successful practitioners who employ it are very few; only a few institutions, such as Binswanger's in Kreuzlingen (on Swiss soil) and Marcinowski's in Holstein, have introduced it. One of the most prominent representatives of analysis, Karl Abraham, at one time an assistant of Bleuler's, maintains himself in the critical atmosphere of Berlin. One might wonder that this state of things should continue unaltered for several years if one did not know that it is merely a superficial appearance. Too much significance should not be attributed to rejection by the official representatives of science and heads of institutions, together with their dependents and followers. It is natural that opponents should raise a clamour while intimidated adherents preserve silence. Some of the latter, after producing contributions to analysis which raised considerable expectations, later withdrew from the movement under the pressure of circumstances. The movement itself advances surely though silently, wins new adherents continually among psychiatrists and laity, brings in a constant stream of new readers for psycho-analytical literature and so compels its opponents to ever more vehement defensive measures. At least a dozen times in recent years, in reports of the proceedings of certain Congresses and scientific assemblies or in reviews of certain publications, I have read 'Psycho-Analysis is dead, at last defeated and finally abolished!' The answer to all this might be like that of Mark Twain in his telegram to the newspapers which falsely reported his death: Report of my death grossly exaggerated. After these announcements psycho-analysis always gained new adherents and co-operators or acquired new means of advancing itself. After all, to be hailed as a corpse is an advance on being received in dead silence.

Hand in hand with this geographical extension of psycho-analysis went an expansion in its content; its application was pushed forward from the field of the neuroses and psychiatry to other fields of knowledge. I shall not treat this aspect of the development of our discipline in much detail, since this has been done with great success by Rank and Sachs in a volume (one of Löwenfeld's *Grenzfragen*) which deals exhaustively with this side of analytical research. Moreover, this branch is still in its infancy; it has been little worked at, consists mostly of attempts and to a certain extent of work which as yet has only been planned. No reasonable person will see any grounds for a reproach in this. An enormous mass of work confronts our little group of workers, most of whom have their main occupation elsewhere and can bring only the qualifications of an amateur to the technical problems of these unfamiliar fields of science. These workers who belong really to psycho-analysis make no secret of their lack of special training; they intend merely to point a way, and to occupy the places of the specialists to whom they recommend analytic technique and principles only until the latter are ready to take up the work themselves. That the results achieved are nevertheless not inconsiderable is due partly to the fruitfulness of the analytic method, and partly to the circumstance that already there are a few investigators who, without being medical men, have taken up the application of psycho-analysis to the mental sciences as their profession in life.

As is natural, most of these branches of study owe their origin to remarks in my earlier analytic writings. Analytic examination of neurotic persons and the neurotic manifestations observable in normal people necessitated conclusions in regard to psychological connections which could not possibly be limited to the field in which they had been discovered. In this way analysis has provided us not only with the explanation of pathological phenomena, but has revealed their connection with normal mental life and disclosed undreamt-of relationships between psychiatry and the most various other sciences dealing with products of the mind. Certain typical dreams, for instance, have yielded an explanation of many myths and fairy-tales. Riklin and Abraham followed this hint and initiated those researches into myths which have found their completion, in a manner complying with all expert demands, in Rank's works on mythology. Further investigation into dream-symbolism led to the heart of the problems of mythology, folklore (Jones and Storfer), and the abstractions of religion. A deep impression was made on all hearers at one of the psycho-analytical Congresses when a pupil of Jung demonstrated the correspondence of schizophrenic phantasy-formations with the cosmogonies of primitive times and races. Mythological material later on received further elaboration, no longer free from objection and yet very interesting, at the hands of Jung, in works attempting to correlate the various neurotic, religious and mythological phantasies.

Another path led from the investigation of dreams to the analysis of works of imagination and of their creators—poets and artists themselves. The first step was taken by the recognition that dreams invented by writers will often yield to analysis in the same way as genuine ones (Gradiva). The conception of an unconscious mental activity made it possible to form a preliminary idea of the nature of poetic creative work; and the realization, gained in the study of neurotics, of the part played by the instincts enabled us to perceive the sources of artistic production and confronted us with two problems: how the artist reacts to these stimuli and what means he employs to disguise these reactions[1]. Most analysts with wide general interests have contributed something to the solution of these problems, which are among the most fascinating in the whole application of psycho-analysis. Naturally, opposition in this direction also was not lacking on the part of those who know nothing of analysis; it took the same form as it did in the original field of psycho-analytic research—the same misconceptions and vehement rejections. It was only to be expected from the beginning that, whatever regions psycho-analysis might penetrate into, it would inevitably experience the same struggles with the occupants in possession. These little invasions, however, have not yet all aroused in some fields the attention that awaits them in the future. Among the strictly scientific applica-

[1] Rank: *Der Künstler;* analyses of poets by Sadger, Reik and others; my little monograph *Eine Kindheitserinnerung des Leonardo da Vinci*; Abraham's analysis of Segantini.

tions of analysis to literature, Rank's exhaustive work on the theme of incest easily takes the first place; its subject will ensure it the greatest unpopularity. Up to the present, little work based on psychoanalysis has been done in the sciences of language and history. I myself ventured the first approach to the problems of the psychology of religion, in 1910, by drawing a parallel between religious ritual and the ceremonials of neurotics. Dr. Pfister, a clergyman in Zurich, has traced the origin of religious fanaticism back to perverse erotism in his book on the piety of Count von Zinzendorf (as well as in other contributions). In the latest works of the Zurich school we find analysis permeated with religious ideas rather than the opposite, as is intended.

In the four essays called *Totem und Tabu* I have made an attempt to deal with the problems of race-psychology in the light of analysis; this line of investigation leads direct to the origins of the most important institutions of our civilization, of state organization, morality and religion, and, moreover, of the prohibition against incest and of the conscience. How far the connections which have come to light in this matter will withstand criticism is probably not ascertainable at the present time.

The first example of an application of the analytic mode of thought to the problems of æsthetics was contained in my book on *Wit*. Everything beyond this is still awaiting workers, who may expect a particularly rich harvest in this field. We are entirely without the co-operation of specialists in all these branches, and in order to attract them Hanns Sachs founded in 1912 the periodical *Imago* which is edited by him and Rank. A beginning has been made by Hitschmann and von Winterstein in illuminating philosophical systems and personalities by analysis, and here both more extended and deeper investigation is much needed.

The revolutionary discoveries of psycho-analysis in regard to the mental life of children—the part played in it by sexual impulses (von Hug-Hellmuth), and the final fate of those components of sexuality which cannot be taken up into the function of reproduction—were bound to direct attention early to pedagogics and to stimulate an attempt to bring the analytic point of view into the foreground in this field of work. Recognition is due to the Rev. Dr. Pfister for having, with sincere enthusiasm, initiated the application of psycho-analysis in this direction and brought it to the notice of ministers of religion and persons concerned with education.[1] He has succeeded in gaining the sympathy and participation of a number of Swiss pedagogues in this matter. Certain members of his own profession are said to share his views but to have elected nevertheless to remain cautiously in the background. In retreating from psycho-analysis, a section of Vienna analysts seems to have alighted upon a kind of medical pedagogy.[2]

With these indications, which are far from complete, I have attempted to give some idea of the innumerable connections, not even yet exhausted, which have evinced themselves between medical psycho-analysis and other fields of science. There is material for a generation of investigators to work at, and I do not doubt that the work will be carried out as soon as the resistances against psycho-analysis are overcome in the field in which it originally appeared.[3]

---

[1] *Die psychoanalytische Methode.* 1913. Vol. I of Meumann and Messmer's Pedagogium.

[2] Adler und Furtmüller: *Heilen und Bilden.* 1913.

[3] See my two articles, entitled *Das Interesse an der Psychoanalyse,* in *Scientia.* XIV. 1913.

To write the story of these resistances would be, in my opinion, both fruitless and inopportune at the present time. The story is not very creditable to the scientific men of our time. But to this I will immediately add that it has never occurred to me to pour contempt upon the opponents of psycho-analysis merely because they were opponents, apart from the few paltry creatures, swindlers and adventurers, who are always found on both sides in time of war. I knew very well how to account for the behaviour of these opponents and, moreover, I had learnt that psycho-analysis always brings to the surface the worst that is in a man. But I made up my mind not to answer my opponents and, so far as my influence went, to restrain others from controversy. Under the peculiar conditions of the altercation about psycho-analysis it seemed to me very doubtful whether either spoken or written debates would avail anything; it was certain which way the majority at congresses and meetings would go, and my faith in the reasonableness and nobility of the gentlemen who opposed me was not at any time great. Experience shows that only very few persons are capable of preserving courtesy in a scientific dispute, to say nothing of keeping to the point, and an altercation about a scientific matter had always been odious to me. Perhaps this attitude on my part has been misunderstood; perhaps I have been thought so good-natured or so easily intimidated that no further notice need be taken of me. This was a mistake; I can rave and revile as well as anybody, but I do not find it so easy to give expression in a manner suitable for publication to the emotions involved and therefore I abstain entirely from the attempt.

Perhaps in many respects it would have been better if I had given free rein to my own feelings and to those of others round me. We have all heard of the interesting attempt to explain psycho-analysis as a product of the peculiar character of Vienna as a city; as recently as 1913 Janet did not disdain to employ this argument, although he himself is undoubtedly proud of being a Parisian. This inspiration runs as follows: psycho-analysis, so far as it consists of the assertion that the neuroses are traceable to disturbances in the sexual life, could only have come to birth in a town like Vienna—in an atmosphere of sensuality and immorality foreign to other cities—and it simply contains a reflection, a projection into theory, as it were, of these peculiar Viennese conditions. Now honestly I am no local patriot; but this theory about psycho-analysis always seems to me quite exceptionally stupid, so stupid, in fact, that I have sometimes been inclined to suppose that the reproach of being a citizen of Vienna is only a euphemistic substitute for another reproach which no one would care to put forward openly. If the premisses on which the argument rests were the opposite of what they are, then it might be worth a hearing. Given a town in which the inhabitants imposed exceptional restrictions upon themselves in regard to sexual gratification, and at the same time exhibited a marked tendency to severe neurotic disorders, that town might certainly give rise in the mind of an observer to the idea that these two circumstances had some connection with each other, and to lead to the inference that one was contingent upon the other. But neither of these assumptions is true of Vienna. The Viennese are no more abstinent and no more nervous than dwellers in other large cities. There is rather less embarrassment—less prudery—in regard to sexual relationships than in the cities of the West and North which are so proud of their chastity. These peculiar characteristics of Vienna would be more likely to mislead the supposed observer in regard to the causation of neurosis than to throw any light on it.

Vienna has done everything possible, however, to deny her share in the origin of psycho-analysis. In no other place is the hostile indifference of the learned and cultivated section of the population so evident to the analyst as in Vienna.

It may be that my policy of avoiding wide publicity is to some extent responsible for this. If I had permitted or given an opportunity for the medical societies of Vienna to busy themselves with psycho-analysis in stormy debates, where violent feelings could come to the surface, and the accusations and abuse which everyone had in his heart could be freely expressed, perhaps the ban on psycho-analysis would have been overcome by now and it would no longer be a stranger in its native city. As it is—the poet may be right when he makes his Wallenstein say:

> But this the Viennese will not forgive me
> That I deprived them of a spectacle.

The task to which I was not equal—that of demonstrating *suaviter in modo* to the opponents of psycho-analysis their injustice and arbitrary attitude—was undertaken and carried out most efficiently by Bleuler in 1911 in his essay *Die Psychanalyse Freuds: Verteidigung und Kritische Bemerkungen*. It would be so natural for me to praise this work which criticizes both sides that I will hasten to say what I deprecate in it. It seems to me in spite of all not truly impartial, too lenient to the faults of the opponents of psycho-analysis and too severe on the shortcomings of its adherents. This trait in it may possibly explain why the opinion of a psychiatrist of such high repute, such undoubted ability and independence, has not had more effect upon his colleagues. The author of *Affektivität* (1906) will not be surprised that the effect of a book is determined not by the strength of its arguments but by the note of feeling in it. Another aspect of the effect of this book—that on the followers of psycho-analysis—was destroyed later on by Bleuler himself, when in 1913 he showed the reverse side of his attitude to psycho-analysis in his *Kritik der Freudschen Theorie.* In this book he demolishes so much of the structure of psycho-analytical theory that our opponents may well be glad of the assistance this champion of psycho-analysis renders them. No new arguments or better observations have served him as a guide to these pronouncements; he takes his stand simply on his own judgement and no longer himself admits, as he did in earlier works, the inadequacy of this ground. It seemed therefore that an almost irreparable loss threatened psycho-analysis here. But in his last publication, *Die Kritiken der Schizophrenie,* 1914, Bleuler summons up all his forces in the face of the attacks made upon him for introducing psycho-analysis into his book on schizophrenia and makes what he himself calls a 'presumptuous claim'. 'But now I will make a presumptuous claim: I consider that up to the present the various kinds of psychology have contributed precious little towards an explanation of the underlying connections in psychogenic symptoms and diseases, but that the psychology of the depths offers something towards a psychology which still awaits creation and which physicians are in need of in order to understand their patients and to cure them rationally; and I even believe that in my *Schizophrenie* I have taken a very short step towards the required understanding. The first two assertions are certainly correct; the last may be an error.'

Since by 'psychology of the depths' he means nothing else but psycho-analysis we may for the present be content with this admission.

III

Mach es kurz!
Am Jüngsten Tag ist's nur ein Furz!
Goethe.

Two years after the first, the second private Congress of psycho-analysts took place at Nuremberg, in March, 1910. In the interval between them, influenced partly by the favourable reception in America, the increasing hostility in German-speaking countries, and by the unforeseen acquisition of support from Zurich, I had conceived a project which with the help of my friend Ferenczi I carried out at this second Congress. What I had in mind was to organize the psycho-analytical movement, to transfer its centre to Zurich and to give it a leader who would look after its future career. As this scheme has met with much opposition among the adherents of psycho-analysis, I will set out my reasons for it in some detail. I hope that they will justify my action, even though it turns out that it was not a very wise one.

I judged that its association with Vienna was no recommendation but rather a handicap to the new movement. A place in the heart of Europe like Zurich, at which an academic instructor had adopted psycho-analysis in his institution, seemed to me much more promising. I supposed too that my own person constituted a second handicap; all estimates of my personality were vitiated by the liking or dislike of the different factions; I was either compared with Darwin and Kepler or was hooted at as a general paralytic. I wished to withdraw myself into the background, therefore, as well as the city where psycho-analysis first saw the light. Moreover, I was no longer young; I saw that there was a long road ahead, and I felt oppressed by the thought that the responsibilities of a leader should fall to me at my time of life. Yet I felt that there must be a leader. I knew only too well the pitfalls lying in wait for anyone who undertakes analysis, and hoped that many of them might be avoided if someone prepared to instruct and admonish could be established in a position of authority. This position had at first been occupied by myself, owing to my fifteen years' start in experience which nothing could make up. I felt the need of transferring this authority to a younger man, who would then as a matter of course take my place after my death. This man could only be C. G. Jung, since Bleuler was my contemporary in age; in favour of Jung were his exceptional talents, the contributions he had already made to psycho-analysis, his independent position and the impression of energy and assurance which his personality conveyed. In addition to this, he seemed ready to enter into a friendly relationship with me and for my sake to give up certain prejudices in regard to race which he had previously permitted himself. I had no inkling at that time that in spite of all these advantages the choice was a most unfortunate one, that I had lighted upon a person who was incapable of tolerating the authority of another, who was still less fitted himself to wield it, and whose energies were ruthlessly devoted to the furtherance of his own interests.

I considered it necessary to form an official association because I feared the abuses to which psycho-analysis would be subjected as soon as it became popular. There should be some headquarters whose duty it would be to announce: 'All this nonsense is nothing to do with psycho-analysis; this is not analysis.' The meetings of the branch societies (which together would form the international association) would provide opportunities for learning and studying psycho-analysis and for the training of medical men, whose work would then have a kind of guarantee upon it. Moreover, it seemed to me desirable, since official science had pronounced its solemn ban upon psycho-analysis and had declared a boycott against medical men and institutions practising it, that the adherents of psycho-analysis should come together for friendly communication with one another and mutual support.

This and nothing else was what I hoped to achieve by founding the International Psycho-Analytical Association. It was probably more than could be attained. Just as my opponents were to discover that it was not possible to stem the tide of the new movement, so I was to find that it would not proceed in the direction I wished to mark out for it. The proposals made by Ferenczi in Nuremberg were adopted, it is true; Jung was elected President and made Riklin his secretary; the publication of a correspondence bulletin which should link the Central Executive with the branch Societies was resolved upon. The objects of the Association were declared to be 'to foster and further the science of psycho-analysis founded by Freud, both as a pure discipline of psychology and in its application to medicine and the mental sciences; and to promote mutual support among the members in all endeavours to acquire and to spread psycho-analytical knowledge.' The scheme, unfortunately, was very violently opposed by the Vienna group. Adler, in great excitement, expressed the fear that 'censorship and restrictions of scientific freedom' were intended. Finally the Viennese gave in, after having secured that not Zurich, but the place of residence of the President, should be the centre of the Association and that he should be elected for two years.

At this Congress three local branch societies were inaugurated: one in Berlin, under the chairmanship of Abraham; one in Zurich, whose head became President of the Association; and one in Vienna, the chairmanship of which I made over to Adler. A fourth group, in Budapest, could not be formed until later. Bleuler had not attended the Congress on account of illness, and later he evinced hesitation about joining the Association on grounds of principle; he let himself be persuaded to do so, it is true, after a personal conversation with me, but resigned again shortly after on account of disagreements at Zurich. This severed the connection between the Zurich group and the Burghölzli institution.

One of the results of the Nuremberg Congress was the founding of the *Zentralblatt für Psychoanalyse*, for which purpose Adler and Stekel joined forces. It had obviously been designed originally as an instrument of opposition, to win back for Vienna the hegemony threatened by the election of Jung. But when the two founders of the journal, labouring under the difficulties of finding a publisher, assured me of their friendly intentions and as a guarantee of their sincerity gave me a right of veto, I accepted the direction of it and worked energetically for this new organ; its first number appeared in September, 1910.

I will now continue the story of the psycho-analytical Congresses. The third Congress took place in September, 1911, in Weimar, and surpassed the previous ones in spirit and scientific fervour. J. J. Putnam, who was present on this occasion, declared afterwards in America how much pleasure it had given him and expressed his respect for 'the mental attitude' of those present, quoting some words I was said to have used in reference to them, 'They have learnt to endure a bit of the truth.' It is a fact that no one who had attended scientific congresses could have failed to carry away a favourable impression of the Psycho-Analytical Association. I myself had conducted the first two Congresses and I had allowed every speaker time for his paper and left discussions to take place in private afterwards among the members. Jung, as President, took over the direction at Weimar and instituted the practice of discussing each paper at the time, which, however, gave rise to no difficulties on that occasion.

A very different picture was presented by the fourth Congress in Munich two years later in September, 1913; it is still clear in the memory of all who were present. It was conducted in a disagreeable and incorrect manner by Jung; the speakers were greatly restricted in time and the discussions overwhelmed the papers. By a stroke of malice on the part of chance it happened that that evil genius, Hoche, had settled in the very house in which the meetings were held. Hoche might easily have convinced himself how ridiculous his notion was of the adherents of psycho-analysis as a fanatical sect blindly submissive to their leader. The fatiguing and unedifying proceedings ended in the re-election of Jung to the Presidency of the International Psycho-Analytical Association, which he accepted, although two-fifths of those present refused their support. We dispersed without any desire to meet again.

About the time of this third Congress the position of the International Psycho-Analytical Association was as follows. The branch societies in Vienna,

Berlin and Zurich had been formed at the Congress in Nuremberg as early as 1910. In May, 1911, a branch at Munich under the chairmanship of Dr. L. Seif was incorporated. In the same year the first American branch society was formed under the chairmanship of A. A. Brill, with the name 'The New York Psycho-Analytic Society'. At the Congress in Weimar the foundation of a second American Society was sanctioned; it came into existence during the following year under the name of 'The American Psycho-Analytic Association', and included members in Canada and the whole of America; Putnam was elected President and Ernest Jones secretary. Shortly before the Congress in Munich in 1913, the Budapest branch society was formed under the chairmanship of S. Ferenczi. Soon after this the first English group was formed by Ernest Jones, who had returned to London. The membership of these branch societies, of which there were now eight, naturally gives no measure of the number of unorganized students and adherents of psycho-analysis.

The development of the periodicals devoted to psycho-analysis also deserves mention. The first of these was a series of monographs entitled *Schriften zur angewandten Seelenkunde* which have appeared irregularly since 1907 and now number fifteen volumes. (The publisher was at first H. Heller in Vienna and later F. Deuticke.) They comprise works by Freud (1 and 7), Riklin, Jung, Abraham (4 and 11), Rank (5 and 13), Sadger, Pfister, M. Graf, Jones (10 and 14), Storfer and v. Hug-Hellmuth. When the journal *Imago*, which will be referred to later, was founded this form of publication ceased to have quite the same value. After the meeting in Salzburg in 1908, the *Jahrbuch für psychoanalytische und psychopathologische Forschungen* was founded, which appeared for five years under Jung's editorship and has now been re-issued, under new editorship and with a slight change in the title, as the *Jahrbuch der Psychoanalyse*. It is no longer intended, as formerly, as an archive for collecting valuable work on psycho-analysis, but its editorial activity is aimed at recording all work done and advances made in psycho-analysis during the year. The *Zentralblatt für Psychoanalyse*, which was set on foot by Adler and Stekel, as already stated, after the foundation of the International Psycho-Analytical Association in Nuremberg, 1910, has in quite a short time had a very unsettled career. As early as the tenth number of the first volume an announcement appeared on the title-page that, on account of scientific differences of opinion with the direction, Dr. Alfred Adler had resolved to withdraw voluntarily from editorship. After this Dr. Stekel remained the sole editor (summer of 1911). At the Congress in Weimar the *Zentralblatt* was raised to the position of official organ of the International Association and made available to all members by increasing the annual subscription. From the third number of the second year (winter, 1912) Stekel alone was responsible for its contents. His behaviour, which is not easy to describe, compelled me to resign the direction and hurriedly to establish a new organ for psycho-analysis in the *Internationale Zeitschrift für ärztliche Psychoanalyse*. The combined efforts of almost all our workers and of H. Heller, the new publisher, resulted in the appearance of the first number in January, 1913, whereupon it took the place of the *Zentralblatt* as official organ of the International Psycho-Analytical Association.

Meanwhile, early in 1912 a new Journal *Imago* (published by Heller), designed exclusively for the application of psycho-analysis to the mental sciences, was founded by Dr. Hanns Sachs and Dr. Otto Rank. *Imago* is now in the middle of its third year and enjoys the patronage of a continually increasing number of readers, many of whom have no concern with medical psycho-analysis.

Apart from these four periodical publications (*Schriften zur angewandten Seelenkunde*, *Jahrbuch*, *Zeitschrift*, and *Imago*) there are other German and foreign journals publishing works which may claim a place in the literature of psycho-analysis. *The Journal of Abnormal Psychology*, directed by Morton Prince, usually contains so many good analytic contributions that it may be regarded as the principal representative of analytic literature in America. In the winter of 1913, White and Jelliffe in New York started a new journal, probably in view of the fact that most medical men in America who are interested in analysis find the German language a great difficulty; it is called the *Psycho-Analytic Review* and is devoted exclusively to psycho-analysis.[1]

* * *

I now have to consider two secessions which have taken place among the adherents of psycho-analysis; the first occurred between the founding of the Association in 1910 and the Congress at Weimar in 1911; the second took place after this and disclosed itself at Munich in 1913. The disappointment that they

[1] [Since this was written, in 1914, there have been further changes, notably the founding of the Internationaler Psychoanalytischer Verlag in Vienna, which took over publication of the four official periodicals mentioned in the text, and the founding of an English branch of it, The International Psycho-Analytical Press, now in London. One of the objects for which the latter was constituted was to publish the second official organ of the International Psycho-Analytical Association instituted for English-speaking countries in 1920, with the title of *The International Journal of Psycho-Analysis*, directed by Prof. Freud and edited by Ernest Jones. Another object was the publication of the International Psycho-Analytical Library, of which the present volume forms No. 7.—Ed.]

caused me might have been averted if I had considered more thoughtfully the reactions of patients undergoing analytic treatment. I knew very well of course that anyone may take to flight on a first approach to the unwelcome truths of psycho-analysis; I had always myself asserted that everyone's understanding will be limited by his own repressions (rather, by the resistances which sustain them) so that he cannot go beyond a certain point in his relation to analysis. But I had not expected that anyone who had reached a certain depth in his comprehension of analysis could discard it again, or ever lose it. And yet everyday experience with patients had shown that total rejection of all analytical knowledge may ensue whenever a strong resistance arises at any deep level in the mind; one may have succeeded in laboriously bringing a patient to grasp some parts of analytical knowledge and to handle them like possessions of his own, and yet may see him, in the power of the very next resistance, throw all he has learnt to the winds and defend himself against it as in the first days of his treatment. I had to learn that just the same thing can happen with psycho-analysts as with patients under analysis.

It is no easy or enviable task to write the history of these two defections, partly because I am devoid of any strong personal motive to do so—I had not expected gratitude nor am I revengeful in any active degree—and partly because I know that by so doing I lay myself open to the contumely of not very scrupulous opponents and offer to the enemies of analysis the spectacle they have so warmly desired—of seeing the psycho-analysts tearing one another to bits. I had to exercise so much restraint to keep myself from entering the lists with opponents outside analysis; and now I see myself compelled to take up arms against former followers of it or those who would still like to be called followers. I have no choice in the matter, however; only convenience or cowardice could prompt one to keep silence and this would do more harm than a frank revelation of the existing evils. Anyone who has followed the growth of other scientific movements will know that the same upheavals and dissensions have commonly occurred in them too. It may be that with them they were more carefully concealed; but psycho-analysis, which repudiates so many conventional ideals, is more honest in these matters also.

Another very disagreeable circumstance is that I cannot altogether avoid some analysis in explanation of these two opposition movements. Analysis is not suited, however, to be used in controversy; it presupposes the consent of the analysed; the situation of analysis involves a superior and a subordinate. Anyone who presses analysis into the service of polemics must therefore expect the person analysed to use the weapon upon him in turn, so that the discussion will reach a state which entirely excludes the possibility of convincing any impartial third person. I shall therefore restrict my use of analytic knowledge, and with it, of indiscreet and provocative statements, as far as is possible; and in addition I will state that no criticism in regard to scientific aspects are based on these grounds. I do not propose to deal with the possible truth in the substance of the theories rejected nor shall I attempt to refute them. This task is left to other able workers in psycho-analysis and has already been performed in part. I merely intend to show that these theories controvert the fundamental principles of analysis (and on what points they controvert them) and that for this reason they should not be known under this name. So I shall only avail myself of analysis in order to explain how these departures from analysis could arise among analysts. At the points of departure, it is true, I must defend the just rights of psycho-analysis by purely critical remarks.

The first task confronting psycho-analysis was to explain the neuroses; it took the two facts of resistance and transference as starting-points, and, giving due weight to the third fact of amnesia, accounts for them with its theories of repression, the sexual propelling forces in neurosis and the unconscious. Psycho-analysis has never claimed to provide a complete theory of human mentality as a whole, but only expected that what it offered should be applied to supplement and correct the knowledge acquired by other means. Now Alfred Adler's theory goes far beyond this point; it seeks at one stroke to explain the behaviour and character of human beings as well as the neurotic and psychotic manifestations in them. It is actually more suited to any other field than that of neurosis, although from motives connected with the history of its development it still places this in the foreground. For many years I had opportunities of studying Dr. Adler and have never refused to recognize his unusual ability, combined with a particularly speculative disposition. As an instance of the 'persecution' that he maintains he has suffered at my hands, I can point to the fact that after the Association was founded I made over to him the leadership of the Vienna society. Not until urgent demands were put forward by all the members of the society was I induced to take the chair again at its scientific meetings. When I had perceived how little gift Adler had in particular for appreciating the importance of unconscious material my view changed to an expectation that he would apply himself to the connections of psycho-analysis with psychology and to discovering the biological foundations of instinctual processes; this idea was justified in a certain sense by his valuable work on the inferiority of organs. He did actually do something of the kind, but his work conveys an impression *as if*—to speak in his own jargon—it intended to prove that psycho-analysis was wrong in everything and that the sexual propelling forces had only been given so much significance by psycho-analysts in consequence of an undue credulity towards the statements of neurotics. Of the personal motive of his work I may also speak publicly, since he himself declared it in the presence of a small circle of members of the Vienna Society. 'Do you think it is much pleasure for me to stand all my life long in your shadow?' To be sure, I see nothing reprehensible in a younger man freely admitting the ambition which in any case one would surmise to be an incentive of his work. But even though a man is dominated by a motive of this kind he should know how to avoid being what the English, with their fine social tact, call 'unfair'—a word which can only be expressed in German by something much coarser. How little Adler was capable of this is shown by the profusion of petty outbursts of malice which disfigure his writings and by the indications they contain of an irrepressible mania on the question of priority. At the Vienna Psycho-analytical Society we once actually heard him claim priority in regard to the 'unity of the neuroses' and the 'dynamic conception' of neurosis. This caused me great astonishment, since I had always believed I had voiced these two principles before I had ever known Adler.

This craving of Adler's for a place in the sun has, however, had one result which is bound to be beneficial to psycho-analysis. When, after irreconcilable scientific disagreements had come to light, I was obliged to bring about Adler's resignation from the editorial staff of the *Zentralblatt*, he left the Vienna society also and founded a new one, which at first adopted the charming title of 'The Society for Free Psycho-Analysis'. Unfortunately, however, the outside world unconnected with analysis is clearly as incapable of appreciating the differences between the views of two psycho-analysts as we Europeans are of detecting shades of difference in the faces of two Chinamen. 'Free' psycho-analysis remained under the shadow of 'official', 'orthodox' psycho-analysis and was treated as an appendage of the latter. Then Adler took a step for which we are thankful and severed all connection with psycho-analysis, designating his theory 'Individual Psychology'. There is room enough on God's earth, and anybody who can is fully entitled to cut any capers he likes on it without interference; but it is not a good thing for people who no longer understand one another and no longer agree together to remain under the same roof together. Adler's 'Individual Psychology' is now one of the many psychological movements adverse to psycho-analysis, and its further development is no concern of ours.

The Adlerian theory was from the very beginning a 'system', which psycho-analysis was careful to avoid becoming. It is also a remarkably good example of 'secondary elaboration', such as occurs, for instance, in the process which dream-material undergoes by the action of waking thought. In Adler's case the place of dream-material is taken by the new material obtained through psycho-analytic study; this is then regarded exclusively from the standpoint of the ego, reduced to terms with which the ego is familiar, translated, twisted, and misunderstood exactly as happens in dream-formation. Moreover, the Adlerian theory is characterized less by what it asserts than by what it denies, so that it consists of three elements of quite dissimilar value: the useful contributions to the psychology of the ego, the superfluous but admissible introduction of a new jargon to describe analytical facts, and the distortions and perversions of these facts when they do not comply with presuppositions in regard to the ego. The first element has never been ginored by psycho-analysis, although it was not one that demanded special attention; psycho-analysis was more concerned to show that all the ego-trends contain libidinal components. The Adlerian theory emphasizes the opposite view, the egoistic constituent in all libidinal tendencies. This would have been an obvious gain if Adler did not misuse this conclusion by throughout denying the libidinal trends in favour of the egoistic component in them. His theory does what all patients do and what our waking thought in general does — namely, makes use of a *rationalization*, as Jones has called it, in order to conceal unconscious motives. Adler carries his theory to such lengths that he regards the ambition to mastery of the woman, to being *above*, as positively the strongest motive in the sexual act itself. I do not know if he has given vent to these monstrous ideas in his writings.

Psycho-analysis recognized early that every neurotic symptom owes its existence to a compromise. Every symptom must therefore in some way comply with the demands of the ego which regulates repression, must offer some advantage, admit of some profitable utilization, or it would undergo the same fate as the original impulse itself which is being kept in check. The expression 'advantage by illness' represents this state of things; one is even justified in differentiating the 'paranosic' gain to the ego, which is operative at the start, from an 'epinosic' aspect of it, which supervenes and relates to other purposes of the ego, when the symptom is required to be permanently maintained. It has also long been known that the withdrawal of this advantage by illness, or a disappearance of it in consequence of some change in external circumstances (reality), constitutes one of the mechanisms of a cure of the symptom. In the Adlerian doctrine the main emphasis falls on these easily verifiable and clearly intelligible connections, while it is altogether overlooked that on innumerable occasions the ego is merely making a virtue of necessity in submitting, because of the use it can make of it, to the very disagreeable symptom which is forced upon it—for instance, in accepting anxiety as a means to security. The ego is here playing the part of the clown in a circus who tries to convince the audience by his gestures that every figure of the *manège* is performed at his command. But only the youngest among the spectators are deceived by it.

The second constituent of the Adlerian theory psycho-analysis must claim as its own. It is actually nothing else but psycho-analytic knowledge, which the author extracted from all the sources open to him during ten years of work in common and has now labelled as his own by changing the terminology of it. 'Insurance' (*Sicherung*), for instance, I myself consider a better word than 'protective measure' (*Schutzmassregel*) which I employ, but I cannot find any difference in their meaning. Again, a host of familiar features come to light in Adler's propositions when one restores the original 'phantasized' and 'phantasy' in place of 'manufactured (*fingiert*), fictive, and fiction'. This identity would be emphasized by psycho-analysis even if the author had not for many years taken part in our common work.

The third element in the Adlerian theory, the distortions and misinterpretations put upon the disagreeable facts of analysis, constitutes that which henceforth definitely separates 'Individual Psychology' from psycho-analysis. As is known, the principle of Adler's system is that the governing motive of self-preservation in the individual, his 'will to power', expresses itself pre-eminently in the form of a 'masculine protest' in the conduct of life, in character-formation and in neurosis. This 'masculine protest', the motive-force at work, according to Adler's theory, is however nothing else but repression detached from its psychological mechanism and, moreover, sexualized in addition—which accords very badly with his vaunted ejection of sexuality from its place in mental life. The 'masculine protest' undoubtedly exists, but in making it the motor of mental life one is treating the observed fact like a spring-board which is left behind as one raises oneself from it. Let us consider one of the fundamental situations in which desire is felt in infancy, that of a child observing the sexual act between adults. When the life-story of those persons who later come into the physician's hands is subjected to analysis it is found that at that moment two currents of feeling took possession of the immature spectator; in the case of a boy, one is the impulse to put himself in the place of the active man, and the other, the opposing feeling, is to identify himself with the suffering woman. Between them these two impulses exhaust the pleasurable possibilities of the situation. The first alone can come under the head of the masculine protest, if this conception is to retain any meaning at all. The second, however, the further course of which Adler either disregards or knows nothing about, is the one that assumes greater significance in the neurosis later. Adler has so merged himself in the jealous narrowness of the ego that he takes account only of those tendencies that are agreeable to the ego and are fostered by it; the situation of neurosis, in which these impulses rise up against the ego, is the very one that lies outside his horizon.

In the attempt—one which psycho-analysis has made necessary—to correlate the fundamental principle of his theory with the mental life of the child, Adler exhibits the most serious departures from actual observation and the most fundamental confusion of concepts. The biological, social and psychological meanings of 'masculine' and 'feminine' are here hopelessly mixed in an inextricable combination. It is quite impossible to suppose—and demonstrably so by observation—that the child—male or female—founds the plan of its life on an original depreciation of the female sex and takes the wish 'to be a real man' as its guiding principle. Children have, to begin with, no idea of the significance of a difference between the sexes; on the contrary, they start with the assumption that the same genital organ (the male) belongs to both sexes; they do not begin their enquiries into sexual problems with the question of sexual differences, while the social underestimation of the female sex is completely foreign to them. There are women in whose neurosis the wish to be a man has played no part. Whatever of the masculine protest can be shown to exist is easily traceable to a disturbance in the primary narcissism due to threats of castration or to early interference with sexual activities. All disputes about the psychogenesis of the neuroses must eventually be decided on the field of the neuroses of childhood. Careful dissection of a neurosis in early childhood puts an end to all misapprehensions about the ætiology of the neuroses and to all doubts about the part played by the sexual impulses in them. That is why, in his criticism of Jung's work 'Conflicts in the Mind of the Child',[1] Adler had to resort to the imputation that the material of the case had been arranged in conformity with some tendency, 'probably by the father'.

I will not dwell any longer on the biological aspect of the Adlerian theory nor discuss whether either actual inferiority of organs or a subjective feeling of it — one does not know which — is really capable of carrying the weight of Adler's system. I will merely interpolate the remark that if it were so neurosis would be a by-product of general decrepitude, whereas observation shows that an impressive majority of ugly, misshapen, helpless and miserable creatures fail to react to their defects by neurosis. Nor will I deal with the very interesting proposition by which inferiority is referred back to feelings of childishness. It shows the disguise in which the factor of infantilism, so strongly emphasized by psycho-analysis, recurs in 'Individual Psychology'. On the other hand, I must point out how all the psychological acquisitions of psycho-analysis have been thrown to the winds by Adler. In his book *Der nervöse Charakter* the unconscious is still mentioned as a psychological peculiarity, without however, any relation to the system. Later on he quite logically declared that it was a matter of indifference to him whether an idea was conscious or unconscious. Adler never from the beginning evinced any understanding of repression.

[1] *Zentralblatt für Psychoanalyse*, Bd. I, S. 122. See also *Analytical Psychology*, by C. G. Jung. 1917. Chap. II. (Translation.)

In abstracting a paper read at the Vienna Society (February, 1911) he writes: 'On the evidence of a case it must be pointed out that the patient had never repressed his libido, against which he was continually securing himself.'[1] Soon after, in a discussion at the Vienna Society, he said: 'If you ask where repression comes from, you are told "From civilization"; and if you ask where civilization comes from, you are told "From repression". You can see therefore it is nothing but playing with words.' A tithe of the acuteness and ingenuity with which Adler has unmasked the defensive devices of the 'nervous character' would have sufficed to show him the way out of this pettifogging kind of reasoning. What it means is simply that civilization is based upon the repressions effected by former generations, and that each fresh generation is required to maintain this civilization by effectuating the same repressions. I once heard of a child that thought people were laughing at it, and began to cry, because when it asked 'Where do eggs come from?' they told it 'From hens', and then when it went on to enquire where hens came from, they said 'From eggs'. But they were not playing with words; on the contrary, they were telling it the truth.

Equally empty and unproductive is all that Adler has to offer about dreams, the shibboleth of psychoanalysis. First he regarded dreams as a turning from the masculine to the feminine side, which is simply a translation of the wish-fulfilment theory of dreams into terms of the 'masculine protest'. Later on he found that the essence of dreams lies in enabling man to realize unconsciously things that consciously he has to go without. Adler must also be credited with priority in confounding the dream itself with the

[1] *Korrespondenzblatt,* Nr. 5. Zürich, April 1911.

latent dream-thoughts, which leads to the discovery of a 'prospective tendency' in them; Maeder followed his lead in this later. In this he overlooks only too readily that every interpretation of a dream that is on the surface entirely incomprehensible is based on the very method of dream-interpretation the assumptions and conclusions of which he disputes. In regard to resistance, Adler informs us that it serves the purposes of the patient's opposition to the physician. This is certainly true; it is as much as to say that it serves the purposes of the resistance. Where it comes from, however, or how it happens that its manifestations are at the disposal of the patient in this way is not enquired into, being a point of no interest to the ego. The detailed mechanism of symptoms and the manifestations of disease, the foundations of the manifold variety of diseases and their forms of expression, are disregarded *in toto*; for everything is pressed equally into the service of the masculine protest, self-assertion and the aggrandizement of personality. The system is complete; to produce it an enormous amount of labour in shuffling interpretations has been expended, while it has not furnished a single new observation. I imagine I have made it clear that it has nothing to do with psycho-analysis.

The view of life which is reflected in the Adlerian system is founded exclusively on the aggressive impulse; there is no room in it for love. It might surprise one that such a cheerless view of life should meet with any attention at all; but we must not forget that, weighed down by the burden of its sexual desires, humanity is ready to accept anything when tempted with 'ascendancy over sexuality' as a bait.

Adler's defection took place before the Congress at Weimar in 1911; after this date the Swiss began theirs. The first signs of it, curiously enough, were some remarks of Riklin's in popular articles in Swiss publications, by which the general public learned earlier than the closest colleagues in the work that psycho-analysis had got the better of some regrettable errors which had previously discredited it. In 1912 Jung boasted, in a letter from America, that his modifications of psycho-analysis had overcome the resistances of many people who had hitherto refused to have anything to do with it. I replied that that was nothing to boast of; the more he sacrificed of the hard-won truths of psycho-analysis the quicker would he see resistances vanishing. This modification which the Swiss were so proud of introducing was again nothing else but a theoretical suppression of the sexual factor. I confess that from the beginning I regarded this 'advance' as too far-reaching an adjustment to the demands of reality.

These two reactionary movements veering away from psycho-analysis, which I must now compare with each other, show another point in common, in that they both court popular favour by means of certain lofty ideas, as if they were *sub specie æternitatis*. With Adler, the relativity of all knowledge and the right of the personality artificially to construe the substance of knowledge in an individual manner plays this part; by Jung the appeal is made to the age-old right of youth to throw off the fetters in which tyrannical age with its hidebound views would bind it. A few remarks must be devoted to exposing the fallacy of these ideas. The relativity of our knowledge is a consideration which may be used against every other science just as well as against psycho-analysis. Its use is prompted by well-known reactionary currents of present-day feeling, which are hostile to science, and it sets up an appearance of superiority to which no one is entitled. No one among us can guess what the ultimate judgement of mankind about our tentative theories will be. There are instances in which rejection by the next three generations has been corrected by the succeeding one and changed into recognition. After he has listened carefully to the voice of criticism in himself and has paid some attention to the criticisms of his opponents, there is nothing for the individual worker to do but to stand fast for his own convictions which are based on experience. One must be content to behave honestly in this matter, not assuming the office of judge which is one reserved to the remote future. It is going very far wrong to stress the question of personal and arbitrary views in a scientific matter; it is clearly an attempt to rob psycho-analysis of its position as a science, after it has indeed already been depreciated by the previous consideration. Anyone who values highly the scientific mode of thought will rather seek all possible means and methods of circumscribing the influence of the personal arbitrary factor wherever it plays too great a part. It must be borne in mind, too, that all eagerness to defend is out of place. These arguments of Adler's are not intended seriously; they are intended only for use against opponents; when confronted with his own theories they keep at a respectful distance. Nor have they hindered his own followers from hailing him as the Messiah for whose appearance expectant humanity has been prepared by any number of forerunners. The Messiah is certainly no longer a relative phenomenon.

Jung's *ad captandam benevolentiam* argument rests on the unduly optimistic assumption that the progress of the human race, of culture and knowledge, has unrolled itself in an unbroken line; as if there had been no epigones, reactions and restorations after every revolution, no generations who have taken a backward step and foregone the gains of their forefathers. Its approximation to the demands of the multitude, its abandonment of an innovation which proved unwelcome, makes it improbable from the start that Jung's revised version of psycho-analysis can justly claim to be a liberation for youth. In the last resort it is not the years of the doer that determine this but the character of the deed.

Of the two movements under discussion Adler's is indubitably the more significant; while radically false, it is marked by consistence and coherence. It is, moreover, in spite of all, founded upon a theory of the instincts. Jung's modification, on the other hand, disconnects the phenomena from their relation with impulse-life; and further, as its critics (Abraham, Ferenczi, Jones) have pointed out, it is so unintelligible, obscure, and confused that it is difficult to take up any standpoint in regard to it. Wherever one lays hold of anything, one must be prepared to hear that one has misunderstood it, and it is impossible to know how to arrive at a correct understanding of it. It is put forward too in a peculiarly vacillating manner, one moment as 'quite a minor deviation which does not justify the fuss that has been made about it' (Jung), and the next as a new message of salvation which is to begin a new epoch in psychoanalysis, in fact, reveal a new aspect of the universe for everything else.

When one thinks of the disagreement displayed in the various public and private expressions of Jung's views, one is bound to ask oneself how much of this is due to his own lack of clearness and how much to lack of sincerity. It must be admitted, however, that the exponents of the new doctrine find themselves in a difficult position. They are now disputing things which formerly they themselves upheld, and not, moreover, on the ground of fresh observations by which they might have been taught something further, but in consequence of different interpretations of the same observations which make the things they see look different to them now from what they did before. For this reason they are unwilling to give up their connection with psycho-analysis, through which they became known to the world, and prefer to proclaim that psycho-analysis has changed. At the Congress in Munich I saw that I must clear up this confusion, and did so by declaring that I did not admit the innovations of the Swiss to be legitimate continuations and further developments of the psycho-analysis that originated with me. Outside critics (like Furtmüller) had already before this perceived the state of things, and Abraham truly says that Jung is in full retreat from psycho-analysis. I am naturally perfectly ready to allow that anyone has a right to think and to write what he likes; but he has no right to put it forward as something which it really is not.

Just as Adler's investigation brought something new to psycho-analysis—a contribution to the psychology of the ego—and then tried to recoup itself all too dearly for this liberality by throwing over all the fundamental analytic doctrines, so in the same way a new contribution formed the base of operations in the campaign started by Jung and his followers against psycho-analysis. They traced in detail (as Pfister did before them) the way in which the material of sexual ideas belonging to the family-complexes and the incestuous object-choice is made use of in representing the highest ethical and religious interests of man—that is, they have explained an important instance of sublimation of the erotic instinctual forces and of their transformation into trends which can no longer be called erotic. This was in complete harmony with all the expectations of psycho-analysis, and would have agreed very well with the view that in dreams and neurosis a regressive dissolution of this, as of all other sublimations, becomes visible. But unfortunately, the world would have risen in indignation and protested that they were sexualizing ethics and religion! Now I cannot refrain from thinking teleologically for once and concluding that these discoverers were not equal to meeting the storm of righteous wrath they saw ahead. Perhaps it even began to rage in their own bosoms. The importance of theological tradition in the former history of so many Swiss is no less significant for their attitude to psycho-analysis than is the socialistic element in that of Adler for the line of development taken by his psychology. One is reminded of Mark Twain's famous story of the vicissitudes his watch underwent and of the remark with which he ends it: 'And he used to wonder what became of all the unsuccessful tinkers, and gunsmiths, and shoemakers, and blacksmiths; but nobody could ever tell him.'

I will now digress into the region of parables: Suppose that in a certain district there lived an upstart who boasted of ancient descent from a noble family living far off. It was proved to him, however, that his parents lived somewhere in the neighbourhood and were quite simple people. There was only one way out of the difficulty and he seized upon it. He could not any longer repudiate his parentage, so he asserted that they themselves were of an ancient noble strain, but that their fortunes had declined; and he proceeded to procure from some obliging office a document showing their descent. I think the

Swiss must have behaved in much the same way. If ethics and religion must not be sexualized, but had been something 'higher' from the start, and yet the descent of the ideas they contain from the family and Œdipus complex appeared undeniable, there could be only one thing to do—these complexes themselves could not from the beginning have had the significance that they seemed to express, but instead must have that higher 'anagogic' meaning (as Silberer terms it) which adapts them for incorporation into the abstract trains of thought of ethics and religious mysticism.

I am quite resigned to being told again that I have misunderstood the substance and tendency of the New-Zurich doctrines; but I must protest from the start against this contradiction of my interpretation of these doctrines (which is formed from the publications of this school) being laid to my door, instead of theirs. In no other way can I make intelligible to myself the whole range of Jung's innovations and grasp all its implications. All the changes that Jung has wrought in psycho-analysis flow from the ambition to eliminate all that is disagreeable in the family complexes, so that it may not evidence itself again in ethics and religion. For sexual libido an abstract term has been substituted, of which one may safely say that it remains mystifying and incomprehensible to fools and wise alike. The Œdipus complex was intended merely as something 'symbolic'; the mother in it means the unattainable, which one must renounce in the interests of civilization; the father who is killed in the Œdipus myth is the 'inner' father, from whom one must become free in order to be independent. Other details of the material of sexual ideas will undoubtedly undergo similar reinterpretation in the course of time. In the place of a conflict between erotic trends obnoxious to the ego and the self-maintenance tendency of the ego there appears the conflict between the life-task and 'psychic inertia'; the neurotic's sense of guilt corresponds to the reproach of not properly fulfilling his 'life-task'. Thus a new religious-ethical system was created, which, just like the Adlerian system, must necessarily lead to new interpretations of the actual results of analysis, or else distort or ignore them. In truth this signifies but that a few of Culture's harmonics in the symphony of life have sounded again, while the dæmonic forces of the instinct-melody have once more passed unheard.

In order to preserve this 'system' intact it was necessary to turn entirely away from observations and from the technique of psycho-analysis. Occasionally enthusiasm for the sacred cause even required a disregard for scientific logic, as when Jung finds the Œdipus complex not 'specific' enough for the causation of neurosis and attributes a specific character to 'inertia', the most universal characteristic of all matter, animate or inanimate! It is to be noted, by the way, that the 'Œdipus complex' represents only the content of the strivings of mental forces in the individual, and is not in itself a force, like 'psychic inertia'. The study of any individual human being has shown and always will show that the sexual complexes in their original sense are active in him. For this reason the investigation of individuals has been neglected and replaced by conclusions arrived at from points arising from study of the race. In the early childhood of every human being there is the greatest risk of coming upon the original, undisguised meaning of these misinterpreted complexes; consequently in therapy the precaution of dwelling as little as possible on this past history has been developed, and the main emphasis is laid on reverting to the current conflict, in which, moreover, not the individual, personal element is the essential thing, but a general feature—'non-fulfilment of the life-task'. We know, however, that the current conflict of a neurotic becomes comprehensible and admits of solution only when it is referred back to the patient's previous history, when one goes back along the path that his libido took in his illness.

How the New-Zurich therapy shapes itself in accordance with these tendencies can best be conveyed in the words of a patient who had to experience it in his own person: 'This time not an atom of consideration was expended on the past or on transference. Wherever I believed I recognized the latter it was explained as a pure libido-symbol. The moral teaching was very fine and I followed it faithfully, but I did not advance a step. It was more annoying for me than for him, but how could I help it? . . . Instead of freedom through analysis, every day brought fresh terrific demands on me, which had to be fulfilled if the neurosis were to be conquered—for instance, inward concentration by means of introversion, religious meditation, resuming life with my wife in loving devotion, etc. It was almost beyond one's strength; it went beyond a radical transformation of one's whole inner nature. I left the analysis as a poor sinner with intense feelings of contrition and the best resolutions, but at the same time in utter discouragement. Any clergyman would have advised what he recommended, but where was I to find the strength?' The patient did in fact mention that he had heard that analysis of the past and of transference must be gone through first. He was told that he had already had enough of that. Since it had not helped him sufficiently, the conclusion seems justified that the patient had *not had enough* of the first kind of analysis. Certainly the subsequent treatment, which no longer has any claim to be called psycho-analysis, did not improve matters. It is remarkable that the men of Zurich should have taken the long road round by Vienna in order to arrive at last at Berne which is so near, where Dubois cures neuroses by ethical encouragement in a less painful manner.[1]

The total incompatibility ot this new movement with psycho-analysis also of course shows itself, first, in the treatment of repression, which is hardly mentioned nowadays in Jung's writings; again in the misapprehension in regard to dreams, which, in complete disregard of dream-psychology, like Adler, he confounds with the latent dream-thoughts; and in a loss of all understanding of the unconscious—in short, in all the essential points I should choose as characteristic of psycho-analysis. When Jung tells us that the incest-complex is merely 'symbolic', that it has no 'real' existence, that a savage feels no desire towards an old gammer but prefers a young and pretty woman, one is tempted to conclude that 'symbolic' and 'without real existence' simply mean what, in virtue of its power of expression and pathogenic effects, is described by psycho-analysis as 'existing unconsciously'—a description that disposes of the apparent contradictions.

When one remembers that the dream itself is something different from the latent dream-thoughts

[1] I know the objections there are to making use of a patient's statements, and I will therefore expressly state that my informant is a trustworthy person, very well capable of forming a judgement. He gave me this information quite voluntarily and I make use of his communication without asking his consent, because I cannot admit that a psycho-analytic technique should claim the protection of secreey.

which it elaborates, something more, there is nothing surprising in patients dreaming of things with which their minds have been filled during the treatment, whether it be the 'life-task', or 'being above or below'. The dreams of people being analysed are undoubtedly open to influence, in the same way as by stimuli produced for experimental purposes. One can determine a part of the material which appears in a dream; nothing in the essence or mechanism of dreams is altered by this. Nor do I belive that 'biographical' dreams, as they are called, occur outside analysis. If one analyses dreams which occurred before treatment, or if one considers the dreamer's own additions to what has been suggested to him in the cure, or if one avoids giving him any such instructions, then one may convince oneself how far removed it is from the purpose of a dream to produce attempted solutions of the life-task. Dreams are nothing but a form of thinking; one can never understand this form by reference to the content of the thoughts; only an appreciation of the work of dream-making will lead to it.

It is not difficult to find an effective refutation of Jung's misconceptions of psycho-analysis and deviations from it. Every analysis conducted in a proper manner, and in particular any analysis of a child, strengthens the convictions upon which the theory of psycho-analysis is founded, and shows the fallacy of the misinterpretations in both Jung's and Adler's systems. In the days before he became so enlightened Jung himself carried out and published such an analysis of a child; it remains to be seen whether he will undertake a new interpretation of its results with the help of a different 'uniform trend of the facts', to use an expression that Adler employs in this connection.

The view that the sexual representation of 'higher' thoughts in dreams and neurosis is nothing but an archaic mode of expression is naturally irreconcilable with the fact that in neurosis these sexual complexes prove to be the channels of such quantities of libido as are withdrawn from utilization in real life. If they were nothing more than a jargon of sexual terms, the distribution of the libido could not have been affected in any way through them. Jung still admits this himself in his *Darstellung der psychoanalytischen Theorie* and formulates the task of therapy as detachment of these complexes from their libido-cathexis. This can never be achieved, however, by turning one's back upon them and urging the patient to sublimate, but only by exhaustive examination of them, so that they may be made fully and completely conscious. The first piece of reality which the patient must deal with is his illness. Efforts to spare him this task point to the physician's incapacity to help him to overcome the resistances, or else to the physician's dread of the results of his own work.

In conclusion I will say that by his 'modification' of psycho-analysis Jung has given us a counterpart to Lichtenberg's famous knife. He has changed the hilt and put a new blade into it; because the same name is scratched on it we are to regard this instrument as the former one.

I think I have made clear, on the contrary, that the new teaching which aims at replacing psycho-analysis signifies abandonment of analysis and defection from it. Some may perhaps be inclined to fear that this defection must have more serious consequences for analysis than if it had originated with persons who had been less closely connected with the movement and had done less to advance it. I do not share this apprehension.

Men are strong as long as they represent a strong idea; they become powerless when they oppose it. Psycho-Analysis will survive this loss and gain new adherents in place of these others. I can only conclude with the wish that fate may grant an untroubled ascension to all who have been discommoded by their sojourn in the underworld of psycho-analysis. May it be vouchsafed to the others to carry their work in the depths peacefully to an end.

February, 1914.